This book is a thoroughly updated and revised edition of Léon Vaganay's *Initiation à la critique textuelle du Nouveau Testament*, which was first published in 1934. It presents a genment documents presented i prior knowledge of the subje over-view, rather than a st tools and skills necessary for iation in the New Testament.

AN INTRODUCTION TO NEW TESTAMENT TEXTUAL CRITICISM

LEON VAGANAY

AN INTRODUCTION TO NEW TESTAMENT TEXTUAL CRITICISM

Second edition revised and updated
by
Christian-Bernard AMPHOUX
Director of Research, CNRS (Montpellier)

Translated into English by Jenny Heimerdinger, MA

English edition amplified and updated by Christian-Bernard Amphoux
and Jenny Heimerdinger

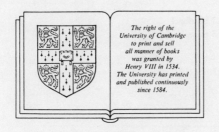

The right of the
University of Cambridge
to print and sell
all manner of books
was granted by
Henry VIII in 1534.
The University has printed
and published continuously
since 1584.

CAMBRIDGE UNIVERSITY PRESS
Cambridge
New York   Port Chester
Melbourne   Sydney

225.6

Published by the Press Syndicate of the University of Cambridge
The Pitt Building, Trumpington Street, Cambridge CB2 1RP
40 West 20th Street, New York, NY 10011-4211, USA
10 Stamford Road, Oakleigh, Victoria 3166, Australia

Originally published in 1986 as *Initiation à la critique textuelle du Nouveau Testament, 2nd edn*
by Léon Vaganay – Christian-Bernard Amphoux
and © Les Editions du Cerf
First published in English by Cambridge University Press 1991 as
An introduction to New Testament textual criticism
English translation © Cambridge University Press 1991

Printed in Great Britain at the University Press, Cambridge

*A catalogue record for this book is
available from the British Library*

Library of Congress cataloguing in publication data
Vaganay, Léon, b. 1882.
[Initiation à la critique textuelle du Nouveau Testament. English]
An introduction to New Testament textual criticism / Léon Vaganay;
translated into English by Jenny Heimerdinger. – 2nd ed. rev. and
updated / by Christian-Bernard Amphoux; English ed. amplified and
updated by Christian-Bernard Amphoux and Jenny Heimerdinger.
     p.   cm.
Translation of: Initiation à la critique textuelle du Nouveau
Testament.
Includes bibliographical references and index.
ISBN 0 521 36433 7
1. Bible. N.T. – Criticism, Textual.   I. Amphoux, Christian-
Bernard.   II. Heimerdinger, Jenny.   III. Title.
BS2325.V3213   1991
225.4'8 – dc 20   90-27539   CIP

ISBN 0 521 36433 7 hardback
ISBN 0 521 42493 3 paperback

20015764

WG

In memory of my tutor, Jean Duplacy

C.-B.A.

Contents

Contents

Illustrations

Foreword to the English translation

Christian Amphoux is employed by the French research body CNRS and is based at the Protestant Faculty of Theology in Montpellier, where he set up the 'Centre de documentation sur les manuscrits de la Bible' in 1984. In 1988 I was privileged to be present at a ceremony held at that institution to mark its change of name to that of the 'Centre Jean Duplacy pour l'étude des manuscrits de la Bible', in memory of the well-known Roman Catholic scholar from Dijon, who had died in 1983, and whose pupil Amphoux had been.

This was more than an ecumenical gesture. It reflected a continuity in textual criticism in France. This continuum is reflected in the present book. Vaganay's *Initiation* appeared in 1934. Duplacy had intended to revise that work but his untimely death prevented this happening. Instead, Christian Amphoux, whose institute has inherited the Duplacy library, eagerly undertook the revision, and it was a happy thought that when he published the work in 1986 it was dedicated to his former tutor. Another ecumenical link is that Amphoux, like Duplacy before him, continues to teach for the Faculté de théologie catholique at Lyons, and that faculty has been a partner in the Montpellier 'Centre' since 1988.

The publication of Vaganay – Amphoux generated a spin-off designed for more popular consumption that appeared in the distinguished monthly magazine *Le Monde de la Bible*. In its January – February 1987 issue it published a lengthy article by Amphoux, 'La Transmission des Evangiles'. In these two publications Francophone students and the interested general public were introduced to the study of textual criticism, to manuscripts, to early translations and to the history of the text. Those whose appetite had been whetted or curiosity aroused by text-critical notes in the *Bible de Jérusalem* and other modern versions or indeed by the critical apparatus of a Greek New Testament now found in the second edition of Vaganay's *Initiation* an easily assimilated and up-to-date assessment of the significance of manuscript variation in the New Testament.

Of course Vaganay – Amphoux's aim to instruct and to inform is not now restricted to readers of French. This translation should open up to a wider audience the latest teaching in France on the subject of the textual criticism of the New Testament. This introduction is indeed an initiation as the French title suggests. The approach is systematic and the author assumes no previous acquaintance with the subject matter. Both author and reviser are conscious of their didactic role as they seek to encourage their readers to see the significance of a subject that all too often, but needlessly, can alienate potential students because of the frequently technical nature of much of the academic discussion in the area.

For those who wish to continue their study in this field, advanced textbooks, some offering more controversial approaches, are available, and these are referred to in the present volume. But the book in hand is a cautious and careful guide for beginners. Issues that are in dispute are carefully explained, and the authors' obvious bias against the 'textus receptus' and their highly critical assessment of many pioneer textual critics are readily recognisable as prejudiced – although these pre-judices are widely shared.

Textual criticism is both a science and an art. The first two chapters are in a sense a description of the 'science' of textual criticism. Verifiable scholarship involves the classifying and collating of the manuscripts. In assessing the results of such 'scientific' work we turn to the 'art' of the subject, and inevitably this is where expert opinions often differ. When we move from the first two chapters which are largely descriptive to chapter 3 we enter into more controversial issues. Readers previously unfamiliar with French scholarship in this subject may perhaps be surprised by some of Amphoux's emphases here. Unlike many textual critics Amphoux is agnostic about finding the original text. Not for him the goal of restoring the wording of the autograph copies. His main concern is to chart the history of the text, attempting to get back to the great recensions and behind these to an early (but not necessarily original) form of the text. His high regard for the so-called 'Western' text, the significance of which is often denigrated by many textual critics, and his belief in its being a representation of a pre-recensional form of the text may surprise many. But this is a point of view that has had adherents in the French tradition, not least Duplacy himself. It is, incidentally, very significant just how frequently the views and works of Duplacy occur in this book.

Idiosyncratic views such as the above are not promoted in a doctrinaire or biassed way, but it should be noted that this approach and his suggested way forward at the end of chapter 4 are not universally followed. Even Amphoux is as aware as anyone that the creation of watertight compartments of text types is not practical, and he stresses quite rightly the great admixture in much of the New Testament textual tradition. His eclecticism and openness are refreshing and commendable.

The essence of Vaganay's original and even from time to time his tone of voice has been preserved; the subject has been brought up to date by a contemporary practitioner; the book is now available and adapted for English readers. Armed with this *Initiation*'s introduction to the sources, methodology and history of textual criticism, it is to be hoped that readers will seek to apply the science and art of textual criticism in the practical way of assessing variants in their reading of a critical edition of the New Testament. If this happens then the value of the original, the revision and now the translation will be fully justified.

It is of particular satisfaction to the undersigned, as I know it is also to Professor Amphoux himself, that this translation has been prepared by Mrs Jenny Heimerdinger, who has been a student of textual criticism under our tuition successively.

J.K. Elliott
University of Leeds

Translator's preface

This English translation of the second edition of Léon Vaganay's *Initiation à la critique textuelle du Nouveau Testament*, revised and updated by Christian-Bernard Amphoux, carries some further modifications made by the reviser and the translator, with the agreement of Les Editions du Cerf. These modifications concern, in particular, the first chapter, where the type of text has been added to the description of the manuscripts, and the Bibliography, which has been considerably amplified and re-arranged. Much help and advice has been gratefully received from Professor J. N. Birdsall whose extensive knowledge and soundness of scholarship have been greatly appreciated in the revisions he proposed on reading the French original. Dr. J. K. Elliott's skilful expertise has been equally valuable. Many thanks are due to him for writing the Foreword to this English edition; and for his patient and thorough reading of the translation and for the amendments he suggested. His encouragement throughout has been highly valued.

Jenny Heimerdinger

Foreword to the first French edition

In every collection of books there are some which get more or less put on one side. If there is one subject which is more austere than any other, even in a library like the 'Bibliothèque catholique des sciences religieuses', it is surely textual criticism. The most cultured minds do not always derive great pleasure from delving into the intricacies of this science. Some professional exegetes happily make do with a mere passing knowledge of it. It is something left to bookworms! Textual criticism is a stern character to whom much homage is paid but with whom close dealings are not often sought. But it also has a habit of paying back those who neglect it: their work always bears the stamp of lazy imprecision. 'Latin without tears' or 'Simple steps in Greek' may be all right but 'Textual criticism made easy' is an impossible challenge and we make no claim to have carried it out.

It has to be said that certain factors have not made the task any easier. There has been the unavoidable necessity of restricting the book to a limited length and of making it available to a wide public. To be honest, there are no gleanings for the specialist in this popularised work other than a few rather unusual ideas which it will amuse him to criticise. A theologian, or even a student of theology, would be right to reject it in favour of that rare species, a good manual. In any case, this work has no ambitions to be that kind of book. We have avoided discussions of too technical a nature and have provided more of a bird's-eye view. We have only given a more detailed account at those places where the information could be useful for future workers in the field. The informed layperson who wishes to have a glimpse of everything without getting stung in the process will probably be the least dissatisfied. He, at least, will not be able to hold it against us that we have presented the topic in a less dull way than usual. He will though, unfortunately, find plenty of things to try his patience. But being well taught himself, he will bear with us kindly as we teach the novices.

The worst problem of all is that there is no subject which dates so quickly as does textual criticism. By the time this work is published valuable new documents may well have come to light. Long before the edition has been sold out, the information will be out of date. The truth of it is that textual criticism is only in the early stages. Whether it be in the area of sources, method or history, the ground is still being cleared. There is just one small comfort for the critic: it is a child's first words which are the most enchanting. His stammerings and stutterings are full of promise, his unformed speech full of hope.

L. V.
Lyons, November 1933

Preface to the second French edition

It is never easy to write a book introducing a subject: it needs to be as complete and as simple as possible all at once. The job is harder still when there is no general work on the subject already, but only a host of smaller works on points of detail which far from cover the whole area, even taken together. Previous attempts by scholars to write an introduction have tended to focus on certain topics (as, for example, Metzger 1968 and Aland–Aland 1982).

In France, Jean Duplacy had gathered together over a period of twenty years or so a good deal of the material necessary for a general introduction to the textual criticism of the New Testament which would have constituted the foundation of a new handbook on the subject. But his work, though extensive, was never completed. Meanwhile, the need for such a handbook continued to be felt, and so when I was approached by Les Editions du Cerf, I agreed to revise and update the *Introduction* by Léon Vaganay.

There were two reasons behind my choice. First, fifty years after its first publication, this book is still the most clear-sighted survey of the subject. There was no point in looking for anything more elaborate which would have required considerable re-working. Secondly, information concerning textual criticism is so diverse and so extensive that it would have been impossible for me to write a completely new book within a reasonable length of time.

I have, therefore, taken up Vaganay's *Introduction*: I have added to it and, in the end, have written or re-written about half of it. I have tried to respect the length and the style of the first edition. But some parts are entirely new. In the chapter on sources, I have taken account of the new discoveries and also of the greater interest that exists today in the manuscripts of the early versions. In the chapter on method, room had to be made for the most recent studies, especially those of E. C. Colwell and J. Duplacy. I have naturally brought the chapter on the history of the printed text up to date. Vaganay's last chapter, which examined some individual variation units, never seemed to me to be very useful and so I have not included it. The most thorough revision, however, concerns the third chapter, on the history of the manuscript text. In the first part of the chapter, I have drawn extensively on my research, initially carried out in collaboration with Duplacy, on the history of the text before AD 200, with the result that I cannot promise that the views expressed there would still be those of Vaganay. There is nonetheless a strong underlying link between my contribution to the book and the work of Vaganay. Vaganay was searching for the original text of the New Testament, which he sensed to be closer to the 'Western' text than to the Alexandrian type. I believe that the research and discoveries made over the last fifty years have confirmed and refined this intuition and I try to take account of that. Furthermore, I was trained in this field by Jean Duplacy who was himself a student of Vaganay. It is, therefore, not surprising that I should generally find myself in close agreement with their ideas.

The current edition is chiefly designed for two kinds of public: on the one hand, all those who have an interest in the Bible and wish to know more about the circumstances in which the text was copied and fixed. On the other hand, it is for students of theology, both those tackling the New Testament for the first time at university level as well as more advanced students who need to know how to make the best use of a critical apparatus for their work in exegesis. In addition, certain pages may be of use to student linguists. These are essentially the people for whom the first edition, too, was written.

In the course of my work, I have drawn on the comments and the advice of certain friends who possess a variety of skills. Amongst them, I would like to mention Maurice Houis concerning questions of oral tradition; Joseph Trinquet, Bernard Outtier, Samir Arbache and Alain Desreumaux concerning the manuscripts of some of the early versions; Gilles Firmin concerning the early editions of the New Testament; Jean Irigoin, Julien Leroy and my colleagues from the 'Institut de recherche et d'histoire des textes' concerning questions of codicology; J. Paramelle who suggested some final corrections after reading the proofs. I express my gratitude to all. But I would in no way want to forget my students, both in Montpellier and in Lyons, who have helped me by their questions and their papers to understand certain points which Vaganay had left in the dark.

C.-B.A.
Montpellier, September 1985

Abbreviations

Anal. Boll.	*Analecta Bollandiana* (Brussels)
ANTF	*Arbeiten zur Neutestamentlichen Textforschung* (Berlin/New York)
BETL	*Bibliotheca Ephemeridum Theologicarum Lovaniensium* (Leuven)
Bib	*Biblica* (Rome)
BRJL	*Bulletin of the John Rylands Library* (Manchester)
CBQ	*Catholic Biblical Quarterly* (Washington, D.C.)
CCG	*Corpus Christianorum, Series Graeca* (Turnhout)
CCL	*Corpus Christianorum, Series Latina* (Turnhout)
CSCO	*Corpus Scriptorum Christianorum Orientalium* (Louvain)
CSEL	*Corpus Scriptorum Ecclesiasticorum Latinorum*, (Vienna)
DBS	*Dictionnaire de la Bible, Supplément* (Paris)
ETL	*Ephemerides Theologicae Lovanienses* (Leuven)
ETR	*Etudes Théologiques et Religieuses* (Montpellier)
GCS	*Die griechischen christlichen Schriftsteller der ersten drei Jahrhunderte* (Berlin)
HTR	*Harvard Theological Review* (Cambridge, Mass.)
JBL	*Journal of Biblical Literature* (Atlanta, Ga.)
JSNT	*Journal for the Study of the New Testament* (Sheffield)
JTS	*Journal of Theological Studies* (Oxford)
LOAPL	*Langues Orientales Anciennes, Philologie et Linguistique* (Paris)
Nov T	*Novum Testamentum* (Leiden)
NRT	*Nouvelle Revue Théologique* (Tournai)
NTS	*New Testament Studies* (Cambridge)
OC	*Oriens Christianus* (Rome)
PG	*Patrologia Graeca* (162 vols.), ed. J.P. Migne, 1857–66, Paris.
PL	*Patrologia Latina* (217 vols.), ed. J.P. Migne, 1844–55, Paris.

PO	*Patrologia Orientalis* (Turnhout)
PS	*Patrologia Syriaca* (Paris)
RB	*Revue Biblique* (Jerusalem)
RHPR	*Revue d'Histoire et de Philosophie Religieuses* (Strasbourg)
RHT	*Revue d'Histoire des Textes* (Paris)
RQ	*Restoration Quarterly* (Abilene, Tex.)
RSR	*Revue des Sciences Religieuses* (Strasbourg)
RTL	*Revue Théologique de Louvain* (Louvain-la-Neuve)
SC	*Sources Chrétiennes* (Paris)
S & D	*Studies and Documents* (Salt Lake City)
SP	*Studia Patristica* (Berlin)
TRNE	*Theological Review of the Near East* (Beirut)
TQ	*Theologische Quartalschrift* (Tübingen)
TRE	*Theologische Realenzyklopädie* (Berlin/New York)
TU	*Texte und Untersuchungen zur Geschichte der altchristlichen Literatur* (Berlin)
TextS	*Texts and Studies* (Cambridge)
VC	*Vetera Christianorum* (Bari)
ZNW	*Zeitschrift für die neutestamentliche Wissenschaft* (Berlin)

Note on the bibliographical references. The Bibliography is divided into seven sections; to assist the reader in following up references, the section number is given as a Roman numeral after each reference by author and date, except when the section is number VII. In the case of section VI, the abbreviation for the manuscript is given as well, where this will assist the reader in finding the manuscript referred to.

Introduction

THE PURPOSE AND THE ARRANGEMENT OF THIS BOOK

By 'textual criticism' is meant any methodical and objective study which aims to retrieve the original form of a text or at least the form closest to the original. Even in a modern book there are nearly always printing errors despite careful checking by the author and proof-readers, so it is not surprising that early writings, copied as they were many times over the centuries, should have frequently undergone alteration. And indeed, from time to time in the old manuscripts of a work different forms of the text can be observed. These different forms are known as 'variants'; they may also be referred to as divergent or erroneous readings.

The goal of textual criticism as applied to the New Testament is thus a very specific one, namely to select from among the many variants transmitted by the manuscript tradition the one which most likely represents the primitive reading. It is only when the contents of the whole text have been established that the other disciplines can operate: literary criticism, to decide the origin of each book and to locate the sources used by the author; historical criticism, to assess the value of the books as historical documents; exegesis, to define the exact meaning of the text. Clearly, on many questions there is interplay between all the different aspects of biblical criticism which often have to lend each other mutual support. Nevertheless, as a general rule, the original reading must be decided upon before anything else. The task of textual criticism may not be a high-ranking one but it is a no less important one for that.

It is, furthermore, a particularly arduous task. The obstacles encountered in seeking to restore a document of any kind are familiar. There is no problem as long as the document is an autograph, however old it may be, such as a private letter written on papyrus; it is simply a matter of indicating the obvious careless slips which the author failed

1

to notice as he was writing. The difficulties begin when the piece of writing was dictated or when there is only a copy of the original text available: account has to be taken of the scribe who may have made many mistakes, from simple slips of the pen to the most glaring faults. The job of discarding the erroneous readings becomes even less straightforward with a work which has been repeatedly copied and the extant copies of which were made a long time after the original: there is no hope of recognising all the errors which may have found their way into a text during a period for which no witnesses remain. Things are more complicated still when there are a large number of late copies with several equally plausible variants for different passages.

This is precisely the situation with New Testament textual criticism. In point of fact, the lapse of time between the original documents and the copies which have been handed down is relatively short: at worst, 250 years or so, since whole manuscripts from the fourth century have survived; and at best, no more than 100 years in the case of papyri dating from around AD 200. In this respect, no other work of early classical literature is in such a favourable position. There is a gap of over 1,000 years between the original composition and the extant manuscripts of the writings of Euripides, Sophocles, Aeschylus, Aristophanes, Thucydides, Plato and Demosthenes. With the Latin authors, the picture is slightly less bleak, but still not nearly as good as the situation of the New Testament writings. The gap is well over three centuries for the writings of Virgil, which are the best preserved.

What constitutes a handicap for New Testament textual criticism are the vast number of witnesses and the enormous number of variants. There are more than 5,000 Greek manuscripts or fragments of manuscripts, counting the lectionaries. And that is nowhere near the number of manuscripts of the versions (that is, the translations into foreign languages), let alone that of the quotations in the writings of the Church Fathers (several million) which help to make up the total sum of witnesses. That being the case, it is not hard to imagine how many thousands of variants there must be. Some say 150,000, others would say nearer 250,000, but the exact number is not really important. The fact is that it would be difficult to find a sentence, even part of a sentence, for which the rendering is consistent in every single manuscript. That certainly gives plenty of food for thought!

It is sometimes said that the greater the number of variants, the greater are the chances of finding the original reading, and attention is drawn to the disadvantageous position of early classical literature

2

for which the original text usually has to be reconstructed from only a small number of copies. In the best cases, for such authors as Euripides, Cicero or Virgil, there are only a few hundred manuscripts.

There is another side of the coin which tends to be forgotten. During the centuries prior to the date of the oldest extant manuscripts the books of the New Testament were copied much more frequently and consequently were subject to many more changes. Another negative factor is that, in the beginning at least, copying was generally carried out by amateur scribes whose skill did not match their enthusiasm. Finally, and most importantly, there are a great many places in the manuscripts of the New Testament (unlike those of more ordinary literature) where the alterations are deliberate and where it is not always easy to see what was the intention behind them. This explains something of the difficulty of New Testament textual criticism.

It would be wrong, however, to paint too black a picture. The great majority of the divergences in readings are to do with details of spelling, grammar or style and do not affect in any way the meaning of the text. True, these minor differences aside, there are a good number of variants which arouse the reader's curiosity by reason of some detail omitted or added to the text. Some are particularly interesting either because they involve a considerable portion of the text or because of their theological significance. In the latter case, though, as would be expected, the substance of Christian doctrine is never affected; rather such variants reflect the diversity of the text as it was known in the first Christian communities. The early papyri attest the overall integrity of the text. The alterations of the most daring revisers are proof of the limits they set themselves. Nevertheless, 'between this general soundness on which historical and theological deductions rely and a text which is perfectly identical to the original one, there is quite a considerable gap' (Lagrange 1929, p. clxv). The aim of textual criticism is to fill this gap.

The first job is to draw up a catalogue of the documents available. Chapter 1 provides a survey of these documents. The next step is to know how to make use of the material to hand and to establish fundamental rules which allow erroneous readings to be discarded; chapter 2 studies this question of method. Using these methodological principles, along with a thorough comparison of the variants, it is sometimes possible for the critic to come to some conclusions about the value of the various witnesses. Although this is a thorny subject, we have nevertheless presented an outline of the history of the text in chapter 3; our lack of knowledge on many of the major points in this area will be obvious but will also help to explain the reason behind changes of opinion amongst scholars. These groping explorations thus quickly lead to fresh questions: What has been done so far to restore the original text? What remains to be done? The answer is to be found in chapter 4: 'The history and the future of the printed text'.

1
The sources of textual criticism

It is usual to classify the witnesses which need to be consulted in order to establish the text of the New Testament into three main types. These are the Greek manuscripts, the versions and the quotations found in early writings. A preliminary task is to examine what might be termed the identifying marks of the witnesses, that is their age and their individual characteristics. That task is the object of this chapter which, by reason of its brevity, can present little more than a dry list and a rather incomplete one at that. But it can still be useful despite these limitations. The chapter begins with some prefatory remarks concerning the manuscripts in general, a natural introduction to the study of New Testament textual criticism.

THE MANUSCRIPTS IN GENERAL
MATERIALS AND FORMS

All kinds of materials have been used for writing on: stone, metals, terracotta, waxed tablets of wood and ivory, even pottery remains ('ostraka'). But the main materials are papyrus, parchment and paper and it is for writings on these that the term 'manuscript' is reserved.

The papyrus plant (πάπυρος) is a fibrous reed which used to grow in abundance along the marshy banks of the River Nile. The Egyptians were using it for writing before 2000 BC, and it appears to have been known to the Greeks in the seventh century BC. It was not, however, until the fifth century BC that it entered into general use, first among the Greeks, and then among the Romans. In the writings of Pliny (*Naturalis historia* XIII, 21–6), there are some indications as to how papyrus was made. The inside of the reed (the pith) was cut lengthwise into thin strips which were laid across each other in two layers at right angles and then pressed together. When the fabric was dry, it was polished and then coated with wax so as to be ready for writing on (χάρτης). Papyrus remained in general use until the Arab conquest of

5

Egypt in the seventh century AD when its importation became practically impossible. The first discoveries of papyrus manuscripts were made in the eighteenth century, since when large numbers of these literary treasures have been found, mostly in Egypt where the dry climate favours the preservation of such fragile materials.

The age of papyrus was succeeded by the age of parchment. Hides of animals had been used for writing since very early times and, outside Egypt, were the chief writing material until papyrus became common in the fifth century BC. The oldest Greek parchment known dates from the end of the third or the beginning of the second century BC and was found at Dura-Europos in the Euphrates valley some seventy years ago. Tradition has it that when one of the Ptolemaean kings refused to send papyrus to the people of Pergamum it was they who invented a method of preparing skins that made writing on them less arduous than it had been previously. The animal skin, usually a sheep's, instead of being tanned was softened in a solution of lime and then scraped with a knife in order to take off the hairy or greasy parts, before being finally polished with a pumice stone. This is how 'parchment', or skin of Pergamum, got its name (περγαμηνή, *pergamena*; also known as μεμβράνα, *membrana*), and it was then that this new material, being strong enough to allow for mistakes to be scratched away, began to compete both with tablets and with papyrus for things like rough work, sketches and anything needing retouching. Later, as it became less expensive, parchment was preferred for literary texts, and for other important work generally. Finally, from around AD 650, when papyrus became rare, parchment predominated until the fourteenth century.

Then it was the turn of paper to take over. Its place and date of origin are somewhat uncertain; it does not seem to have been known in Syria or Egypt until after the taking of Samarkand by the Arabs in AD 707. Distinction can be made between, on the one hand, oriental paper or 'bombycine' which is of Arab invention and manufacture, and, on the other hand, paper of different sorts manufactured in the West. Of the latter, the earliest was that made in Spain from the tenth century, which resembles the paper of Arabic origin; but later types have their own characteristic format (e.g. Catalan paper, mid-twelfth century). The Italian paper (early thirteenth century) which was the first to have watermarks (1280, in Fabriano) replaced all the other Western papers from the fourteenth century. The fragile nature of paper, its high cost and its Arabic origin prevented it from being widely known for a long time. It was parchment which continued to be generally used for finer

6

copies, particularly for the sacred books. Paper finally took over completely with the invention of printing.

As to the form of the manuscripts, they were either made as a scroll (*volumen*) or as a square book (*quadratus*), the scroll being the older of the two forms. One individual sheet of parchment or papyrus could be used only for short documents such as letters or contracts, and so, for longer texts, the sheets were joined together so as to make a scroll about ten metres in length. The much longer papyrus scrolls which have been found in tombs appear to have been made *ad hoc*. It was usual to attach a roller to the end of the scroll and sometimes even to the beginning as well, so enabling the scroll to be rolled up as the reading of it progressed.

Towards the end of the first century AD the codex entered into use. It had already been customary to fasten several waxed tablets together with one or more threads and this practice was later extended to the tying together of sheets of parchment or papyrus. These would be folded and sewn together in quires. This is the origin of the modern book. It was much easier to handle a codex than a scroll and, in addition, a codex could hold more than a scroll; yet despite these advantages it was only gradually that it replaced the scroll, such is the force of habit. It is interesting to note that the Christians were among the first to use the papyrus codex, when they came to write their sacred books. The oldest New Testament papyrus fragment, dating from the first half of the second century, comes from a codex (P^{52}). From the same period, there is a copy of Numbers and Deuteronomy which is a combination of a papyrus scroll and a parchment codex. From the fourth century onwards, the codex form became general.

WRITING

Writing instruments

For writing on waxed tablets the stylus (στῦλος) was used, a pointed stick usually made of metal and with a flattened end for making erasions. For writing on papyrus or parchment a reed cut like a quill (κάλαμος, *calamus*), was the usual instrument. Later quills were made from bird feathers, particularly goose feathers. Black ink was ordinarily used (μέλαν, *atramentum*), though red ink (*rubrica*) was also known. Writing with metal inks, that is silver or gold, on purple-dyed parchment was reserved for *de luxe* editions.

The form of the letters

This is a question of great importance from a palaeographic point of view. There are essentially three main types of writing. The capital letters are tall, regular and separated from one another as in inscriptions. The majuscule letters differ from them in that some of the letters have a more rounded shape and the writing of the majuscules was performed with greater speed; they are often referred to as uncials, a hyperbolic allusion to their size as if they were an inch high. Five main types of uncials are found in Greek New Testament manuscripts, varying according to their date: Roman (second – third century); biblical (fourth – fifth century); Coptic (sixth – seventh century); ogival (fifth century onwards); round liturgical (eighth century onwards). It is more difficult to classify the various kinds of minuscule letters, which vary greatly in shape according to the geographical origin and even the contents of the texts, and do not always correspond to an exact period. The general characteristics are that they are small and joined up; this latter feature has given rise to the designation 'cursive' (running hand), but this is not an entirely accurate label: the joining of the letters is not always a feature of the minuscules and, furthermore, it is sometimes present in the majuscules.

In writings on papyrus the minuscule was used for documents concerning daily life, whereas for literary documents the majuscule was usually – but not always – used, either detached or joined. In parchment manuscripts, scribes used only uncial letters until the ninth century; from then on they began to use minuscules and finally minuscules took over completely in the eleventh century. As for capitals, apart from some Latin manuscripts, they were hardly used at all except for the titles of books. As a final note, it may be added that a number of manuscripts display a curious mixture of uncial and minuscule letters, an indication of the transition which was taking place from capitals to a freer style of writing.

Presentation and punctuation

As a general rule, in the uncial manuscripts the words are not separated from each other but the writing is continuous (*scriptio continua*). It is not until the eleventh century, and then only in the Latin manuscripts, that there exists any kind of systematic separation of words or sections of the text. There is, however, a sign, which takes on a variety of shapes, to indicate the end of a paragraph (παράγραφος, *paragraphos*).

8

Punctuation and accentuation were not unknown in ancient manuscripts but were of a very elementary nature until the seventh century. In the later manuscripts, abbreviations abound. The information provided in the title (*inscriptio*) is often reproduced or added to in a final note (*subscriptio*). It sometimes happens, too, that mention is made of the number of lines (στίχος, *stichos*, a line of sixteen syllables) contained in the book, a commercial procedure known as stichometry, used as a means to calculate the payment due to the scribe.

In books that were meant to be read in public the text was sometimes divided up into sections according to sense, a procedure followed by the schools of rhetoric, whereby a new line was started after each group of words which could be spoken together. Phrases may be long (κῶλον, *colon*) or short (κόμμα, *comma*), hence Jerome's description of division *per cola et commata* (Preface to the translation of Isaiah).

Palimpsests (πάλιν, *'again'*; ψάω, *'to rub'*)

This is the word used to describe manuscripts on parchment, very occasionally on papyrus, which have been rubbed clean of their writing in order to be written on a second, or even a third time. It was quite a common practice between the sixth and ninth centuries when papyrus and parchment were in short supply. The original text of a palimpsest is often of great value for the history of classical literature or the study of the Bible. They were initially read with the help of chemical substances such as gall-nut which used to cause serious damage to the manuscripts. These chemicals have now been replaced by ultra-violet rays.

DATE AND PLACE OF ORIGIN

A note written by the scribe at the end of a manuscript indicating its date and country of origin, known as a *colophon*, is a custom going back to very early times, but unfortunately it is only found in a few manuscripts and at certain times, such as during the Carolingian period or in the fifteenth-century Renaissance. Where any such indication is absent the date and place of origin of a manuscript are determined, with a varying degree of precision, by examining the manufacture of the book (codicology), or the details of the writing and copying (palaeography), or the characteristic aspects of the text it contains. The smallest details can be important: the material used for writing on, the type of binding and the end leaves, the stitching; the format, the arrangement of the quires, and their ruling and numbering; the page lay-out, the shape and beauty of the letters, the abbreviations; the colour and quality of the ink, the decoration of the illuminated bands, titles, initial letters, and the illustrations; any writing not in the actual text such as titles, red letters, glosses and notes in the margin, inscriptions of dedication or concerning the owner; and finally, in the text itself, the order of the contents, the divisions of the text, the variant readings, the missing words ('lacunae'), the punctuation, the accentuation, even the musical notation. None of these details is irrelevant to the philologist. For the purposes of gathering together information about as many manuscripts as possible, there are computer databases which either exist already or are in the process of being set up.

Anyone who is interested in these questions, and who is unable to gain easy access to the libraries, could consult some of the specialised works which include a great variety of samples of literary manuscripts, both secular and biblical. Particular mention may be made of the collection made by H. Follieri (1969) and also *La Paléographie grecque et byzantine* (International CNRS Colloque 559 (Oct. 1974), Paris 1977). For further works, see the bibliography in Dain 1975 and Reynolds – Wilson 1974).

THE GREEK MANUSCRIPTS

A list of the Greek manuscripts was first compiled at the beginning of the century by C. R. Gregory and later continued by E. von Dobschütz. More recently, it has been brought up to date and revised by K. Aland (1963 (V)) with additional supplements which continue to be published periodically (1969, pp. 22 – 37; 1972, 1974, 1977, 1982, 1985, 1988 (V)). But Aland's list is not entirely exhaustive; new manuscripts sometimes come to light in private collections, or as a result of archaeological discoveries as was the case at Mount Sinai in 1975 (see B. Aland 1985, Junack *et al*. 1989, Politis 1980; see also below p. 163). The manuscripts can be divided into four categories, of somewhat unequal importance, according to the material from which they are made, their type of script and the use for which they were intended: these are the papyri, the uncials, the minuscules and the lectionaries. These will now be discussed in order, with a paragraph at the end on ostraka and talismans.

Chapter one

THE PAPYRI

There are ninety-six known New Testament papyrus manuscripts, designated by the letter P followed by a superscript number. Most of them come originally from Egypt although, for obvious reasons, the exact location of their discovery is kept a careful secret by their vendors. They are now scattered in libraries throughout Europe and America.

These Greek papyri, some of them bilingual in Greek and Coptic, such as P^6 (see p. 38 on Coptic versions), cover a wide span of time (second to seventh century). They are, for the most part, the remains of books, although a few, for example P^{18} and P^{22}, are fragments of scrolls. Some are so short as to comprise only one leaf, or even one verse, such as P^{12} which contains Hb 1:1. More usually, they consist of several leaves which may have been brought to light over a period of many years, as was the case with P^5. The longest are the Chester Beatty papyri in Dublin ($P^{45\ 46\ 47}$) and the Bodmer papyri in Cologny/Geneva ($P^{66\ 72\ 74\ 75}$) which deserve special mention. Another important papyrus is P^{13}, containing about a third of the Epistle to the Hebrews. With the exception of two of Paul's letters (1 – 2 Timothy) almost all the New Testament books are represented on the papyri. Two recent works with lists of the New Testament papyri may be usefully consulted: Aland 1976 (V) and van Haelst 1976 (V). The latter gives details of papyrus and parchment manuscripts which are not in Aland's list but which, in part of their contents at least, have passages from the New Testament. A second edition of van Haelst's catalogue is being prepared.

The Chester Beatty papyri

The New Testament section of these papyri, P^{45}, P^{46} and P^{47}, has been published by F. G. Kenyon 1933 – 7 (VI). There are several fragments from three distinct manuscripts. All three are in codex form, which is a point of great importance for the history of the Bible and of books generally (see p. 7 above). They are also all from the third century and together they present a witness to the four major elements of the New Testament (the Gospels, Acts and the Catholic Epistles, the Pauline Epistles, Revelation) and in this respect are unique up to the fourth century. Individually, however, each manuscript is incomplete, with many sheets missing and with those remaining damaged to a greater or lesser extent.

The earliest manuscript, P^{45}, contains the four Gospels and Acts.

There are only thirty leaves remaining out of about 110: Matthew (two), Mark (six), Luke (seven), John (two), Acts (thirteen). The Gospels appear to have been arranged in the order Matthew – John – Luke – Mark, but it is uncertain. The book was made up of separate sheets folded in two. One of the thirty leaves is kept in Vienna. Text type: Caesarean (see p. 104).

The second manuscript, P^{46} (about AD 200) was discovered in several stages. There are in all eighty-six leaves out of an original 104 which were made by folding in half fifty-two larger sheets placed together, to form one quire. The outside leaves from the beginning and the end of the book are the ones which are missing. P^{46} contains the Pauline Epistles in a special order: Romans – Hebrews – 1 Corinthians – 2 Corinthians – Ephesians – Galatians – Philippians – Colossians – 1 Thessalonians ... (the rest have disappeared). Thirty leaves of the manuscript are kept at Ann Arbor (Mich.). Text type: Caesarean (see p. 104).

The third manuscript, P^{47} (end of the third century), consisting of ten leaves, contains a large section of Revelation (9:10 – 17:2).

The Bodmer papryi

The Bodmer collection consists of papryi in Greek and Coptic, both biblical and other. There are five which have parts of the New Testament. P^{73} is a small fragment of Matthew which was discovered stuck between two leaves of P^{74}. The other manuscripts contain a large part of the Gospels, Acts and the Catholic Epistles, sometimes in excellent condition. They have been published in Cologny/Geneva by V. Martin 1956, 1958, 1962 (VI); M. Testuz 1959 (VI); V. Martin and R. Kasser 1961 (VI); R. Kasser 1961 (VI).

P. Bodmer II (P^{66}) contains almost all of John's Gospel up to chapter 14 (only 6:12 – 34 is missing) and fragments of the rest of it. The book has traces of a binding and was made up of quires of unequal size (four to eight double sheets) with the well-preserved leaves being from the first five quires. A fragment of a leaf is in the Chester Beatty Library. P^{66} is the oldest of the biblical Bodmer papyri (towards AD 200, perhaps earlier). Text type: pre-Alexandrian (see p. 107; see also p. 97).

P. Bodmer VII – IX (P^{72}) contains in their entirety three Catholic Epistles, 1 – 2 Peter and Jude. The book was made at the beginning of the fourth century by gathering together a mixture of texts which had been copied in the third century for private use. Jude and 1 – 2 Peter have, respectively, seven and thirty-six numbered pages out of an original total of about 180. The book is made up of quires consisting of four sheets folded together, known as *quaternions*, with two sheets folded separately at the end of the book. Text type: Caesarean (see p. 105).

P. Bodmer XIV – XV (P[75]) contains the Gospels of Luke and John with lacunae. As with P[46], the sheets were placed on top of each other and folded together to form one quire. There were thirty-six sheets, or seventy-two leaves, originally, but only fifty-one are left and some of those are in a very fragmentary state. The manuscript dates from the first half of the third century. It has an elongated format (26 x 13 cm) in contrast to the almost square format of P[66] (16 x 14 cm). Text type: Alexandrian (see p. 107).

P. Bodmer XVII (P[74]) is much more recent (seventh century) and of less interest. It contains Acts in quite good condition and fragments of the Catholic Epistles. Of the original 132 leaves, scarcely half have preserved their text intact. While it is true that manuscripts in this period are rare, yet its text is close to that of the uncials from two or three centuries earlier. Text type: Alexandrian (see p. 109).

Thus, apart from this last manuscript, and in spite of the frequent lacunae, the Chester Beatty and Bodmer papyri represent documents of the greatest importance for the study of the New Testament text as it was known in Egypt at the end of the second century and in the third century.

THE UNCIALS

General survey

There are 299 known uncial manuscripts or fragments of manuscripts on parchment. Most of the fragments come from different manuscripts but twenty-four of them have been wrongly counted as separate from the actual manuscript they belong to. There are for example nine numbers which all represent MS 070 (Schmitz 1982). In the list of manuscripts used today, the redundant numbers are written in brackets and the number which has been retained is given instead. For the time being, it is best to leave the naming of the uncials as it stands.

For a long time, the system used for identifying the manuscripts was a complicated one. The manuscripts were divided according to their contents into four groups: Gospels (e), Acts and the Catholic Epistles (a), the Pauline Epistles (p) and Revelation (r). Then, in each of these groups, each manuscript was assigned a capital letter (Latin, Greek or Hebrew), the letters being repeated for the four groups. It is not difficult to see how inconvenient such a system was. Not only is the same letter used to refer to different manuscripts which then have to be further identified by a secondary annotation (D^c, D^p, E_1, E_2, E_3), but in addition, in the first group, there were too many manuscripts for the letters available and indices had to be used. Both these problems lead to confusion but it was the system used by C. Tischendorf, and by C. R. Gregory at first until he devised the current system.

H. von Soden suggested a new system of numbering but it was not generally adopted, being too complicated. It is nevertheless worthwhile to be familiar with his system so as to be able to make use of his edition (see pp. 155 – 8). The revised system of Gregory is the one which is used today. Each manuscript or fragment is designated by a number in arabic figures preceded by a nought. However, in the case of the first forty-five uncials, they continue to be known by the capital letters which they were assigned in the initial system. In order to avoid getting totally lost, the beginner would do well to study carefully the introductions and the appendices to the contemporary editions of the New Testament (United Bible Societies 1983[3a] = UBS[3a]; see 1966 – (III); Nestle – Aland 1979[26] = Nestle – Aland[26]; see 1898 – (III). We advocate the designation of an uncial by its number preceded by a nought, with its letter first and possibly, though not necessarily, a full stop between the letter and the number; thus, for Codex Vaticanus, B.03 or B03, but not B on its own.

It is curious that, among all these uncial manuscripts, no more than five should contain either at present (S.01) or originally (A.02, B.03, C.04, Ψ.044) the whole of the New Testament. All the other witnesses contain only a part of it and even then often in a mutilated condition. Moreover, there are only nine complete copies of the Gospels, seven of Acts, nine of the Catholic Epistles, seven of the Pauline Epistles, and four of Revelation. The great majority of the uncial manuscripts, almost 200 of them, are no more than fragments, in some cases of only a few verses. As would be expected, the Gospels are by far the best represented (138 witnesses) whereas Revelation has only nine witnesses. Some of the manuscripts are bilingual (Greek – Latin, Greek – Coptic, etc.), with the translation in either a parallel column or on a facing page, more rarely in interlinear form. There are numerous traces of corrections and these are indicated in the apparatus by a number or letter in superscript following the manuscript letter, an asterisk indicating an original reading (B* B^c C* C^2 C^3).

It is usually difficult to establish where exactly the uncials came from originally because they often travelled around a great deal before finally arriving in the libraries. The exact year of their writing is likewise only known in exceptional cases, in fact even the century may not be certain especially for the very short fragments. Generally speaking, they date from the fourth to the tenth century, there being about twenty, in addition to B.03 and S.01, from the fourth century itself (057, 059, 0160, 0162, 0169, 0171, etc.) or earlier still (0189, 0220). Before the discovery of the papyri, it was the uncials which, thanks to their antiquity, were regarded with particular favour and affection. Nowadays scholars are more critical, and it is commonly accepted that the date of a manuscript is of much less importance than the text which it represents.

Particular manuscripts

The description in this section of the more significant manuscripts will be limited to some remarks concerning their external features and a brief note on the type of text they represent. More information on the text types can be found in the later section dealing with the different New Testament recensions (pp. 98 – 110).

Codex Sinaiticus (ℵ or S.01), of the fourth century, was discovered by Tischendorf in St Catherine's Monastery on Mount Sinai (1844 – 59). It was taken to Leningrad and transferred to the British Library in London in 1933. In addition to the New Testament, it contains almost all of the Old Testament (some of the missing leaves were found at Sinai in 1975), the Epistle of Barnabas and about a third of *The Shepherd* of Hermas. The text was written in four columns and was amended by seven correctors. There is a facsimile edition of the New Testament by K. Lake (1911; S.01 (VI)). Text type: Alexandrian (see p. 108 and see also p. 97).

Codex Alexandrinus (A.02), of the fifth century, was written in Egypt and, after being in the possession of the Patriarch of Alexandria since 1098, was brought to London in 1628, where it is now kept at the British Library. It is written in two columns and contains the Old and the New Testaments as well as the two Epistles of Clement of Rome, though with large parts missing. There is a reduced facsimile edition of the New Testament by F. G. Kenyon (1909; A.02 (VI)). Text types: Syro-Byzantine and Alexandrian (see p. 109 and p. 108).

Codex Vaticanus (B.03), of the fourth century, is one of the most valuable uncial manuscripts and has been kept in the Vatican Library in Rome since some time between 1475 and 1481. It contains, set out in three columns, the Old and the New Testament, although both of them are damaged, the former at the beginning, the latter at the end. There exists a facsimile edition of the New Testament (Milan, 1904; B.03 (VI)); and a colour reproduction of the manuscript, with an introduction by C. M. Martini, was prepared for the bishops at the Second Vatican Council (1968; B.03 (VI)). Text type: Alexandrian (see p. 108).

Codex Ephraemi rescriptus (C.04), of the fifth century, originated in Egypt and was brought by Catherine de Medici to Paris where it is kept in the Bibliothèque Nationale. A palimpsest manuscript, it originally contained the whole Bible which was replaced in the twelfth century by a Greek version of several of Ephraem's treatises. It now consists of no more than some portions of the Old Testament and about two thirds of the New Testament. There is a rather poor edition of the manuscript by C. Tischendorf (1843–5; C.04 (VI)). Text types: Alexandrian and Caesarean (see p. 108 and p. 105).

Codex Bezae Cantabrigiensis (D.05 Greek/d Latin), is from the fourth/fifth century. It was kept in Lyons from the ninth century until 1562, receiving mention by the Council of Trent in 1546 for the interest of its variant readings. In 1562, it was acquired by Théodore de Bèze (Beza) who gave it to the University of Cambridge (1581) where it has remained ever since. It is a bilingual Greek and Latin manuscript containing the four Gospels (in the order Matthew–John–Luke–Mark) and Acts, which have been preserved with lacunae in both the Greek and the Latin texts, and also the Catholic Epistles of which only the end of 3 John remains. On the question of the origin of this manuscript see the article by J. N. Birdsall (1986). There is an excellent facsimile edition (1899; D.05 (VI)) as well as a transcript edition by F. H. Scrivener (1864, reprint 1978; D.05 (VI)). It has a 'Western' text (see p. 110 and pp. 91–7).

Codex Claromontanus (D.06 Greek/d Latin), of the sixth century, was bought by Beza from the monastery of Clermont in Beauvaisis (France) and is now kept in the Bibliothèque Nationale in Paris. Like the previous manuscript, it also has a bilingual Greek–Latin text but contains only the Pauline Epistles with lacunae. Between the Epistles to Philemon and to the Hebrews there is a stichometric list of sacred books. An old edition of the manuscript exists by Tischendorf (1852; D.06 (VI)). Text type: 'Western' = Caesarean (see p. 106).

Codex Freerianus or the Freer Codex (W.032), of the fifth century, originated in Egypt but was bought from an Arabian merchant by C. L. Freer in 1906 and is now in Washington (Freer Gallery of Art). This is a highly valuable manuscript consisting of twenty-six quires of unequal size (four to eight leaves, see p. 7); it contains the four Gospels, once again in the order Matthew – John – Luke – Mark, with some lacunae. After Mk 16:14, there is a curious addition sometimes known as the 'Freer logion'. An excellent facsimile edition exists, by H. A. Sanders (1912; W.032 (VI)). It displays various text types (see p. 97, p. 104, p. 108 and p. 109).

Codex Koridethi (Θ.038) is of uncertain date, possibly the ninth century, and is kept in Tbilisi (Georgia, USSR) but notes in the margin make frequent mention of Koridethi. The copyist of the manuscript was, in all probability, Georgian. It contains the four Gospels almost in their entirety. There is a good edition by G. Beerman and C. R. Gregory (1913; Θ.038 (VI)). See also a note by J. N. Birdsall (*Classical Review* 33 (1983), p. 305, n. 5) for some suggestions about the palaeography of Codex Koridethi. Text type: Caesarean (see p. 104).

Finally, mention may be made of Codex Ψ.044 of the eighth/ninth century and kept on Mount Athos (Monastery of The Great Lavra). It contains the Gospels, Acts and the Epistles with few lacunae. Text type: Alexandrian (see p. 108).

Of the other uncials which are of any considerable length, the following are the more significant for textual criticism:

1. Manuscripts of the Gospels: first, the group composed of L.019, T.029, Z.035, Δ.037, of an Alexandrian text type (see p. 108); secondly, the series E.07, F.09, G.011, H.013 on the one hand, and on the other the series S.028, V.031, Ω.045, which are of a Syro-Byzantine type (see p. 109) and frequently stand together, in agreement with the mass of the minuscules but against the preceding group; thirdly, the purple manuscripts N.022, O.023, Σ.042, Φ.043, which have more than one variant in common with Θ.038 (see p. 104).

2. A manuscript of Acts: Codex Laudianus (E.08/e), a bilingual Greek – Latin manuscript from the sixth century, kept in the Bodleian Library in Oxford. 'Western' text (see p. 97).

3. Manuscripts of the Pauline Epistles: Codex Augiensis (F.010/f), kept in Trinity College, Cambridge and edited by F. H. Scrivener (1859), and Codex Boernerianus (G.012/g), kept in Dresden (facsimile

ΚΑΙ   ΚΩΛΝ

CΗΜΕΝωΝΠΟΙωΘΑΝΑΤωΔΟΞΑCΕΙΤΟΝΘΝ
ΚΑΙΤΟΥΤΟCΕΠΙωΝΛΕΓΕΙΑΥΤωΑΚΟΛΟΥΘΕΙΜΟΙ
ΕΠΙCΤΡΑΦΕΙCΔΕΟΠΕΤΡΟCΒΛΕΠΕΙΤΟΝΜΑΘΗΤΗΝ
ΟΝΗΓΑΠΑΙΗC ΑΚΟΛΟΥΘΟΥΝΤΑ
ΟCΚΑΙΑΝΕΠΕCΕΝΕΝΤωΔΕΙΠΝω
ΕΠΙΤΟCΤΗΘΟCΑΥΤΟΥ ΚΑΙΕΠΕΝΑΥΤω
ΚΕ ΤΙCΕCΤΙΝΟΠΑΡΑΔΙΔωΝCΕ
ΤΟΥΤΟΝΟΥΝΕΙΔωΝΟΠΕΤΡΟCΛΕΓΕΙΑΥΤωΙΗΥ
ΚΕ ΟΥΤΟCΔΕΤΙ ΛΕΓΕΙΑΥΤωΟΙΗC
ΕΑΝΑΥΤΟΝΘΕΛωΜΕΝΕΙΝΟΥΤωC
ΕωCΕΡΧΟΜΑΙΓΙΠΡΟCCΕ CΥΜΟΙΑΚΟΛΟΥΘΕΙ
ΕΞΗΛΘΕΝΟΥΝΟΥΤΟCΟΛΟΓΟCΕΙCΤΟΥC
ΑΔΕΛΦΟΥC ΚΑΙΕΔΟΞΑΝΟΤΙΟΜΑΘΗΤΗC
ΕΚΕΙΝΟCΟΥΚΑΠΟΘΝΗCΚΕΙ ΚΑΙΟΥΚΕΠΕΝΑΥΤΟ
ΟΙΗC ΟΥΚΑΠΟΘΝΗCΚΕΙC ΑΛΛΑΕΑΝΑΥΤΟΝ
ΘΕΛωΜΕΝΕΙΝ ΕωCΕΡΧΟΜΑΙΠΡΟCCΕ
ΟΤΟCΕCΤΙΝΟΜΑΘΗΤΗC ΟΜΑΡΤΥΡωΝ
ΠΕΡΙΤΟΥΤωΝ ΚΑΙΟΓΡΑΨΑCΤΑΥΤΑ
ΚΑΙΟΙΔΑΜΕΝΟΤΙΑΛΗΘΗCΕCΤΙΝΑΥΤΟΥ
ΗΜΑΡΤΥΡΙΑ ΕCΤΙΝΔΕΚΑΙΑΛΛΑΠΟΛΛΑ
ΟCΑΕΠΟΙΗCΕΝΟΧΡCΙΗC ΑΤΙΝΑ
ΕΑΝΓΡΑΦΗΤΑΙΚΑΘΕΝ ΟΥΔΑΥΤΟΝ
ΟΙΜΑΙΤΟΝΚΟCΜΟΝΧωΡΗCΕ
ΤΑΓΡΑΦΟΜΕΝΑΒΙΒΛΕΙΑ

ΕΥΑΓΓΕΛΙΟΝ ΚΑΤΑ

ΙωΑΝΗΝ ΕΤΕΛΕCΘΗ

ΑΡΧΕΤΑΙ ΕΥΑΓΓΕΛΙΟΝ

ΚΑΤΑ ΛΟΥΚΑΝ

1 An uncial manuscript, D.05. The Greek page is on the left, the Latin on the right. This is the famous Codex Bezae which probably has the text closest to the original of the Gospels and Acts. Here, the end of John's Gospel can be seen.

ɔҽɕ ɪoɦaꝶ

SIGNIFICANSQUAMORTEHONORIFICAbITDM
EThoccumdIXISSETdICITILLISEGUEREME
CONUERSUSAUTEMPETRUSUIDETdISCIPulum
quemdILIGEbATIHS SEQUENTEM
quIETRECUbUITINCENA
SUPERPECTUSEIUS ETdIXITILLI
dME QUISESTQUITRADIDITTE
huNCERGOUIDENS PETRUSdICITADIHM
dME hICAUTEMQUId · dICITILLIIHS
SIEUMUOLOGICMANERE
USGUEdUMUENIO QUIdADTETUMESEGUERE
EXIUITERGOhICUERbUS APUTFRATRES
ETPUTAUERUNTQUONIAMdISCIPULUS
ILLE NONMORITURETNONdIXITILLUd
IHS NONMORIERIS SEdSIEUM
UOLOMANERE USGUEdUMUENIOQUIdADTE
hICESTdISCIPUS QUITESTIMONIUMdAT
dEhIS ETQUISCRIPSIThAEC
ETSCIMUS QUONIAMUERUMEST EIUS
TESTIMONIUM SUNTAUTEM ETALIAPLURA
QUAEFECITXPSIHS QUAE
SISCRIbANTUR SINGULARITERNECIPSUM
FACILEPUTOMUNDUM CAPERE
QUISCRIbUNTURLIbRI

EUĀNGELIUM SECŪNd
IOhĀNEN EXPLICIT
INCIPIT EUĀNGELIUM
SEC LUCĀN

2 The same. The subscription also introduces the beginning of the Gospel of Luke; in this manuscript, John is the second Gospel and Mark is the fourth. (Photos taken from the facsimile edition by F. H. Scrivener, 1899.)

19

edition 1909); both are ninth century, bilingual manuscripts whose readings often agree with those of Codex Claromontanus (D.06, see p. 104). Apart from these there is also Codex Coislinianus (H.015), of the sixth century and in such a bad condition that its forty-one leaves are scattered in seven libraries, twenty-two of them in the Bibliothèque Nationale in Paris under two different numbers. There is an edition by M. H. Omont (1889; H.015 (VI)). According to a note in the manuscript, the text was collated at Caesarea with a copy written by Pamphilus although it appears to have an Alexandrian text type (see p. 108).

4. Two manuscripts of Revelation: Codex Vaticanus (046, formerly B^r), of the eighth century, not to be confused with the famous B.03 mentioned above (which no longer has Revelation); Codex Porphyrianus (P.025) of the ninth century, which contains in addition Acts and the Epistles; it is kept in Leningrad and has a special text type (see Schmid 1955–6).

As for the other uncials, the study of their text is making good progress. The most interesting are mere fragments: 0169, fourth century, the remains of a small book (9.5 x 8 cm) with Rv 3:19–4.3 (see Metzger 1981, pp. 72–3); 0171, around AD 300, a fragment of Luke's Gospel (22:44–56, 61–3), whose text is close to that of Codex Bezae (see Aland–Aland 1982, Eng. trans. (1989), p. 104); 0188, seventh century, a leaf of Mark's Gospel, (11:11–17) with an unusual text (see Salonius 1927, pp. 100–2, and Treu 1961); 0121a (1–2 Corinthians), 0121b (Hebrews), 0243 (1–2 Corinthians), tenth century, have an early form of the Pauline Epistles.

THE MINUSCULES

According to current figures, there are 2,811 minuscule manuscripts or fragments of such. J. J. Wettstein, in 1751 (III), was the first to designate them with Arabic numerals (see p. 141) but his system was somewhat complicated. As with the uncials, the minuscule manuscripts were divided into four groups according to their contents: the Gospels (e), Acts and the Catholic Epistles (a), the Pauline Epistles (p) and Revelation (r), and the numbers repeated for each class. This was the system used by C. Tischendorf, and also C. Gregory at first, but it had two major drawbacks. On the one hand, if a manuscript contained the whole of the New Testament it sometimes had four different numbers assigned to it. And on the other hand, the same number could refer to several different manuscripts. A further problem was that the German and English scholars could not even agree on the numbering.

H. von Soden proposed a new system in 1902 but it failed to work (see p. 155). By common consent, it is Gregory's revised system of 1908 which is used today. In this, there is one number for each manuscript and one manuscript for each number. For some strange reason, there are five exceptions to this rule, namely numbers 1, 2, 4, 7 and 36 which are each used for two manuscripts with different contents. The simplest and most practical way round the problem is to add a small index letter (e, a, p or r) after the number to show which Codex is meant in each case. The current list has some other irregularities: twenty-five manuscripts have a number which has already been assigned to another manuscript and therefore have the mention 'abs' (= copy) or a further letter (b, c, d, e) added to the number, and fifty further manuscripts have been given a number when, in fact, they are part of another numbered manuscript. Finally, three numbers have never been used (1825, 2171, 2395). The result is that there are in reality a total of about 2,785 separate minuscule manuscripts.

Only about fifty of these ever contained the whole of the New Testament. Like the uncials, most have only the Gospels, and Revelation is represented least. On the other hand, they have, more often than the uncials, additions of various sorts such as a catalogue of the seventy disciples, a biography of the Apostles, a summary of Paul's journeys. Where these are present, they suggest that the manuscript is of a later date.

In fact, the minuscule manuscripts do not appear until the ninth century. The oldest dated minuscule, 461 (Uspenski, a text of the four Gospels kept in Leningrad), has the date: 7 May 6343 (the year 835 in our calendar) and is thus older than some of the uncials. There are only a few minuscules which date from as early as the ninth century, less than twenty in fact for the New Testament. From the following century, however, there are nearly 130. The majority of the manuscripts were copied in the twelfth, thirteenth and fourteenth centuries, the age when production was at its height.

For too long the minuscules overall were neglected by scholars who seemed to be more interested in the older manuscripts simply because of their age – as if the value of a text could be determined by the age of the manuscript without any regard for the quality of the text it contained! The last fifty years, however, have seen a change in attitude.

The minuscules are nowadays regarded as representing a late text of the type current in the East in the early Middle Ages, but it is recognised that there are exceptions to this rule. An attempt has been made to collate the minuscules and to classify them by families, but work is slow. The relationships between the manuscripts may vary from one part of the text to another and so the manuscripts have to be examined in their entirety; and the number of manuscripts is so great that two thirds of them have not yet been studied at all. Nestle – Aland[26] (see 1898 – (III)) lists 200 minuscules which are used more or less regularly in the critical apparatus, to which it adds a further 600 which form the mass of the minuscules and which have the usual Byzantine text. These figures give the impression that one in four minuscules is of textual interest and is likely to have some early readings. But there remain something like a further 2,000 minuscules about which very little is known, to say nothing of the passages which have not been collated in the manuscripts which are used. (It must be noted, however, that the 128 minuscules used in the critical apparatus to Luke's Gospel prepared by the IGNTP (1984, 1987 (III)) are, in fact, only a selection of the total number of minuscule manuscripts examined in the course of compiling the apparatus.) The job of classifying the New Testament minuscules is thus very much an unfinished task. The chief results of the work which has been done so far are briefly described here.

The Gospels

Family 13 or the Ferrar Group contains at least a dozen manuscripts (13, 69, 124, 174, 230, 346, 543, 788, 826, 828, 983, 1698), most of them made in Calabria. The variants characteristic of this group are: Mt 16:2 – 3 omitted; pericope of the woman taken in adultery (Jn 7:53 – 8:11) transposed to the Gospel of Luke after 21:38; the episode of the sweat of blood (Lk 22:43 – 44) transposed to the Gospel of Matthew after 26:39.

Family 1, first assembled by K. Lake, includes ten manuscripts: 1[eap], 22, 118, 131, 209, 872, 1278, 1582, 2193 and, according to IGNTP, 205 (see above). It is closely related to the previous family and to certain uncials and some of the other minuscules: W.032 (for Mk 5.31 – 16:8), Θ.038, 0188, 28, 565, 700. This group is recognised as one of great importance.

Codex 565 (ninth century) and a few others (157, 262, 1071, etc., and also the uncial Λ.039) have different texts but all bear a final note stating that they were copied from manuscripts kept in Jerusalem.

Another curious group is that composed of 4ᵉ, 273, 566, 899, 1424 and many others which, in Matthew, have variants in the margin which refer in Greek to τὸ ἰουδαϊκόν, 'the Jewish (Gospel)' (the Gospel to the Hebrews).

Codex 1424 (ninth/tenth century) together with about thirty others, form, in Huck – Greeven's *Synopsis* (1981[13] = Huck – Greeven[13]; see 1892 – (III)) a group which von Soden put together and subdivided into various smaller groups. M.021 and 945 are examples of this group.

Codex 33 and 892 (ninth century), 579 and 1241 all represent an Alexandrian type of text, something which is rare among the minuscules (see p. 108).

The rest of the New Testament

The minuscules containing the remaining parts of the New Testament have been less well studied even though there are fewer of them. As far as Acts and the Pauline Epistles are concerned, it is the diversity of the text in the papyri and the uncials which has attracted the interest of most scholars. In 1983, however, a project was begun in Abilene (Texas) under the direction of C. Osburn, where a fresh collation is being made of virtually every Greek manuscript of Acts with a view to the publication of a new critical edition of Acts (International Project on the Text of Acts). For the Catholic Epistles, efforts to classify the minuscules have been made over the last ten years in America, Germany and France. The results tend to confirm the groups discerned by von Soden (1902 – 13).

Codex 33, 81 and 104 have an Alexandrian type of text (see p. 108).

Codex 2138, dated 1072 and kept in Moscow, is the oldest of about twenty minuscules[1] which display an affinity with a Syriac version of the seventh century (see pp. 34 – 5 and p. 97, and Amphoux 1981a and 1981c). Of this group, minuscule 614 (thirteenth century, kept in Milan) was collated for Acts together with 876, 1581 and two others of the same group (383, 431), originally by H. von Soden (see p. 155); it was later used in the editions published by J. H. Ropes (1926 (III)), A. C. Clark (1933 (III)), A. V. Valentine-Richards (1934; 2138 (VI)), and finally M. E. Boismard and A. Lamouille (1985 (III))

---

[1] 206, 429, 522, 614, 1108, 1292, 1448, 1505, 1518, 1611, 1758, 1799, 1831, 1890, 2138, 2495 and, to a lesser degree, 876, 1765, 1832, 1852, 1891, 2147, 2652.

with other additional minuscules. The text of the group is a 'Western' text (see pp. 109 – 10).

Codex 1739 (from around 950 and kept on Mount Athos) not only has a text which, according to the copyist, agrees with that of Origen, but it also contains notes in the margin with quotations from the early Church Fathers. In certain places in Acts, it is related to Codex Bezae, while in the Pauline Epistles it is close to the great uncials. In the Catholic Epistles it has more of a Caesarean type of text (Duplacy – Amphoux 1980). A text related to some degree to that of 1739 is found in about ten minuscules including 323, 945, 1241, 1243, 1735, 2298, 2492 (see Birdsall 1959; Amphoux – Outtier 1984).

In the rest of the minuscule manuscripts it is the Byzantine text which largely dominates, but that does not prevent the occasional occurrence of an older reading which belongs to one of the groups mentioned in this section.

THE LECTIONARIES

By lectionaries are meant those manuscripts which, instead of presenting a complete and continuous text of the New Testament, have only those passages which were selected for public reading in church services according to a daily calendar of the ecclesiastical year. They are, as such, liturgical books. A lectionary usually has two parts, one known as the 'synaxarion' or 'temporal', the other as the 'menologion' or 'sanctoral'. The first part contains the readings for each day (or sometimes just for Saturdays and Sundays) of the liturgical year which begins on Easter Day. The second part gives the references of those readings, as well as some additional readings, which occur on the Saints' days, following the civil year which begins on 1 September. The exact contents vary very much according to local practices.

Apart from a few papyrus fragments (P^3, P^4, P^{44}), the lectionaries were written on parchment (sometimes on paper from the thirteenth century onwards) in either uncial or minuscule script. But in the case of lectionaries, the manuscripts are classified not according to their style of writing but according to their contents. Each set of daily readings has one passage from the Gospels and another from either Acts or the Epistles. An 'Evangeliary' (l) contains only the readings from the Gospels: John over the Easter period, then Matthew, Luke and Mark from Whitsuntide to Holy Week in the following year. An 'Epistolary' (l^a) has only the readings from Acts or the Epistles: Acts during Easter and then the Epistles of Paul. There exist several systems for selecting the readings: Saturday and Sunday each have their own series of passages, whereas the rest of the week uses the same series each day. The most popular system, and probably the most recent, selects readings from the Catholic Epistles during the weeks preceding Lent. The other system, and that used on Saturdays and Sundays, only uses the Pauline Epistles which are read through more slowly. Certain lectionaries are complete (l^{+a}), containing both the evangeliary and the epistolary readings.

The list of lectionaries today goes from *l*1 to *l*2280. In order not to confuse them with the minuscules, an *l* in italic script is placed before the number in arabic figures. Taking into account the irregularities of the numbering (thirty-seven numbers used twice, forty-five numbers covering more than one manuscript and eleven numbers not used) it can be said that some 2,200 distinct lectionaries or fragments of lectionaries are known at the present time. The great majority of these are Evangeliaries (almost 1,700). Complete lectionaries are, on the other hand, few in number (around 200). All of these manuscripts are of a relatively late date: apart from two very early fragments (*l*1604, fourth century, with a Caesarean type of text, see p. 104, and *l*1043, fifth century, with an Alexandrian type of text, see p. 108), the oldest copies are from no earlier than the sixth century (*l*1347, kept in Verona, an Evangeliary and Psalter) with only about thirty, including fragments, from before the ninth century. Among the most recent, *l*547 (thirteenth century, kept at the Vatican) is worthy of note because it belongs to Family 13 (see p. 22 and 104).

There was a renewed interest in the lectionaries about twenty years ago (see Duplacy 1970), but progress has been slow. Only rarely are they used in the critical apparatus. In UBS[3a] (see 1966 – (III)), with a limited apparatus, 149 are used with varying frequency; Huck – Greeven[13] (see 1892 – (III)), although only listing one in the Introduction, does in fact cite another 143 in the apparatus (see Elliott 1986, p. 573); the critical apparatus to Luke's Gospel prepared by the IGNTP uses forty-one; Nestle – Aland[26] (see 1898 – (III)) only refers to five. Duplacy's study of the lectionaries shows that these witnesses are not without textual interest. But nine tenths of the work is still to be done and the results will have to be patiently awaited.

THE OSTRAKA AND TALISMANS

The writings on these objects are more of a curiosity than directly useful for textual criticism. Among the ostraka (see p. 00) which have so far been discovered, only a few bear anything from the New Testament, and when they do it is usually just a few verses from the Gospels. Of special note is the uncial 0153 which is not a codex but a group of twenty ostraka published by G. Lefebvre 1904 and listed by K. Aland (1963 (V)) with a Gothic 'O' and a number 1 – 20: they are inscribed with a fairly complete narrative of different scenes of the Passion.

The talismans are amulets made out of a wide variety of materials: wooden or clay tablets, or pieces of papyrus or parchment. Some of them bear inscriptions from the New Testament such as the Lord's Prayer, the beginning of the four Gospels or a verse to do with the healing of the sick (Mt 4:23 – 4). Of the few that exist, nine are grouped under the uncial number 0152 (listed by K. Aland as T 1 – 9) and two appear in the list of papyri, P^{50}, P^{78} (J. van Haelst (1976 (V)), nos. 482 and 558).

THE VERSIONS

It is the versions which, after the Greek manuscripts, constitute the most valuable source of documentation for the history of the New Testament. Primary importance is traditionally accorded to three groups: the Latin, Syriac and Coptic translations, which will be examined first. But there are other versions, usually regarded as of secondary interest, which require equally careful study: they are the Gothic, Armenian, Georgian, Ethiopic, Arabic and Slavonic versions. After a description of those, brief indication will finally be given of some further versions which exist. There is an excellent book on the subject by B. M. Metzger (1977); this can be supplemented by a collection of articles edited by K. Aland (1972) as well as by various dictionary articles (see especially 'Bible' (Articles), 1960, 1980 in Bibliography VII).

THE LATIN VERSIONS

These can be divided into two classes, the Old Latin texts on the one hand, and the Vulgate, commonly attributed to Jerome, on the other.

The Old Latin versions (it)

The exact number of these versions is not known: some of them have been handed down in the form of manuscripts, very varied in many respects; others are in the form of quotations (see pp. 49 – 50 above). No Old Latin manuscript has the complete text of the New Testament. Some Vulgate manuscripts have occasional Old Latin readings which should be added to the ninety or so (partial) Old Latin manuscripts which are listed. These writings are amongst the oldest of the copies of the New Testament, sometimes dating back to the fourth century. They are designated by a small letter (as in Nestle – Aland[26]; see 1898 – (III)) which is sometimes added in superscript to the abbreviation 'it' (UBS[3a]; see 1966 – (III)). But as there are not enough letters for all the manuscripts, the Vetus Latina Institut in Beuron (Germany) has made a new list using Arabic numerals starting with 1. Once this system has entered general use, the problem of using the same letter for different manuscripts will be avoided (e.g. 'e' means Codex Palatinus for the Gospels, the Latin side of Codex Laudianus for Acts, and Codex Sangermanensis for the Pauline Epistles). In the following comments on the main manuscripts, the new Beuron number is used and then the old letter given.

Codex Bobbiensis (1, k), from the fourth to the fifth century, was initially kept at the monastery at Bobbio in northern Italy but is now in Turin. It contains only Mk 8:8 – 16:8 (with the short ending, that is without verses 9 – 20), and Matt 1:1 – 15:36 with some lacunae. There is a facsimile edition by C. Cipolla (1913; it (1, k) (VI)). The text of this manuscript may be based on a recension made in Africa (in present-day Tunisia) in the third century. It is close to the text of Cyprian's quotations, having what is known as an 'African' type of the Old Latin text (see p. 101).

Codex Palatinus (2, e) from the fourth to the fifth century, is a *de luxe* copy with gold and silver letters on a purple background. It probably originated in northern Italy and was first kept in the Bibliotheca Palatina in Vienna but is now in Trent (except for two leaves, one in Dublin, the other in London). It contains the four Gospels (in the order Matthew – John – Luke – Mark) with lacunae. Like the previous manuscript, it has an 'African' type of text but it has undergone other influences which bring it closer at times to what is called the 'European' type of text (see p. 102).

Codex Vercellensis (3, a), from the fourth century, is also a purple manuscript and is kept at Vercelli. It contains, once more, the four Gospels in the order Matthew–John–Luke–Mark with lacunae. Together with the next manuscript, it is the main representative of the 'European' text type for the Old Latin versions.

Codex Veronensis (4, b), from the fourth to the fifth century, is another purple manuscript, kept in Verona. It contains the Gospels in the same order as before, with lacunae, and with a text very similar to that of the previous manuscript.

Codex Bezae (5, d) is a Greek–Latin bilingual manuscript (see p. 16 above). The Latin side is generally quite a close translation of the Greek (with some exceptions) and represents a different type of text from the others found among the Old Latin versions, belonging to the 'Western' text (see pp. 109–10).

Codex Colbertinus (6, c) is from the twelfth century; it was copied in Languedoc and is now in the Bibliothèque Nationale in Paris. It contains the whole of the New Testament but only the Gospels have an Old Latin text, especially in Mark and Luke where the influence of the 'African' type can be noticed (see p. 101).

For the Gospels, mention must also be made of Codex Corbeiensis II (8, ff^2, fifth century), Brixianus (10, f, sixth century) and Rehdigeranus (11, l, seventh/eighth century), all of a 'European' type of text (see p. 102).

Codex Laudianus (50, e) is a Greek–Latin manuscript of Acts (see p. 17 above).

Codex Gigas (51, gig), from the thirteenth century, was kept first in Prague but has been in Stockholm since 1648. It gets its name from its enormous size. It contains the whole Bible as well as other works but only Acts and Revelation have an Old Latin text, which may well represent a version from before AD 350.

Codex Floriacensis (55, h) is a palimpsest of the sixth century which was first at Fleury-sur-Loire and is now in Paris (Bibliothèque Nationale). It contains fragments of Acts, the Catholic Epistles (1–2 Peter, 1 John) and Revelation. The text of Acts is very close to the Old Latin text (the 'African' type, see p. 101) found in Cyprian's writings.

Codex Corbeiensis (66, ff), from the ninth century, was initially kept in Corbie, then in Saint-Germain-des-Prés, and finally today in Leningrad. It has an Old Latin text of the Epistle of James, different from that of the next manuscript but both types within the 'Western' text distinct from that of 2138 (see p. 23 n. 1) and of the Harclean Syriac sy^h (see pp. 34–5).

Codex Legionensis (67,1) from the seventh century is kept at Leon, Spain (MS 15). It has an Old Latin text of Acts and the Catholic Epistles of the Spanish type. It has been edited by B. Fischer (1963) (see Thiele 1965, pp. 166f.).

For the Pauline Epistles, attention may simply be drawn to the Greek – Latin manuscripts already mentioned (see pp. 17 – 20): Codex Claromontanus (75, d) and its copy Codex Sangermanensis (76, e, ninth century), Codex Boernerianus (77, g) and Codex Augiensis (78, f). It is worth adding to these, first, the fragment kept at Monza (86) and Codex Budapestiensis (89), and also the *Liber* or *Speculum de divinis scripturis* (PS-AU spe, m); this is a work in several codices which is attributed to Augustine (PS-AU = Pseudo-Augustine) and which contains passages from almost all the books of the New Testament, though it is in no way a biblical manuscript. The text type of these quotations is Spanish (see on 67,1 above and p. 102).

All of these manuscripts have been published, and some of them reproduced in facsimile (see Bibliography VI). There is available at present an edition of the four Gospels based on the principal Old Latin manuscripts, which sets out the variant readings of each in such a way as to allow the distinction between the European and the African text types to be seen clearly: Jülicher 1963, 1970, 1972 and 1976 (see 1938 – (III)). The Old Latin text of Acts is also considered in some detail in the work by M. E. Boismard and A. Lamouille (1985 (III)), in the Introduction (vol. I, pp. 37 – 67) and in the apparatus to their critical edition (vol. II). But by far the most important work is that which has been carried out since 1949, by the Vetus Latina Institut in Beuron. The goal of the authors is to publish, in twenty-six volumes, the Latin Bible as it was before the Vulgate, drawing on as exhaustive a list of documents as possible (not only Old Latin manuscripts but also Vulgate manuscripts with Old Latin readings, as well as quotations from the Latin Church Fathers collected from a thorough reading of their works). From 1983, the Centre de Recherches sur la Bible Latine in Louvain-la-Neuve has also been working on this edition of the Latin Bible. On the New Testament side, the work started with the publication of the Catholic Epistles and the shorter Pauline letters (edited by H. J. Frede (1962 – 4, 1966 – 71, 1975 – 82, 1983) and W. Thiele (1956 – 69); see 1956 – (III)). In 1987, work was begun on the Epistle to the Hebrews. By classifying the variants and by determining their age, the editors are able to display several types of text, setting them out in horizontal lines one above the other with the oldest type of text at the top and the Vulgate at the bottom. It thus becomes clear that there is not only one type of African text but two at least (not counting that of Tertullian which stands on its own); that the oldest forms of the text are only preserved in the form of quotations; that there is not only one type of European text either but rather four or five, several of them from Spain. Furthermore, it is often in the oldest layers of the Old Latin text that variants are found which also appear in certain Greek or Oriental witnesses. With factors such as these emerging, it cannot be stressed too much that the Old Latin tradition is extremely important for uncovering the earliest New Testament text.

The Vulgate attributed to Jerome (vg)

The manuscripts of the Vulgate present a very different picture. In the first place, they are very numerous (more than 10,000). Secondly, they are for the most part quite recent (after the ninth century) and well-preserved. Some of them, though, are older (sixth – ninth century) and one of them was even copied from another which goes back to within a century of the original, which is very remarkable for a manuscript. They used to be designated by the first letters of their names but, in order to avoid any confusion, Gregory classified them using Arabic numerals. Greek and Latin capital letters are still used, however, for the most important Vulgate manuscripts.

On account of its textual value, the Vulgate deserves a separate study all of its own, but within the limited scope of this book it is of less interest than the Old Latin version and so only a few details will be given here about the manuscripts. They can be divided into five main groups according to where they were copied: Italy, Great Britain (although originating in Italy), Spain, Ireland and France; there are, in addition, the recensions of Alcuin and Theodulf. The best manuscripts belong to the first two groups and the following are worthy of special mention: the Amiatinus (A), from the eighth century and containing the whole Bible; the Fuldensis (F), written between AD 541 and AD 546 on the instructions of Victor of Capua, and containing the New Testament with the Gospels laid out in the form of a harmony; the Mediolanensis (M) and the Harleianus (Z), both manuscripts of the Gospels from the sixth century; finally, and above all, the Sangallensis (S or Σ) whose date of origin (around AD 500) and text are altogether remarkable.

Of this latter manuscript, edited by C. H. Turner (1931), with supplements by P. Lehmann 1933, A. Dold 1933 and 1941, and B. Bischoff

1946 and 1966, only portions remain amounting to about half the Gospels. Indeed, in the Middle Ages it was taken apart and used, as were so many works, to supply end pages for new books. The first critical edition of the Vulgate was the great work begun by J. Wordsworth and H. I. White and completed by H. F. D. Sparks and A. W. Adams (1889 – 1954 (III); vg^{ww}). Before that, the main edition available was that ordered by Pope Clement VIII at the end of the sixteenth century (1590 (III), 3rd edn. 1598) and known as the Clementine Vulgate (vg^{cl}). A popular critical edition of the whole Bible appeared in 1969 (3rd edn. 1983; see 1969 – (III)) edited by R. Weber assisted by B. Fischer, J. Gribomont, H. F. D. Sparks and W. Thiele; it is referred to as the Stuttgart Vulgate (vgst). In 1907, a Benedictine Commission was given, by Pope Pius X, the task of reconstituting the Bible of Jerome, a work which was completed at St Jerome's Abbey in Rome in 1989 (III) (vg^{r}).

THE SYRIAC VERSIONS (sy)

The Aramaic language can be divided into two main groups: 1) Eastern Aramaic, which includes in particular the Syriac dialect, also known as Edessenean. Most of the Syriac versions of the New Testament (the Diatessaron of Tatian, the Old Syriac versions, the Peshitta version and the Philoxenian and Harclean versions) are written in this dialect. 2) Western Aramaic, the language spoken by the Jews in Palestine at the time of Jesus and including, among other dialects, Christo-Palestinian in which another Syriac version of the New Testament (Syro-Palestinian) was written. These five Aramaic versions pose a number of unresolved problems.

The Diatessaron of Tatian (Diat)

The origin of this harmony, which brings together parallel passages of the four Gospels, has been lost. But it has left its mark, more or less clearly, on manuscripts written in up to twenty languages or dialects. The subject of the Diatessaron is thus very complicated and no-one has yet produced a complete critical edition. And yet the Diatessaron occupies an important place in New Testament textual criticism, partly because of its early date and also because of the agreement of some of its readings with a variety of other early manuscripts all with a 'Western' text (see pp. 109 – 10). The following may be mentioned among the indirect witnesses of the Diatessaron:

a leaf of text in Greek discovered in 1933 at Dura-Europos, dating from the first half of the third century and classified among the New Testament uncial manuscripts (0212). It has been edited by C. H. Kraeling (1935; 0212 (VI));

a commentary by Ephraem (Diat^e) preserved in two manuscripts in Armenian, and discovered in Syriac (with lacunae) in 1957 in a Chester Beatty manuscript. Edited by L. Leloir (1963; Diat^e (VI)) and translated by the same author (Leloir 1966);

one, or two, Arabic versions (Diat^a) preserved in six manuscripts, and a harmony in Persian (Diat^p) translated from a Syriac original which was independent to some degree of the Diatessaron;

quotations by Syriac or Armenian writers, in particular Aphraates, Ephraem and the *Liber graduum*;

Codex Fuldensis of the Vulgate (Diat^f, see p. 30) which would appear to have been copied from an Old Latin harmony (possibly translated from the Diatessaron), whilst aligning the text with the Vulgate. There is a twofold interest in this manuscript: on the one hand, it presents a plan of the Diatessaron which corresponds to that of the preceding witnesses; on the other hand, it is very likely to be behind a number of Western medieval harmonies which follow the Vulgate text. It has been edited by E. Ranke (1868; Diat^f (VI));

the Diatessaron of Liège (Diat^l) which is the oldest of the harmonies in Middle-Dutch and which may well also be based on an Old Latin text. The critical edition by D. Plooij, C. A. Phillips and A. H. A. Bakker (1929 – 1970; Diat^l(VI)) is the best edition currently available for the study of the Diatessaron;

the Venetian Diatessaron (Diat^v) which, in just one manuscript, preserves a text which is older and more independent of Codex Fuldensis than the Tuscan Diatessaron (Diat^t). It also has some readings in agreement with the quotations of Aphraates. It has been edited by V. Todesco, A. Vaccari and M. Vattasso (1938; Diat^v (VI)).

The present situation is that the arrangement of the Diatessaron is fairly well established but the actual text is far from certain. The Gospel of Thomas (Coptic) appears to have certain textual affinities with the Diatessaron, slightly more so with the Arabic version than with the other witnesses. On the question as to whether it was originally written in Greek or Syriac, scholars are still divided.

Chapter one

The Old Syriac versions

One version of the Gospels has been preserved in two manuscripts. The first is from the fifth century and was discovered in 1842 in a monastery of the Nitrian desert (Egypt) by W. Cureton; it is kept in London (several leaves which probably belong to it are in Berlin) and it is known as the Curetonian Syriac (sy^c). This manuscript contains, with lacunae, the Gospels in the order Matthew – Mark – John – Luke. The best edition is that by F. C. Burkitt (1904 (III)) which has an English translation and a rich critical apparatus. The second manuscript is from the end of the fourth century and is a palimpsest which was found in 1892 by Mrs A. Smith Lewis and Mrs M. Dunlop Gibson in the library of St Catherine's Monastery on Mount Sinai; it is known as the Sinaitic Syriac (sy^s). In its primary text the manuscript contains the four Gospels in the usual order with lacunae. There is a critical edition by A. Smith Lewis (1910; sy^s (VI)) and a defective facsimile reproduction by A. Hjelt (1930; sy^s (VI)). The texts of the two manuscripts are different but related, and they have a number of agreements with Codex Bezae and the Old Latin text. Between them, they contain almost all of the Gospels. They each bear the words: 'evangelion da-mepharreshe', that is 'The Gospel of the separated [books]', as opposed to Tatian's harmony, which was known in the East as 'The Gospel of the mixed'.

There is also an Arabic palimpsest from Mount Sinai which has been examined by A. S. Atiya (1967), and whose primary text has a version of Matthew, John and Mark distinct from that of the Peshitta.

For Acts and the Pauline Epistles, there apparently once existed another Old Syriac version of which no actual manuscript remains but which is partially preserved in the works of the Church Fathers. For Acts, there are (1) two Armenian manuscripts edited in Venice which attest a *catena* or chain; (2) an Armenian version of the fifth century of a commentary on Acts by Ephraem which exists in three manuscripts edited in Vienna (Eng./Lat. trans. by F. C. Conybeare, in Ropes 1926 (III), pp. 373–453); and (3) quotations in Aphraates and the *Liber graduum* (see Kerschensteiner 1964). The version of Acts used is the same in each case and is closely related to the text of Codex Bezae. As for the Epistles of Paul, the same Syriac version is attested by quotations in about fifteen authors, in particular in a commentary by Ephraem published in Vienna (Armenian text 1836, Latin translation 1893; see Kerschensteiner 1970). The text of this version is especially close to Codex Boernerianus (G.012/g, see pp. 17–20).

The Peshitta version (sy^p)

Gregory listed in a somewhat confused fashion almost 250 manuscripts of this version. It is very likely that there are hundreds more in the libraries of the Near East. More than a dozen of those listed are of great antiquity (fifth – sixth centuries) and are very close to the original. But there is little to be gained from going into the details of the various manuscripts because whether they be ancient or recent they present very few variants (Vööbus 1954, pp. 88 – 103). It is precisely that fixed nature of the text which characterises the Peshitta manuscripts, a feature derived from the Massorah, a system of writing and phonetics taught in the Syrian schools either at Edessa or Nisibis to ensure the correct writing and pronunciation of the sacred text. The Peshitta does not contain all of the New Testament but, in accordance with the Syrian canon, omits the four smaller Catholic Epistles (2 Peter, 2 – 3 John and Jude) and Revelation. It further omits certain passages: Mt 27:35; Lk 22:17 – 18; Jn 7:53 – 8:11; Ac 8:37; 15:34; 28:29; 1 Jn 5:7 – 8. These verses have been added later in certain manuscripts. There is no critical edition of this version except for the Gospels (Pusey – Gwilliam 1901 (III)). The complete New Testament has been edited, without an apparatus, by the British and Foreign Bible Society, 1905 – 20 (III). See also B. Aland 1986. The text type of this version is Syro-Byzantine (see p. 109 and pp. 118 – 19).

The Philoxenian (sy^{ph}) and Harclean (sy^h; marginal notes: sy^{hmg}) versions

These versions, unlike the Peshitta, contain the whole of the New Testament and are represented by 130 listed manuscripts (J. D. Thomas, 1979 (V)), though there are no doubt still more. There is as yet no critical edition of them but they can be consulted in an old edition made in Oxford by J. White from just one manuscript with reference, where necessary, to two others also in Oxford (*Sacrorum Evangeliorum versio syriaca philoxenia*, 1778; *Actuum et Epistolarum tam Catholicarum quam Paulinarum versio syriaca philoxenia*, 1799 – 1803). The text is that of a scholarly version which slavishly follows a Greek model, with variants in the margin and others in the text indicated by diacritical signs.

The question of how to differentiate between the different versions within the one text was only recently given a satisfactory answer in an excellent study by S. P. Brock 1981. Brock compares both the text of the quotations of Philoxenus in his *Commentary on John's Prologue* (edited by A. de Halleux, *CSCO* 380 – 1, 1977) and, on the other hand, the text edited by White, with the Peshitta and is thus able to show that the text of Philoxenus is different from that of White and that it is an intermediary text between White's text and the Peshitta: it emerges that the Philoxenian version is that of the quotations and that White's text represents the Harclean version. The former moves away from the Peshitta in its theological preoccupations; it is then revised by the latter with a concern to stick as closely as possible to the Greek (Brock 1981, p. 337). This provides a basic criterion for distinguishing which elements of the manuscripts belong to one or the other version. White's model was purely Harclean; others (and Brock gives an example) have possibly retained traces of the work ordered by Philoxenus of Mabbûg. Establishing just how far this is so will be one of the tasks to be undertaken by a critical edition when it is eventually produced.

The Harclean version has not aroused as much interest as the other versions, perhaps because of its relatively late date. Polycarp, working for Philoxenus, carried out his work between AD 507 and 508, and Thomas of Harkel made his revision in AD 615–6. Nevertheless, White maintains that the latter is of primary textual interest. In Acts especially, the marginal variants and occasionally its other readings make it one of the closest texts to that of Codex Bezae (see p. 110). For certain Catholic Epistles (James, 1 Peter), it displays a close textual relationship with the Greek minuscule 2138 and others like it (p. 23 and p. 97).

The Syro-Palestinian version (sy^pal)

The unpublished thesis of A. Desreumaux on the Syro-Palestinian manuscripts (1979) provides a very clear survey of the manuscripts in this Aramaic dialect (though an inventory of certain important collections, such as that of Leningrad, is missing). There is an Evangeliary which is attested by three manuscripts (eleventh/twelfth century) with a good edition by A. Smith Lewis (1899; sy^pal (VI)). There is also a lectionary containing passages from the Old Testament, Acts and the Epistles (see A. Smith Lewis, 1897; supplements, 1907; sy^pal (VI)). Two palimpsests use leaves of parchment which come from different books, five of them containing texts from the New Testament: firstly, Codex Climaci rescriptus (edited by A. Smith Lewis, 1909; sy^pal (VI)) is written over about eighty leaves from an Evangeliary, a 'praxapostolos' (second half of the New Testament) and a Bible; secondly, the 'great Georgian palimpsest' (incomplete edition, H. Duensing, 1906; sy^pal (VI); private collection Krauss), consisting of about twenty leaves from two Gospel manuscripts. Finally, there are fragments from about thirty books, containing either liturgical passages or continuous Biblical text (sixth – tenth centuries); some of them have not been published but many have been, and particular mention may be made of a short fragment of Acts (10:28 ... 41), published in an important article by C. Perrot (1963); it attests the same text type as that of Codex Bezae (see p. 110). The catalogue of Desreumaux completes that of Bar-Asher (1977).

THE COPTIC VERSIONS

Coptic (from the Arabic 'qubṭi', derived in turn from αἰγύπτιος, 'Egyptian'), was the language written and spoken in Egypt following the introduction of Christianity into the country. The oldest documents which have been preserved are from the third century. The language is written using Greek characters with some additional signs. It is split into several dialects whose main differences are phonetic. A large number of biblical manuscripts and religious works, both Christian and pagan, exist in Coptic, but the language owes its fame chiefly to the discovery of the library of Nag-Hammadi in 1945 with its thirteen papyrus books containing Coptic (especially Sahidic) versions of forty-nine Gnostic writings including the Gospel of Thomas. The main literary dialect is Sahidic, possibly originating in Upper Egypt (some scholars would argue for a northern origin; see Kasser 1965). The liturgy, on the other hand, from the sixth century onwards, prefers Bohairic, the dialect from the Nile Delta (Western side). These are the two dialects used for most of the biblical manuscripts in Coptic. But other dialects are also important for the New Testament Achmimic, sub-Achmimic, Fayyumic and also Memphitic or Middle-Egyptian. The documents adopt a wide variety of forms: continuous texts or lectionaries, codices or scrolls, manuscripts on papyrus, parchment, paper, ostraka. Gregory's listings need to be brought up to date but in the meantime the following articles may be consulted in Bibliography V: for the Sahidic, Vaschalde 1919 – 22; for the other versions, *Le Muséon* 1930 – 3; Bouvarel-Boud'hors 1987, Schmitz-Mink 1986 – 9, Till 1959. For the text type of the Coptic versions, see p. 105.

The Sahidic versions (sa)

There are a number of collections of Sahidic texts. The most well known are those of Pierpont Morgan (New York), Chester Beatty and Bodmer.

What is striking is the fragmentary state of the manuscripts, very few of them preserving an entire book. On the whole, the codices are very old; several go back to the fourth century or even before. The critical edition by G. Horner (1911 – 24 (III)), though it was excellent in its time, is now out of date following the discovery of new documents of which the most important are:

Codex Crosby, from the end of the third century, kept at the University of Mississippi, is a papyrus of fifty-two leaves forming one quire (like P^{46}, see p. 12); it contains the whole of 1 Peter in the middle of non-biblical works. There exists a description of it by W. H. Willis (1961);

a papyrus codex, from the fourth century, kept in Berlin, of which there remain thirty-five leaves in a fragmentary state, containing Acts with a 'Western' text. It has been edited by F. Hintze and H. M. Schenke (1970; sa(2) (VI));

Codex Bodmer XIX, from the fourth/fifth century, on parchment, of which there is left half of Matthew (14:28 – 28:20) and Romans 1 on separate pages. Edited by R. Kasser (1962; sa(3) (VI));

Codex P Palau 181 – 182 – 183, from the fifth century, on parchment and kept in Barcelona. It contains the whole of Luke, Mark and John. Edited by H. Quecke (1972 Mark, 1977 Luke; sa(4) (VI); 1984 John; sa(5) (VI)) with an apparatus showing the variant readings of Codex A and B (Chester Beatty) and of M 569 (Pierpont Morgan);

Codex Chester Beatty A (from around AD 600) and B (from the seventh century), both on parchment, the first containing the whole of Paul's Epistles, with Hebrews after 2 Corinthians (the usual Sahidic order), and the second containing the entire Book of Acts. It has been edited by H. Thompon (1932; sa(6 – 7) (VI));

five Pierpont Morgan Codices, from the eighth/ninth century (see Aland – Aland 1982, Eng. trans. (1989), p. 201), on parchment: one with the four Gospels (M 569), one with the Gospel of John (M 5), two with the Epistles of Paul (M 570, M 571) and one with the Catholic Epistles (M 572; see Schüssler 1969).

In comparison with these manuscripts which are of some length, the documents available to Horner were no more than a collection of odd fragments with which it was impossible to establish a unified text.

The Bohairic versions (bo)

The manuscripts in Bohairic are in a much better condition. Several contain, if not the entire New Testament, large sections of it. Most of the witnesses are relatively recent (ninth – sixteenth centuries) and present a fairly homogeneous text in which sometimes even the corrections are carefully noted. In the last fifty years, however, some very much older manuscripts have been discovered, including fragments from the Epistles of Paul. Of special note is:

Codex Bodmer III, from the fourth century, on papyrus and containing John's Gospel (incomplete) and the first chapters of Genesis. The language of the manuscript is more archaic than that of the medieval documents and is sometimes called 'proto-Bohairic'. It has been edited by R. Kasser (1958; bo(1) (VI)).

The best edition of the Bohairic version dates from before the discovery of these older manuscripts. It is again that of G. Horner (1898 – 1905 (III)).

The other Coptic versions

In the other dialects the manuscript tradition is not nearly as rich and not even all of them put together contain a complete New Testament. But there are nonetheless some early documents, among which the most important are:

a bilingual codex in Greek and Achmimic (ac), from the fourth century, on papyrus, kept in Strasbourg and containing John (chs. 10 – 13) and James, as well as 1 Clement. It has been edited by F. Rösch (1910; ac(1) (VI)). It corresponds to the Greek papyrus P^6;

a papyrus discovered at Qau in sub-Achmimic (ac^2), from the fourth century, kept in Cambridge University Library (British and Foreign Bible Society) and containing almost all of John's Gospel (2:12 – 20:27); of the original fifty leaves there remain forty-three. It has been edited by H. Thompson (1924; ac^2(1) (VI));

a codex in Fayyumic (fay), from the beginning of the fourth century, on papyrus, kept an Ann Arbor (Mich.) and containing, with many lacunae, John 6 – 15. The manuscript was made in one single quire. There is a rather poor edition by E. M. Husselman (1962; fay(1) (VI));

Codex Scheide in Middle-Egyptian (mae), from the fourth/fifth century, on parchment, kept in Princeton and containing all of Matthew's

Gospel on 238 small-size leaves. The text of this manuscript, whilst generally close to that of the great Greek uncials, displays at the same time an affinity with the Western type of text. It has been edited by H. M. Schenke (1981; mae(1) (VI));

Codex Glazier (mae/G^{67}), from the fifth century, on parchment, kept in New York (Pierpont Morgan Library). With its 107 leaves of the Book of Acts (1:1 – 15:3) this manuscript is the most noteworthy one of all for its text (see p. 105). It is soon to be published; meanwhile, a number of studies have been made of it (see Petersen 1968; also Haenchen and Weigandt 1968);

a codex on papyrus (mae), from the fifth century, kept in Milan, of which only fragments remain but which originally contained the Epistles of Paul, with Hebrews after 2 Corinthians (like Chester Beatty A; see p. 37). It has been edited by T. Orlandi (1974; mae(3) (VI)).

THE OTHER VERSIONS

There are several more versions in languages other than Latin, Syriac or Coptic which play an important part in New Testament textual criticism either because of their early date or because of their conservative character. The study of these versions is not as far advanced as that of the others and, consequently, it is not possible to make more than a few comments on each.

The Gothic version (goth)

The interest of this version derives from the fact that it originally comes from a fourth-century community in what is now Romania (see Gryson 1990). The manuscripts are few in number (about six) but they are relatively early, going back in the main to the sixth century. Mention may be made of the following:

Codex Argenteus, from the sixth century, on purple parchment with gold and silver letters; it was copied in Northern Italy and is now kept in Uppsala. This *de luxe* manuscript initially contained the four Gospels (in the order Matthew – John – Luke – Mark) and had 336 leaves, of which 188 are left. There is a facsimile edition (1927; goth(1) (VI)). All that remains otherwise of the Gospels are fragments of the end of Matthew and of Luke;

Codex Ambrosiani, consisting of four palimpsests which are kept in Milan. Two of them have a primary text of parts of all the Pauline Epistles (without Hebrews). There is a facsimile edition by J. de Vries (1936; goth(2–5) (VI)). Apart from these copies of the Epistles, there are only fragments of Romans, Galatians and Colossians.

R. Gryson 1990 argues that the type of text found in the Gothic version is 'Western' but of a different strand from those of the Old Latin versions (see also p. 120).

The Armenian versions (arm)

The importance of works in Armenian has already been seen in connection with the Diatessaron and the Old Syriac version of the Pauline Epistles (see p. 33 above). The New Testament manuscripts in Armenian are among the most numerous: the catalogue of E. F. Rhodes (1959 (V)) is incomplete but the list already stands at 1,244. They are all relatively recent manuscripts, however, the oldest being a copy of the four Gospels dating from AD 887, and kept in Moscow. The most important manuscripts, which are in Armenia, form a homogeneous group and belong to the tenth/eleventh century. Most of the manuscripts, though, are spread out between the twelfth and the seventeenth centuries and have very few variants between them. For Acts, the Epistles and Revelation, the oldest manuscript is a bilingual Greek–Armenian copy (Greek minuscule 256) dating from the eleventh/twelfth century, and kept in Paris. Many of the manuscripts have a 'colophon' as well as various preliminary pages.

For the study of the text in Armenian there is at present only an old edition available, by J. Zohrab (1789 (III)), but work is being done on a critical edition in Erevan, the capital of Soviet Armenia. The interest of the Armenian text lies in the fact that there are a number of variant readings from several ancient text-types, especially that of the great uncials (Alexandrian type, see pp. 107–9) and that of Codex Koridethi for the Gospels; and for the Pauline Epistles, that of Codex Claromontanus (Caesarean type, see p. 104). As far as the Gospels are concerned, it seems that it is not the version transmitted by the manuscripts which is the oldest. In the quotations of the early writers an older version is attested which is said to be particularly close to the Diatessaron and the Old Syriac (Lyonnet 1938). For the quotations of Matthew's Gospel, see Leloir 1967.

The Georgian versions (geo)

There are far fewer New Testament manuscripts in Georgian than in Armenian but the exact number is not known. The manuscripts fall into two groups, those representing old translations, with many early variant readings, and those (more numerous and more recent) representing the Georgian Vulgate, with a text close to that of the mass of Greek minuscules. The oldest of the Georgian witnesses are fragments: they can be recognised by the use of a prefix ('ḫan' until the seventh century and then 'hae') which disappears later on. There are about sixty such fragments, preserving passages from the Gospels and the Pauline Epistles. With one exception, the longer manuscripts scarcely go back beyond the tenth century. A selection of some of them is given here, using the numbering of the list of Old Georgian manuscripts compiled by B. Outtier (1988 (V); see p. 121):

the ḫan-meti palimpsest of the Gospels (1), recently reconstituted and published in Tbilisi (L. Kazaia, 1984; geo(1) (VI)) where it is kept. It has 126 folios and is the oldest Georgian witness of any length (fifth/sixth century). It has the same text type as that of the Adysh manuscript which had hitherto been the only one of its kind. The secondary text consists partly of a commentary by John Chrysostom (eleventh century) and partly of an Evangeliary (eleventh/twelfth century);

the Adysh manuscript (2, geo[1] in UBS[3a], dated 897) is the next oldest manuscript, containing the complete Gospels. It comes from the Monastery of Shatberd and is now in Tbilisi. It has the same type of text as the previous manuscript except for Luke where the text agrees with two other manuscripts from the same monastery, Codex Džruč (6, dated 936) and Codex Parḫal (7, dated 973). There is a facsimile edition by A. S. Khakhanov and E. S. Takaischvili (1916; geo(2) (VI)) and a Latin translation with parallel texts by J. Molitor (1953–9). An edition has been made of the Old Georgian text based on the Adysh manuscript by R. P. Blake and M. Brière (1929–55; geo(4–5) (VI));

Codex Ksani (3, from the tenth century and kept in Tbilisi) also has the four Gospels but they are not complete (240 fols.). An edition was made in Tbilisi (I. Imnaisvili, 1949–50; geo(3) (VI)); its text lies between the oldest type of text, the Adysh type, and that of the other Old Georgian manuscripts;

the Opiza manuscript (4, geo[a] in UBS[3a] dated 913, kept on Mount Athos at the Iberon Monastery) and the Tbet' manuscript (5, geo[b], 995, previously in Leningrad and now in Tbilisi) are amongst these other manuscripts. They also contain the four Gospels but in a newer recension which differs from both the preceding ones. The variant readings of their text as compared with that of the Adysh manuscript appear in the critical apparatus of Blake–Brière (see the Adysh manuscript above);

an Iberon manuscript (georg. 62, eleventh century) contains the four Gospels in yet another recension, that of St George the Athonite;

another Iberon manuscript (20, georg. 42, from around 960) is the oldest Georgian manuscript of the Acts and the Epistles of Paul;

the Sinai manuscripts (23, georg. 39, dated 974; and 22 which is divided into three, georg. 58 – 31 – 60 and dated 977) also preserve the text of Acts and the Pauline Epistles. They were used as the basis for the edition of Acts by G. Garitte, 1955 (III);

a codex from the Monastery of Kranim (24, dated 978 and kept in Tbilisi) is the oldest Georgian witness to Revelation. There is a Latin translation by J. Molitor (1966 – 8);

the Kala-Lectionary (50, tenth century) is, in spite of its being incomplete, the most remarkable of the manuscripts which have the Catholic Epistles, partly because of the age of its variants and partly because of its system of readings. It is used in the edition by M. Tarchnischvili (1959), which, unfortunately, only gives the beginning and the ending of the readings. In the Latin translation by J. Molitor (1965 – 6), it is referred to by the letter **B**.

Mention may finally be made of the Georgian editions in the collection *Monuments of the Old Georgian Language* (1945 – 56 (III): vol. II, the Gospels (A. Šandize, 1945), vol. VII, Acts (I. Abuladze, 1950), vol. IX, the Catholic Epistles (K. I. Lort'k'ipanidze, 1956).

The Arabic versions (ar)

This is a very complex field, again largely uncharted. The number of manuscripts is very high (see the list compiled by G. Graf 1944 (V)), and their origins extremely varied. There are bilingual manuscripts where the Arabic exists alongside Greek, Latin, Coptic, or Syriac. The Arabic versions are of unequal value for textual criticism but several of them, both in the West and in the East, preserve a certain number of Caesarean or 'Western' variants (see pp. 103 – 5 and pp. 109 – 10). The manuscripts tend to be relatively recent (ninth century onwards); of the older ones, the following are of particular note:

a manuscript from the Monastery of Mar Saba (Jerusalem) dating from the eighth/ninth century and kept in the Vatican library (ar^{vat}), is quoted by Tischendorf in his critical edition of the New Testament. There are 178 leaves remaining, with the Pauline Epistles. The text has some variants of the Caesarean text type (see pp. 103–5), possibly through a Syriac intermediary;

two fragments of a bilingual Greek (0136 and 0137) – Arabic uncial from the ninth century. It consists of four leaves with passages from Matthew. The Arabic text has been edited by A. Smith Lewis (1894; 0136–0137 (VI));

a manuscript kept on Mount Sinai (arab. 151), dated 867. It has many exegetical notes in the margins and represents the oldest Arabic manuscript of Acts and the Catholic Epistles. It also has the Epistles of Paul, some of which have been edited with an English translation by H. Staal (1969; ar(2) (VI));

another manuscript from Mount Sinai (arab. 72), dated 897, containing the four Gospels in their entirety. The text is that of a Caesarean version, made from a Greek manuscript (see Arbache 1975). It has a number of early variant readings and is one of the more interesting Arabic manuscripts for the study of the New Testament text.

In addition, the writers in Arabic, be they Muslim or Christian, give many early readings in their biblical quotations which are also found in an Old Syriac type (Vööbus 1954). No critical edition of the Arabic text exists but it would be very useful if it did (although no easy task to undertake) in view of the textual importance of its oldest witnesses.

The Ethiopic versions (eth)

The work on the Ethiopic text is likewise not very advanced. There are a great many manuscripts (several hundred in the libraries of the West) but mainly of recent date, that is later than the thirteenth century. There are a few known exceptions:

three manuscripts from the Abba Garima Monastery in Aduwa (Ethiopia) dated tenth and eleventh centuries, and containing the Gospels (see Metzger 1977, pp. 224–5). According to R. Zuurmond (1989 (III)), these manuscripts attest the earliest forms of the type 'Aa', probably the oldest type, whereas manuscript 2 is of the type

'Ab' which is also attested by Codex Zotenberg 32, kept in Paris. Zuurmond refers to a total of more than 250 manuscripts which have been analysed according to this classification.

The contents of the Ethiopic New Testament manuscripts are not known in detail but a centre was created some ten years ago in the United States with the aim of compiling a complete film library of all the Ethiopic manuscripts known world-wide (Hill Monastic Manuscripts Library, Collegeville, Minnesota). Once this information has been collected, it should be possible to produce a critical edition of the New Testament. At present, the most up-to-date edition available is that of F. de Bassano (1920–6 (III); 2nd edn. 1934); alternatively, the older editions may be consulted: Rome 1548–9 (III) (eth[ro] in UBS[3a]) and T. Pell Platt, 1826 (III) (eth[pp]). Certain Ethiopic variants belong to several ancient text types: that of the great uncials and, at the same time, that of Codex Bezae (Alexandrian, see pp. 107–9 and 'Western', see pp. 109–10). They are of sufficient value in themselves to assure the lasting interest of this version.

The Slavonic versions (slav)

The first Slavonic version is attributed to Cyril and Methodius in the ninth century, a date later than that of the other versions. The manuscripts run into hundreds; the oldest ones go back to the tenth century but even they attest different types of text which suggests that there were several versions already in existence:

Codex Zographensis, from the tenth century, was written in Macedonia and is kept today in Leningrad. It contains the four Gospels (from Mt 3:11 onwards) and has a text which is often 'Western' (see p. 110). There exists a rather poor edition by V. Jagić (1879; sl(1) (VI) reprint 1954);

Codex Marianus, from the beginning of the eleventh century, was also copied in Macedonia and is kept in Moscow (two leaves are in Vienna). The text of the four Gospels in this manuscript, unlike that of the previous one, is the usual one of the Greek minuscules. It has been edited by V. Jagić (1883; sl(2) (VI) reprint 1960);

the oldest manuscripts of Acts and the Epistles are from the twelfth century, and of Revelation, the fourteenth century. J. Vajs, in his research and in his critical edition of the first Slavonic version of the Gospels (1927–36 (III)), comes to the conclusion that the text has been heavily influenced by the 'Western' text (see p. 110). F. Pechuska, writing about Acts (1948 (III)), arrives at the same conclusion, but the view is not generally accepted.

Versions which have (almost) disappeared

Mention must be made of three more versions from the East of which there remains but a trace:

the Nubian version (a language spoken in the south of Upper Egypt) counts a mere ten leaves; eight of those belong to the same manuscript, an early lectionary, published by G. M. Browne (1982 (III)); see also Browne – Plumley 1988. Variant readings of a 'Western' or Caesarean type have been noted (see Metzger 1977, pp. 273f). Nubian is the only native African language in which there remain any biblical manuscripts;

there may well have existed a version in Middle Persian, of which nothing is left. The Persian manuscripts which have survived attest a more recent version (later than the year 1000) of which the Gospel text is edited in Walton's Polyglot Bible of 1657 (III; see p. 137). There is evidence of some early variant readings;

the Sogdian version (a language of Iran which became the main language of communication in all of Central Asia from the seventh to the eleventh centuries) is represented by thirty or so leaves of which twenty-three are from a tenth-century Evangeliary. Once more, alongside readings shared by the Peshitta, there exist variants which are also found in the Old Syriac version and the Diatessaron, that is of the 'Western' text (see p. 110; and Metzger 1977, p. 281).

Non-Latin Western versions

As far as biblical texts are concerned, this last group of early versions is largely uncharted territory.

Nothing is left of a version which may have been written in Celtic.

In the Germanic dialects, manuscripts have been preserved in Old English, Old Saxon and Old High German.

In the Romance dialects, the versions seem to be of a rather late date.

QUOTATIONS MADE IN EARLY WRITINGS

After the Greek manuscripts and the versions, the quotations from the New Testament found in ancient writings are of the greatest interest to textual criticism. These include the writings not only of the Church Fathers but also of other ecclesiastical writers, orthodox or heretical, and even of pagan authors, all of which may be able to give some clues as to the form of the text used in early times.

The quotations from the Fathers must, of course, be taken from a critical edition, and there are a number of collections available today, details of which are given in the Bibliography, section 4. Most of the volumes in the modern collections have an index of the New Testament passages. These collections, however, are unfortunately not yet complete; where a work is not available, the older editions of J. P. Migne can be consulted.

It is only within the last twenty-five years that work has been done to bring together all the biblical Patristic quotations. The Centre d'analyse et de documentation patristique (CADP), set up in Strasbourg, is building up a collection of quotations on microfilm, classified verse by verse; several tens of thousands a year are being produced. An index is also being published under the name of *Biblica patristica*, four volumes of which have appeared since 1975 (V).

GREEK WRITERS

Between 1969 and 1981, an international team under the direction of J. Duplacy produced *L'Inventaire général des citations patristiques de la Bible grecque*, (a general catalogue of Patristic quotations from the Greek Bible). More than 500,000 references were listed and are in the process of being entered onto microfilm and published in indexes at the Strasbourg-based Centre (CADP – see above). At the same time, there has been an increase in the number of critical editions, with the result that today there is a large amount of valuable documentation to hand which has only just begun to be put to use. (The catalogue, for example, is mentioned and, to some extent, used, in Nestle–Aland[26] (1898 – (III)). A brief indication of the editions available is given here:

The Apostolic Fathers: edited by F. X. Funk–K. Bihlmeyer (1956[2] (IV); *SC* 10 bis (1958), 33 (1951), 53 bis (1968), 167 (1971), 172 (1971). These are the first authors to quote from the writings of the New Testament but they can scarcely be used as witnesses to the text, for the references are more allusions than actual quotations and as such may well derive from oral tradition (see pp. 89 – 90) rather than the written text itself. No agreement with any particular type of text can be observed.

The Apologists: it is quite another matter with these writers belonging to a generation later: edited by I. C. Th. Otto (1851 – 81 (IV)); *TU* 4, (1888 – 93); and *SC* 20 (1948), 123 (1966). The quotations are more substantial, especially those of Justin, and have attracted the attention of several scholars because of the number of 'Western' readings they contain (see p. 97). But the whole question still needs further study. Among these Fathers, particular note may be made of Tatian, the author of the Diatessaron (see pp. 100 – 1).

Work on the text of Marcion's Bible is a little further advanced (see pp. 99 – 100). It is true that all that remain of it are small scraps, preserved in the arguments of ecclesiastical authors against Marcion, more particularly those of Tertullian and Epiphanius. But these have been collected and examined in an excellent work by A. von Harnack (1924). H. von Soden's short study of them can also be consulted (1927).

Irenaeus of Lyons: lived in Lyons from AD 177, died possibly around AD 202; edited by W. W. Harvey (1857 (IV)) and *SC*, ten vols. published. The volume of his work is considerable and some valuable studies, although by now a little old, have been produced: Sanday – Turner – Souter 1923; Kraft 1924. The text of Irenaeus is very fragmentary and so care must be exercised when interpreting the many quotations of his work which have been handed down in translation only (Latin or Armenian). As was noted in the case of Justin, so with the writings of Irenaeus, the Western variants predominate on the whole; they seem to be influenced neither by Tatian's Diatessaron nor by the Old Latin versions.

Moving on to Egypt: Clement of Alexandria (about AD 150 – 215, *GCS* 12, 17(2) and 52, and *SC*, nine vols. published) is the subject of a greater number of studies of more recent date: Mees 1970; and Zaphiris 1970. Careful reviews of these works have been produced by Duplacy (in his 'Bulletins de critique textuelle' of 1972 and 1973). Clement's text offers readings belonging to several types, 'Western', Caesarean and Alexandrian (see p. 97, pp. 103 – 4 and pp. 107 – 8), although the authors noted above are not in agreement as to the proportions of each. This mixture of text types is typical of manuscripts of Clement's time, in particular P^{66}.

Because of the extent of his work, the study of the text of Origen

(AD 185 – 254, *SC*, twenty-eight vols. published, the rest to be found in *GCS* 3, 30 and 33) is a much lengthier task. But it is a task of particular importance, first, because Origen lived both in Alexandria (until AD 231) and in Caesarea (AD 215 – 19 and after AD 231), and secondly, because his text was used by later generations of Church Fathers (e.g. Jerome) and also appears in the margin of certain manuscripts (e.g. 1739). Furthermore, the text is likely to represent an intermediary stage between the first Caesarean recension and that of Pamphilus (see pp. 103 – 4). The main thing to bear in mind about Origen's text is that its readings are generally Alexandrian but with a certain proportion of Caesarean variants for the Gospels and the Pauline Epistles, which probably increases after AD 231. There are no, or very few, 'Western' readings.

Rather less is known about the quotations of the other Fathers, such as Hippolytus of Rome (? – AD 235), Eusebius of Caesarea (? – AD 239), Athanasius of Alexandria (AD 295 – 373), Gregory of Nazianzus (? – AD 389), Gregory of Nyssa (? – AD 394), Didymus of Alexandria (? – AD 398), John Chrysostom (? – AD 407; for Chrysostom's text of Acts see the interesting study by Boismard – Lamouille (1985 (III)), Cyril of Alexandria (AD 380 – 444) or Theodoret of Cyrrhus (AD 393 – 460), to name but a few of the more familiar names. It would be unwise to discount the witness of such authors. Early readings sometimes end up in strange places: for example, in the work by a certain pseudo-Andrew of Crete, *An eulogy of James, the brother of the Lord* (edited by J. Noret, 1978), there are quite a few Caesarean variant readings of the Epistle of James. This was a work written (according to Noret, p. 100) between AD 610 and 640 in Palestine. And John Damascene in the century following (? – AD 749) has readings which are related to the 'Western' text. Mention may also be made of Basil of Caesarea (AD 330 – 79) who was responsible for the division of the Gospel text as it is preserved in part in the *Regulae morales*, a work which provides an insight into the problems which were beginning to arise when a writer wished to make reference to the biblical text.

As for the biblical quotations found in the 'catenae', the difficulty in using them, when a critical edition is not yet available, is a well known one. For the Pauline Epistles, there is the work by K. Staab (1933 (IV)), which is a collection of all the fragments of the commentaries written by Didymus, Eusebius of Emesus, Acacius of Caesarea, Apollinaris, Diodore of Tarsus, Theodore of Mopsuestia, etc. For the Gospels, Staab's work has been continued by J. Reuss (1941 – 84 (IV)).

It could also be of interest to examine the quotations made by pagan writers, such as Celsus, Porphyry or Julian. A start has been made, with the work of Porphyry, by A. von Harnack (1916a, pp. 105f.).

LATIN WRITERS

A great deal more is known today than previously about both Latin and Greek Patristic quotations, thanks to the Vetus Latina Institut in Beuron (see p. 29). The older Fathers, such as Tertullian or Cyprian, retain their place of importance for what they reveal about the New Testament of the African Church in the first half of the third century or even earlier. But as the later quotations are systematically listed and examined, the text type of the quotations can be determined for an increasing number of writers.

The quotations of Tertullian (about AD 150 – about AD 220, *CSEL* 20 and 47, *CCL* 1 – 2), were (inadequately) studied by H. Rönsch (1871) but have been partially re-examined, notably by H. von Soden (1927) and by H. J. Frede (*Vetus Latina*, (1962 – 89 (III)) vols. 24 – 5). In the opinion of Frede (Introduction, p. 30), as far as the Epistle to the Ephesians is concerned, Tertullian translates for the most part directly from the Greek; von Soden believes that he uses an assortment of Latin translations. Whatever the case, Tertullian is important both as an original and as an early witness.

The quotations of Cyprian (about AD 200 – 258, *CSEL* 3, *CCL* 3) have been the subject of some excellent monographs: Corssen 1892; Heidenreich 1900; von Soden 1909. They represent a type of text also attested by several manuscripts and known as the 'African' type (see p. 101). It is a text which, without a doubt, was used in the third century in what is now Tunisia; it is of a 'Western' type but distinct from the Bezan text type (see p. 110). It represents one of the very first translations made of the New Testament (see p. 102). It may also be added that Zeno of Verona (d. before AD 380, *CCL* 22), in the Epistles at least, attests the same type of text as that of Cyprian.

For the purposes of determining the text of the Roman Church of the same period, the importance of the quotations of Novatian (d. about AD 251, *CCL* 4) is undeniable. Some brief studies were made of them some time ago: d'Alès 1923; Baumstark 1930. For the Pauline Epistles, however, it is more a matter of allusions than quotations, which do not reflect any particular text type (see *Vetus Latina*, vols. 24 – 5).

The text of the great travllers such as Hilary of Poitiers (d. AD 367,

CSEL 22 and 65, *CCL* 62) and his contemporary Lucifer of Calaris (d. AD 370, *CSEL* 14, *CCL* 8) certainly merits attention. The first major studies were made some time ago: Bonnassieux 1906; Vogels 1922. According to Frede (*Vetus Latina*), the text of Hilary displays a relationship in some of its readings with that of Cyprian but it is not characteristic of any particular text type. Lucifer, on the other hand, is the best Patristic witness of the text type **D** for the Pauline Epistles, which is the text type of Codex Claromontanus (see p. 16).

Special mention must be made of Priscillian, Bishop of Avila (d. AD 385, *CSEL* 18) who is the first witness of the Spanish type of the Old Latin text (**S**, cf. p. 102), again close to Cyprian's text (cf. Thiele, *Vetus Latina*, vol. 26). Other witnesses of this type would be: the *Speculum*, attributed to Augustine (*CSEL* 12), and Bachiarius (Spain, about AD 400).

The commentaries of Ambrosiaster (d. AD 384, *CSEL* 50 and 81, *CCL* 9) and Pelagius (d. AD 418, *Text S* 9(12) on the thirteen Epistles of Paul (excluding Hebrews) contain many Scriptural quotations. The text of the former is a witness to the Old Latin type **I** (see pp. 101 – 2) which is found in some manuscripts (Beuron 61, 86) but is also bears a resemblance to that of Marius Victorinus (d. AD 363, *CSEL* 83, *SC* 68), a type close to **D** (see p. 102). The text of the latter, in contrast, follows a clear Vulgate type (see Frede 1961).

Similarly, there are many quotations in the commentaries on Revelation written by Tyconius (d. AD 390, *TextS* 3(1)) and Primasius (d. AD 552, *PL* 68). Several valuable studies have been made of them: Hausleiter 1891; Vogels 1920.

On the text of Augustine, there is no shortage of introductory studies, as, for example, that of S. H. Milne (1926); and special mention should be made of the studies by Dom D. Bruyne (1921 and 1931). Augustine uses a rather mixed Old Latin text. All kinds of influences can be detected, from the substrata of Cyprian's African type right through to the type of the Vulgate (see *Vetus Latina*, pp. 29 – 30).

There are many other Patristic writings in Latin not covered by this brief list; and the references to *Vetus Latina* are only valid for the Epistles. A great deal of work clearly remains to be done, even in the area of the Latin text, in order for a useful description of the quotations of every author to be provided.

Chapter one

SYRIAC WRITERS

Attention has been focused mainly on Ephraem of Nisibis (AD 306 – 73) or Ephraem the Syrian, who wrote commentaries on nearly all the New Testament. It is chiefly his quotations from the Gospels which have been studied in two works of the highest value, by F. C. Burkitt (1901 (IV)) and J. Schäfers (1917). Note should also be made of L. Leloir's work (1958).

Certain passages quoted by other Syriac writers are to be found in F. C. Burkitt's critical edition of the Old Syriac (see p. 33). It is especially useful for Ephraem's text and also that of Aphraates. A. de Halleux's edition of the commentary on John's Prologue by Philoxenus of Mabbûg is of fundamental importance for distinguishing between the Philoxenian text and the Harclean (see pp. 34 – 5). There is also the list of the Syriac Patristic quotations from the Epistles of Paul by J. Kerschensteiner which can be consulted (see p. 33), as well as studies by Baarda (1975).

Work on authors in other languages has made even less progress than that on the Greek, Latin or Syriac writers. Almost the only study to mention is that of L. Leloir (1967, already indicated p. 40).

This short summary of the most important works dealing with the New Testament quotations should not lead to precious information elsewhere being overlooked – either, on Latin writers, in Sabatier's book (see p. 144) or, on the Patristic writings generally, in the critical apparatus of the main editions of the New Testament text, that is, that of Griesbach (see p. 141) or Tischendorf (see pp. 147 – 8). As long as these sources are used with care, they can continue to be of great value.

To sum up the situation, with the Greek manuscripts, the versions and the quotations of the early writers, New Testament textual criticism is richly equipped with useful tools. In order to establish the biblical text in its authentic form, the scholar is most fortunate in being able to draw on early and abundant sources. But he must use them correctly. For that, it is essential to know the rules to be followed for the elimination of corrupt readings. There is such a mass of material to sort through that this is often no easy task. A well-defined method is therefore all the more necessary.

2

The method of textual criticism

The guiding principles of textual criticism are the same for all writings, whatever type, although in practice their application varies according to the number, variety and quality of witnesses available. In this sense, then, it is correct to speak of a method of New Testament textual criticism. But that does not mean that it is a fixed method. On the contrary, it is one of the points over which scholars most disagree. They may well generally agree about there being several stages to be worked through by the critic in order to reach the correct reading, but they agree rather less about the order and significance of the stages. The aim here is not to enter into detailed discussion about the various theories nor to lay down any rigid order of procedure. Verbal criticism, external criticism and internal criticism will sometimes be seen to work hand in hand. The chief purpose of this chapter will be to establish points of reference in what is a very complex issue.

VERBAL CRITICISM

In order to re-establish in its original purity an ancient text which has been handed down to us in a more or less altered state, the critic must first of all study the sources of corruption in manuscripts. This is what is called verbal criticism. For secular writings in Greek and Latin, lists have been drawn up with the most common errors together with their most likely corrections, all catalogued in alphabetical and methodological order. It is lists of this kind, such as are found in L. Havet's *Manuel de critique verbale* (1911, reprint 1967) for Latin texts, which prove to be the most helpful mentor for learning how to restore a document to its original form.

For the New Testament, however, verbal criticism is rarely conclusive. Some scholars, such as J. Duplacy, would even advocate doing away with verbal criticism altogether. While there are undoubtedly involuntary, one could say mechanical, errors on the part of the scribes, in the biblical manuscripts just as in any other, the problem is that it cannot be always said for certain that a variant is definitely an accidental error. There is an even greater number of intentional variants most of which are closely tied in with the very nature of the New Testament writings; they therefore need to be examined according to the critical procedures which are explained in later sections of this chapter. The present section, therefore, will simply present the main types of involuntary alterations, since it can be useful to be familiar with them.

INVOLUNTARY VARIANTS

Involuntary variants are always with us, for no copyist is infallible. It is only natural, therefore, that they should crop up in the manuscripts of the New Testament, for its books were copied over and over again, all too often by amateur scribes. But accidental slips are not the most difficult errors to correct. Attempts have been made to classify them according to the reason which produced them in the first place. Thus there is A. T. Robertson's classification (1925, pp. 150 – 5) which, to use his own terms, consists of errors of the eye, of the ear, of memory, of the judgement, of the pen and of speech. Unfortunately, this kind of classification is not as easy to apply as it looks, and it is better to use a less technical grouping.

Additions

The most common error is dittography, that is the repetition by mistake of a letter, a syllable, a word, a group of words or even part of a sentence. Usually this type of error hits the reader in the eye for it spoils the meaning. So, for example, on the Latin side of Codex Laudianus (E.08/e) in Ac 2:4 the scribe has written: 'et repleti sunt et repleti sunt omnes spiritu sancto'. Similarly, in Jn 13:14 in Codex Vaticanus (B.03) the scribe has written twice the words from εἰ to διδάσκαλος. But, in fact, it will be seen that this kind of error is not always so easy to detect.

Omissions

This is the price which has to be paid for distraction. There is first of all straightforward haplography, that is writing only once letters, syllables or words which should have been repeated. Next, and above all, there is omission by *homoioteleuton*, that is the confusing of words,

53

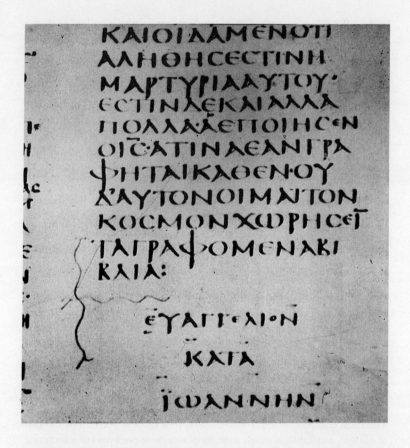

3 Codex Sinaiticus, S.01 (fourth century), has two endings to John's Gospel.
Here the manuscript is seen in natural light; the Gospel ends correctly with v. 25
of chapter 21.

lines or parts of sentences which have the same ending. What happens
in this case is that the eye of the copyist goes from the first occurrence
to the second so that part of the text, sometimes even an entire sentence,
gets left out in the process of copying. For example, Lk 18:39 is missing
from some manuscripts (33, 57, 130, it^b), no doubt because the verse
has the same ending as the previous one.

This error is not, in fact, always obvious. For instance, in Ac 4:17
some manuscripts (S.01, A.02, B.03, D.05) have ἀπειλησώμεθα,

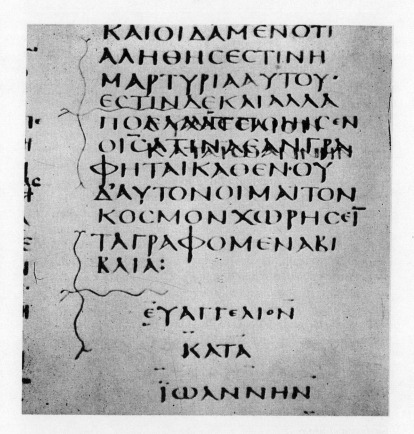

4   In this photograph, the manuscript is seen with the help of ultra-violet rays.
It has been corrected by the scribe himself who erased the original subscription
and 'paragraphos' (the wavy line) and added in their place the final verse which
he had omitted in his first copy. The erased parts have left marks in the parchment which can be made visible using an ultra-violet lamp. These lamps are also
used for the reading of palimpsests. (Photos H. M. Teeple, 1961.)

'let us warn', whereas most read ἀπειλῇ ἀπειλησώμεθα, 'let us warn
with threats', which gives greater force to the prohibition. Grammati-
cally, both forms are correct and there may either have been homoioteleuton in the case of the former reading or dittography in the case of the
second. It is clear that, even for the most simple mistakes, a hastily
formed judgement about their cause could lead to wrong conclusions.

Confusion of letters

The letters most commonly confused were those with either a similar sound or a similar shape. For the vowels, first of all, the majority of the errors are due to itacism, that is the tendency to pronounce certain vowels or diphthongs, like η ει υ οι, like an iota, and therefore to replace them with an iota. This type of variant is common in the manuscripts, and it is not always possible to affirm that it occurred in the process of dictation: the very act of copying involves an element of 'interior dictation' (A.-M. Desrousseaux; quoted by Dain 1975, p. 41) which is sufficient to explain the confusion of sounds. Other interchanges also happen between such letters as ε and αι, ε and η, ο and ω. Although these errors are usually trivial, they have more than once altered the meaning of a phrase: for example, in 1 Pet 2:3, some manuscripts (K.018, L.020, etc.) replace χρηστός 'gentle' by χριστός 'Christ'.

Consonants with near identical sounds were likewise confused in some districts: τ and θ, π and β, κ and χ; κσ and πσ were also confused with ξ and ψ. But confusion between consonants generally arose from the similarity of form of certain of the capital letters: E and C, O and Θ, Γ and T. Hence in 1 Cor 6:20, instead of δή some manuscripts have ΑΡΑΓΕ 'therefore' (minuscule 1611, Methodius), and from that arises perhaps the reading ΑΡΑΤΕ 'carry' in several other manuscripts (Chrysostom; and in Latin: it[fg], vg, Marcion according to Tertullian, Cyprian, etc.).

Confusion of words

Apart from the abbreviations which added enormously to the difficulty of reading the manuscripts, most of the mistakes of this kind are rightly attributed to poor writing (see p. 8). A few examples will demonstrate the problem. In 1 Tm 3:16, certain manuscripts, such as D.06, have ὁμολογοῦμεν ὡς, 'we confess that', instead of ὁμολογουμένως, 'without contradiction'. In Jn 1:13, 18; 7:37 – 38, the meaning depends on the punctuation, which was not used in the first copies; and it has not been inserted in the same way in the different manuscripts. In 1 Tm 3:16, K.018, L.020, P.025, etc. have taken ΟΣ (= ὅς), 'who' for the abbreviated form ΘΣ (= Θεός), 'God', which is also found as a correction in S.01[c], A.02[c] and C.04[c].

Other changes

There are many other kinds of unintentional variants. It would be impossible to list all the incidences of 'lapsus calami', such as the changes of the order of letters, or of syllables, or of words, as in the different position of πάλιν in Mk 14:40. Or again, the grammatical faults, or spelling mistakes, especially in proper names which were not very common: Ναζαρά, Ναζαράτ, Ναζαρέθ, Ναζαρέτ, Ναζαρέδ, in Lk 4:16. There must also be a great many mistakes which were not directly the fault of the scribe: he may have had to decipher poor writing, or copy from a papyrus damaged by age, or else he may have been led astray by marginal or interlinear notes. It simply has to be accepted that in many cases of textual corruption the reason for the change cannot be known.

INTENTIONAL VARIANTS

These are sometimes difficult to distinguish from involuntary variants. In particular, certain spellings could be deliberate just as well as the result of negligence or distraction. In any case, the intention behind deliberate alterations is not necessarily bad. The high esteem in which the sacred text was held was itself sufficient reason to correct it if there was any cause to suspect that it had been tampered with. 'Where there was any doubt about the original text, since the final text which was going to be read, studied and taken as the rule of faith and life had to be absolutely perfect, corrections were made boldly, things were added and things were omitted, but all was done out of the conviction that it was right to do it, and the purer the intentions the more it was done' (Lagrange 1933, p. 495).

Corrections of spelling, grammar and style

Variants of this kind can, on the whole, be put down to the work of amateur scholars who are the more dangerous because, under the pretext of retrieving the original, they in fact deform it. Their attempts to correct the copy they have before them are made under the guise of restoring it to its early state. So they change the spelling of proper names (καπερναούμ replaces καφαρναούμ in certain manuscripts of Mk 1:21); or they alter the dialectical forms of verbs (the Hellenistic endings of ἦλθαν, εἶπαν are replaced by classical ones: ἦλθον, εἶπον). In the same way they correct what they imagine to be grammatical mistakes.

In Lk 4:1, after the verb of movement ἤγετο, 'he was led', several manuscripts (A.02, N.022) prefer the accusative εἰς τὴν ἔρημον, 'into the desert', to the dative ἐν τῇ ἐρήμῳ (S.01, B.03, D.05), even though in the Koine ἐν is usual to mean 'into'. Some go a step further and try to improve the quality of the style, providing, for example, a more logical link between sentences by inserting connectives: that no doubt explains the presence of γάρ in several manuscripts of Mk 4:24 (713, it[b]). Or else they replace an ordinary word by a clearer or more elegant synonym: thus, in Mk 7:5, A.02, L.020, it[bc], etc. read ἀνίπτοις χερσίν, 'with unwashed hands', in place of κοιναῖς χερσίν, 'with common (= impure) hands' in S.01*, B.03. Conflated readings (see p. 60) of this verse also occur: P[45] κοιναῖς χερσὶν καὶ ἀνίπτοις, or f[13] κοιναῖς χερσὶν ἀνίπτοις.

Corrections for the sake of harmony or conformity

These are alterations made in order to suppress any divergences between parallel passages, a temptation which faces all editors.

Agreement between parallel passages of the New Testament

The work of assimilation is especially apparent in the Gospels and above all in the Synoptics where attempts are made to do away with the slightest variation. Jerome's complaints concerning the Latin copies of the Bible (*Epistola ad Damasum, praefatio in quattuor evangelia*) are relevant here. He pointed out that the numerous errors contained in the manuscripts then in use had arisen partly from the practice of filling out separate Gospel accounts of an incident with details from parallel passages. He also blamed the method used to deal with variant readings, which was simply to take the first manuscript to hand as the norm and to correct all the other manuscripts accordingly. The same kind of confusion is found in the Greek manuscripts. Often, the easiest way to harmonise was to place end to end parallel or even diverging texts, so producing what are known as conflated readings. This accounts for Jn 19:34 inserted after Mt 27:49 in S.01, B.03, C.04.

In some instances, one passage is made to agree with another from the same book or from the same author. For example, there are three accounts of the conversion of Paul in Acts. In the first account, certain manuscripts contain information borrowed from the other two accounts. So, in Ac 9:5 in E.08, A.02, vg, there is the additional expression 'it hurts you to kick against the goads', which has been borrowed from

Ac 26:14. It is not rare to come across the same sort of thing in the Pauline Epistles. Thus, in Gal 4:17 a number of manuscripts (D.06*/d, F.010/f, G.012/g...) add 1 Cor 12:31. Attempts to create uniformity generally were given free rein.

Agreement between Biblical quotations in the New Testament and the text of the Old Testament

There are many passages from the Old Testament quoted in the New Testament, often rather freely. Again, attempts have been made to iron out divergences by aligning the quotations with the Septuagint text. So, where Mt 15:8 gives a free quotation of Is 29:13, the exact text has been reproduced in some manuscripts (C.04, E.07, F.09 and others). Where necessary, the reference itself is corrected, as in Mk 1:2 where many manuscripts (A.02, E.07, F.09 and others) have 'as it is written in the prophets' instead of 'as it is written in the prophet Isaiah' (such as in S.01, B.03), because in fact the quoted words are from several of the prophets.

Agreement between New Testament texts and liturgical texts

The books of the New Testament were used for public reading from an early date and certain passages such as the Lord's Prayer were specially adapted for liturgical use. This use of New Testament passages, with the various alterations that it entailed, did not fail to have an effect on the Scriptural text. As an example: several manuscripts of Mt 6:13 (E.07, G.011, K.017, L.019, among others) add to the end of the Lord's Prayer the words: 'For thine is the kingdom, the power and the glory for ever. Amen', the reason being that public prayers often ended with such a doxology.

Exegetical corrections

Too often, when faced with passages difficult to interpret, copyists or revisers would try to make the passage more complete, more exact, less offensive or less obscure. This accounts for a good many variants where the early reading has been altered by interpolations, deletions and other changes of all sorts.

Interpolations

First, there are the simple explanatory glosses which seek to make the text easier to understand. Hence, in 1 Cor 7:14: 'for the unbelieving husband is consecrated by his wife', several manuscripts (D.06/d,

F.010/f, G.012/g, vg, for example) add the phrase τῇ πιστῇ, 'believing', to describe the wife. Then, there are also marginal notes which a later copyist is reluctant to leave out and so incorporates into his text. This probably did not happen as often as has been said; it certainly is difficult to prove. But there is an example in James 1:5: in the margin beside 'If any of you lacks wisdom', some reader of Codex 1518 has written: πνευματικῆς καὶ οὐκ ἀνθρωπίνης, 'spiritual, not human', a gloss which emerges in the text of 603. Finally, and above all, there are the conflated readings (see p. 58) where two or more variants for a particular passage have been quite simply run together so as to avoid the risk of omitting the authentic reading. In Mt 26:15, most manuscripts speak of the 'thirty pieces of silver' but some (for example D.05, it[ab]) read 'thirty staters', which in its turn produces the conflated reading 'thirty staters of silver'.

Deletions

These were apparently less numerous than the additions but they were used to get over some historical difficulty or correct an awkward expression. In Mt 23:35, where there is a mention of Zacharias, several manuscripts (such as S.01*) omit the genealogical detail 'son of Barachias' so as not to contradict 2 Ch 24:20 where Zacharias is said to be the 'son of Joida'. In Lk 23:32, 'two other criminals were led away with him (Jesus)', the word 'other' is left out in some manuscripts (it[c e ff2], sy[s]) as it could be felt to be offensive.

Tendentious alterations

Some revisers of the text made only very slight changes, on occasion nothing more than one word, but behind these modifications can sometimes be discerned a certain theological tendency. That could account for the variant of sy[c] in Mt 1:21, which, instead of 'he will save his people from their sins', reads 'he will save the world ...' so as to avoid what the copyist felt was too strong a Jewish emphasis.

Doctrinal corrections

Variants of dogmatic origin are rarer than those of the preceding group although more common than is usually admitted. This is not the place to go into alterations that the heretics are said by the Church Fathers to have introduced into the New Testament text. There are perhaps traces of them in certain manuscripts, but they are not as a rule very obvious, and indeed it often happens that a variant turns out to be earlier than the doctrinal purpose which it later serves. In order to make accurate analyses of such variants, the critic must first develop a very sound methodology.

On the other hand, doctrinal corrections inspired by the wish to strengthen a proof or answer enemies are not always very hard to spot. In Mk 13:32, 'But of that day or that hour no one knows, not even the angels in heaven, nor the Son, but only the Father', several manuscripts (X.033, 983, 1689) delete 'nor the Son'. Similarly, in the childhood narrative in Luke, certain expressions used about Jesus: 'his parents' (2:41), 'his mother and his father' (2:33), have been corrected to 'Joseph and Mary' (1012, it[abc]), 'Joseph and his mother' (A.02, E.07, G.011, it, and others). There are a number of other passages which could be cited where variants have arisen in an attempt to bring the text more into line with the standard teaching of the Church.

These then are the preliminary steps to be taken in New Testament textual criticism: to find out how the changes to the original could have come about. But verbal criticism on its own is inadequate for determining with certainty the quality of many variants. Too many plausible hypotheses can be advanced to explain the sources of corruption. As K. Lake so well puts it (1933, p. 5): 'The critic has always to be ready to revise his judgement. He ought to be suspicious of readings but far more suspicious of his own conclusions.' In fact, verbal criticism, which examines so to speak the diseases of the text, is often powerless to discover its hidden illnesses. It enjoys more success with the involuntary variants than with the intentional ones. Its powers of diagnosis are neither penetrating enough nor sure enough always to uncover the primitive reading from amongst the various corrupted forms of a text. It is, in short, insufficient by itself.

It must be said, however, that a methodical list of the different types of textual error is not without its usefulness. When the later stages of criticism, both external and internal, are reached, it is good to be able to recall these faults readily. The critic is then on his guard and his eyes are open – a necessary condition for making the best use of the facts.

EXTERNAL CRITICISM

When the student consults for the first time a good critical apparatus, that is an exact and methodical, if not complete, collection of the New Testament variants, he may well be rather overwhelmed by the sheer number of sigla used to designate the manuscripts for each reading. But it is on this apparatus that external criticism is based in its pursuit of the original form of the text. Once the examination of the errors of textual transmission has proved inconclusive, the next step which must be taken is to study the respective value of the witnesses (manuscripts, versions, quotations) where the variants are found. This is called external criticism because it relies solely on the authority of the document itself rather than on the intrinsic value of the particular readings, and it has long been predominant. Its guiding principles need to be examined and the results they produce evaluated.

THREE DEFECTIVE PRINCIPLES

In order to choose the correct reading from amongst the different variants, it used to be customary, and indeed it too often still is customary, to appeal to the number, the age and the general character of the witnesses; these are three criteria which, whether taken singly or together, are insufficient to justify a choice of reading.

The number of the witnesses

A hundred manuscripts which are copies one of another constitute but one authority, whereas two independent manuscripts should be reckoned as two. Moreover, even when faced with a real majority, care must be taken not to assume automatically that the majority is right without further examination. All copies do not have the same value. It is the question of the nature of the text which is important, not the quantity of its representatives. *Non numerantur sed ponderantur*. 'A fault may be copied as many times as you like, you will never make a correct reading out of it' (Collomp 1931, p. 35). The beginner is naturally inclined to find safety in numbers and needs to be on his guard against this trap. Universal suffrage has no place in textual criticism.

It is, of course, true that the presence of a large number of documents can sometimes be a useful signpost but it can never be adequate on its own for drawing firm conclusions. As will be seen, copies have to be considered as representatives of a group and not as separate witnesses. That immediately weakens any argument based on their number. But there is more to it than that: even when the main manuscript groups agree on a variant, it is still essential to check whether there is not a divergent reading attested by any of the other documents of authority; for it is a simple fact that the original reading may be found in only a few scattered documents while what the majority contain is an early correction.

The age of the witnesses

This is no better a guide. A codex of the sixth century may be the copy of a good second century manuscript which has been lost but which was a first-hand copy of the original. A fourth-century codex could be a poor copy of a defective third-century manuscript with a dozen intermediaries separating it from the original. It would therefore be wrong to trust the latter more than the former. Important lessons can be learnt from recent discoveries. For example, there is a reading (1 Pet 2:20) which hitherto was known only from the relatively late uncial (Ψ.044) and some minuscules (including 1739, tenth century) and which has now been found in a papyrus (P^{72}) from the beginning of the fourth century. Certain readings in the uncials S.01 and B.03, also of the fourth century, which had previously gone uncontested are now in question. The authority which tends to be attributed to an early codex rests on a foundation which is sometimes deceptive: its nearness to the original. The factors which carry more weight are the number of witnesses, and more especially the quality of the copies made between the original and the manuscript in question. In a word, it is the age of the text and not the age of the manuscript which must be considered, for there are relatively recent manuscripts with a very early text and early manuscripts with a corrupted text.

Of course, the age of a witness is never to be completely overlooked. It would be right to be wary of a variant which does not emerge until the fifteenth or sixteenth century, for example, and to pay more attention to a variant in a papyrus from around AD 200. But, once again, it would be wrong to be hypnotised by the papyri and the uncials. There are minuscules which date from before the uncials. There are even minuscules whose text is better than that of some papyri or uncials.

The general character of the witnesses

Again, this is not a decisive criterion. Certainly, it is tempting to prefer a manuscript which displays a certain accuracy to one which is full of obvious faults, but, unfortunately, a correct manuscript may present a faulty text if it faithfully reproduces a manuscript which is itself the result of a bold revision, full of tendentious alterations. Conversely, a novice scribe may produce numerous faults of detail and yet present, in spite of that, an excellent text.

A manuscript is frequently called 'good' without too much thought and the label should not be taken as an accurate guide. The contents of the parcel cannot be judged by its wrapper. A good textual witness is one which inspires confidence by its habitual accuracy and competence, qualities which cannot be recognised by external criticism alone. It is, on the contrary, the intrinsically superior quality of its readings which allow a manuscript to be judged worthy of esteem. So caution must be exercised: manuscripts may often not live up to their reputation, and, if he is not on his guard about that, the editor of a text may well find himself repeatedly not being as careful as he would have hoped to be.

To summarise, when weighing up the value of a variant it would be wrong to say that the number, the age or the external accuracy of the witnesses are without importance. These criteria may, on occasions, be useful. But it would be naive to think that they alone are sufficient to determine the original form of a text. By themselves, they can lead to no definite conclusions. It is sometimes said in commentaries that some reading or other has the support of the most, the oldest and the best manuscripts. It is clear that when all things are properly considered this is actually no proof at all. But it would be wrong to criticise too harshly: may he who has never practised this simplistic kind of textual criticism throw the first stone! But it is better avoided. Once again, it is the text which lies behind the manuscripts which has to be studied.

CLASSIFICATION OF TEXTS

It is now more than two centuries since philologists, anxious to produce a good edition of the texts of Classical Antiquity or of the Middle Ages, first began to discard these defective principles in favour of a new method which consisted in grouping manuscripts according to the textual variants – a method which entailed the classification of the different forms of a text. It produced, in particular, the famous 'stemma codicum', the (reconstituted) genealogical tree of the manuscripts which, at the time, represented a step forward. It ceased to be of value when it was applied to situations for which it was not suitable. This is in fact what happened in the case of the New Testament; see the important article by J. Duplacy (1975) which not only provides a historical survey of the genealogical method, but goes on to give some illustrations of it using a new statistical process (see pp. 71 – 3 below), and also includes a useful bibliography.

Before looking at the method in more detail, it would be helpful to remember the various secondary factors which are sometimes useful to the codicologist (and the palaeographer) in establishing relationships between manuscripts and in distinguishing the different forms or families. A fairly complete account, though now rather old, can be found in A. C. Clark (1918); more recent specialised works have already been referred to (p. 10). In short, two series of characteristic details can be distinguished. The first group is wholly to do with things outside the text: drawings in illuminated manuscripts, glosses in the local language, the numbering of the pages, regional (or national) peculiarities of the writing, and, for the New Testament manuscripts, the grouping of extra-biblical material such as summaries, prefaces, and so on. The other group of details has more to do with the text itself: blemishes, holes, tears (creating gaps), leaves displaced (causing the text to be out of order), similarities in the arrangements of lines or columns indicating a common model. All of these things, together with those described above (pp. 9 – 10), are helpful and even of great value in classifying the manuscripts. The Ferrar group (f^{13}, see p. 22), for example, is sufficiently specific for the codicologist to be able to identify its members without any further examination of the text. Codicology is a science which is making progress at present and it may well, one day, be able to help sort out the complicated tangle of the relationships which exist between the different types of the New Testament text. No-one, however, would claim to be able to construct on this slender basis a whole genealogy, the stemma, or to obtain in any way the original text. In order to achieve that, several systems have been put forward.

Bengel: a geographical classification

J. A. Bengel (1734; see p. 140) was the first to attempt to group the manuscripts into families according to geographical factors. But it was his successors, J. S. Semler and J. J. Griesbach (see pp. 141 – 2) who were the first to use (although more or less as a simple convention) the terms 'Alexandrian', 'Byzantine' and 'Western', terms which are still used today.

Lachmann: the system of common faults

This was a system developed in Germany, around 1830 – 50, the major contributor being K. Lachmann who was well known as much for his work in the Classical field, with his edition of Lucretius, as in the biblical field (see pp. 146 – 7). The principle behind the system is a familiar one: all the copies which contain the same faults in the same places were copied from each other or are all copies of the one manuscript containing those faults. Obviously, the faults in question must not be simple errors such as spelling mistakes, which could even have existed in the original, or which could be a coincidence, without a common origin. But as long as the faults are well selected, the principle rests on the unlikelihood of several copyists making exactly the same mistakes independently of each other. A series of common errors is an indication of a common ancestor. This, in outline, is the basic rule which enables copies to be divided into families and the genealogical tree of the manuscripts to be constructed.

A stinging criticism of Lachmann's method was made by J. Bédier (Préface, 1913, and 1928). He shows that in nearly every case the stemma which emerges makes all the known copies descendants of two ancient families and two only. He takes great delight in ridiculing this curious law by which hidden forces, confined in the depths of the sub-conscious, have exerted their influence. In plain terms, the method of common faults is almost bound to result in a final classification into two families. For those philologists with a text to edit, it is appealing as a means of accounting scrupulously for the origin of all the variants, and also perhaps as a means of satisfying their subconscious desire to reserve the final choice between two alternatives for themselves.

Bédier's criticism apart, this method is in any case not always valid since independent copyists may find themselves making the same mistake, especially in the case of rare words, which are a trap for any copyist. It is also incomplete: it can ascertain the presence of a relation-ship but not the absence of one. Above all, it cannot be applied to contaminated texts, which arise when a manuscript has been copied from more than one model. It is impossible in such cases to unravel the web of genealogies, for it varies from passage to passage, and often the different threads cannot be disentangled. In the end, if Lachmann's method is taken to its logical conclusion, it leads too frequently to fanciful constructions, and to hypotheses which may indeed be plausible, but none more plausible than another; for it is so easy to modify 'those little conjectural combinations which we call classification of manuscripts' (Bédier 1929, p. 17).

What is to be made of this system when it is applied to New Testament textual criticism? It may help sometimes to establish links between manuscripts but there can be no question of constructing a genealogical tree, not even within the restricted limits of one family. There are too many missing elements for that, not least the main witnesses, those closest to the original. Lachmann himself was aware of this problem (see pp. 146 – 7). What is more, the text of the Bible is a living text where the ideas of the reviser (or of the scribe) intrude too frequently for the textual critic to be able to rely on the laws which can be observed in the mechanical reproduction of texts. Almost all the manuscript witnesses are the result of revisions based on several models, so that in every line a conscious choice has taken place, and this renders useless any calculations based on the laws of probability. The construction of family trees according to the presence of common faults is thus quite useless for the purposes of establishing the original form of the text of the New Testament.

Dom Quentin: the 'iron rule'

Some seventy years ago, Dom H. Quentin put forward a new method for classifying the manuscripts which rectified some of the faults associated with the former method. It is explained in his *Mémoire sur l'établissement du texte de la Vulgate* (1922) and in his *Essais de critique textuelle* (1926); the method was applied for the first time to the text of Genesis in the Vatican edition of the Vulgate commissioned by Pope Pius X (see p. 31).

Here is an extract from the account given by the Benedictine scholar himself:

From the very first, I reject all thought of the primitive reading. I do not think in terms of errors, or common faults, or good or bad readings, but only in terms of different forms of the text. Working with those alone, and applying a method based strictly on statistics, I define the parameters of the families and then I classify the manuscripts within each family, and finally the families themselves. From this classification results a critical canon which lays down an iron rule for the establishing of a text, and using this, I am able to reconstitute the archetype which, in effect, is the nearest form of text to the original which can be reached with the extant manuscripts. It is then, and only then, that I allow myself to think about the original. I examine the text from that point of view; and in those parts where the archetype is obviously faulty, I correct it using the resources of internal criticism; I always, however, take care to indicate with some clear sign that at such and such a place I have departed from the text which resulted from the strict application of the critical canon.

(Quentin 1926, p. 37)

This method has aroused a lively debate. Mention will only be made here of the general criticism made by J. Bédier (1928) with his usual degree of perspicacity. The eminent critic shows, with reference to the manuscript tradition of the *Lai de l'ombre*, that Dom Quentin's procedure would allow a dozen or so genealogical schemata to be constructed, each as plausible as the other. And he goes on: 'there are no doubt still other combinations which should be considered; I regret that it is only my insufficiently fertile imagination which prevents me from seeing them all.' In short, Dom Quentin's method is no more capable than the old one of delivering a sure classification of the manuscripts because there are too many possible genealogies, and each variant may cause them to be modified. When all is said and done, a family tree that is only probable is inadequate as a foundation for determining the text even of an archetype.

Meanwhile, it is interesting to note that Dom Quentin does not appear ever to have applied his system to New Testament Greek. For, as will be seen (pp. 116–18), the manuscript tradition of the original Greek text is very different from that of the Vulgate. While it is true that it is possible to distinguish a certain number of families, within those families so much freedom was exercised by the scribes and the revisers that it becomes impossible to determine the relationship between the members of the families. Not one of them has been preserved in its pure state and, through the course of the centuries, sometimes even from the very beginning, there has been a lot of cross-fertilisation from one family to another. Revised and contaminated texts abound everywhere. Given such poor conditions, what hope is there of retrieving the archetype of every family, when even the slightest deliberate correction or the least element of contamination amplifies, entangles and complicates any genealogy?

And, supposing the thing were possible, of what help would Dom Quentin's 'iron rule' be? For it consists, in fact, in nothing more than the application of the principle of the majority to the chief witnesses. Would it lead to discovery of the common ancestor, the text which served as a basis for all these different recensions? Not at all, because the 'iron rule' would mean putting on one side the right variant every time it happened that the majority of the 'heads of families' had made an identical correction to the reading. Under the guise of escaping from the dangers of subjective criticism the student would be blindly following the doubtful opinions of the early revisers. Furthermore, reaching this underlying common text would mean going back only as far as the middle or the beginning of the third century. That would still be too far from the original date of the New Testament for the 'iron rule' to be of very much use.

Colwell and Claremont: the selection of variation units

After the Second World War, the International Greek New Testament Project (see Colwell 1968) was set up with the aim of producing a full critical edition of the New Testament, starting with the Gospel of Luke. It is within that context that E. C. Colwell and others relaunched the study of the comparison of text forms. The main articles explaining Colwell's method are to be found in *Studies in methodology in textual criticism of the New Testament* (1969). There are other articles on the subject by G. D. Fee (1968) and E. J. Epp (1967); cf. B. Ehrman (1987b).

Initially Colwell, together with M. M. Parvis, devised what was known as 'the method of "Multiple Readings."' It assumes as its starting point a certain classification of the most well-known manuscripts, especially the uncials, and then goes on to ask the following question: given this classification, how is each new manuscript to be placed in one of these basic groups? The answer comprises three stages: the number of agreements between the new manuscript and each of the others for specific variation units which produce a clear demarcation between the groups of the first classification; the number of agreements between the new manuscript and the group closest to it, based this time on an examination of only the singular readings of the group; still within the group, a comparison of the text of the various manuscripts for the other variation units. This system raises at least as many questions as it answers, and Colwell is to be congratulated for having tackled some of them, such as how a variation unit is to be defined, and what to do about those variants with only one witness. By far the most interesting idea to come out of his method, and one that will be returned to later, is that of collecting significant variation units, that is those units with variants which enable the groups to be clearly distinguished one from another.

The problem with this method was the weight of material involved. How could it be applied to a long text or to hundreds of manuscripts? How could all the different results be weighed up? With the minuscules particularly in mind, Colwell (with a new team) subsequently streamlined his method by removing the final step so as to make it less clumsy. It became known as the 'Claremont Profile Method' (CPM). The aim now was to devote attention only to those new manuscripts whose text was significantly different from any previous ones. The first step was to determine to which group the new manuscript belonged; the second step was designed to act as a double-check, and this became the most important part of the method. If, on the sole basis of the singular readings of a group, a new manuscript has a text very close to the others, then the variants peculiar to that manuscript are considered as secondary and as nothing to do with the problem of classification. In this way the text forms are classified by their 'profile'.

The same criticism could be levelled against this method as against the two previous ones: there is nothing in the results which have been published which does anything to change what was already known about the manuscript tradition. Compared with Dom Quentin's method, Colwell's method even takes a backward step in one respect, for it assumes, as its starting point, that a certain grouping of the manuscripts can be taken for granted. But this grouping has no firm foundation, for it rests on generalisations formulated on the basis of a few tests. Consequently, the selection of the manuscripts which has been made does not present a faithful picture of the wide variety of existing witnesses (by no means all of which are known), but rather demonstrates how incomplete our initial knowledge of the manuscripts is. It was this partial knowledge which from now on became a guiding influence on the work of the philologist from the beginning to the end of his research. The best example of this is the classification of the Greek manuscripts of the Epistles of John by W. L. Richards (1977), who concluded, on the basis of what was known initially about the manuscripts, that there existed two types of text, whereas, in fact, the percentages of agreement indicate the clear existence of three distinct groups (see Amphoux 1981/2).

Despite these shortcomings, the CPM and the Multiple method do mark a significant advance on one point which was neglected by Dom Quentin: the selection of variation units. The criticism made by J. Bédier did have some effect. It is not possible to treat all the many kinds of agreement and disagreement between the manuscripts in the same way. Many of them arise, in one way or another, from the problems of copying. Only some are relevant for the classification of text types. The agreements to be reckoned with are those which occur at the places where there are distinctive variants.

Another step forward is that the method is less ambitious. It no longer seeks to achieve a reconstruction of the archetype of the family genealogies. The forms of the text are rather classified according to how close they are to each other; no attempt is made to work out an order of descent from that classification, for it is recognised that much more information would be needed. And America now has at its disposal valuable new technology in the form of computerised information which, using the CPM, has allowed an experimental classification of the minuscules of Luke's Gospel to be made (Wisse 1982) for the critical apparatus prepared by the IGNTP (1984, 1987 (III)).

Duplacy: how to select the different forms of a text for classification

Another project for a large critical edition of the New Testament was embarked upon in Europe at the end of the sixties: 'Novi Testamenti graeci editio maior critica', with K. Aland, J. Duplacy and B. Fischer as co-directors. It was within this framework that Duplacy set out to tackle the methodological questions raised when confronted with the large volume of manuscripts to be analysed for the purposes of compiling a critical apparatus. With the help of other studies (cf. Duplacy 1975, already referred to, p. 65), especially that of Dom J. Froger (1968) and those of J. G. Griffiths (1969 and 1973), Duplacy brought to completion the work started by his predecessors.

Like Colwell, he was interested in the selection of variation units and their boundaries. Ideally, only the significant variants should be retained, a selection which can be carried out only bit by bit and once the variation units have been made in some way comparable one with another. At that point, the agreements between the different text forms can be counted and a provisional classification obtained. But Duplacy demonstrates that agreement between two forms of a given text can vary greatly from one chapter to the next. So the provisional classification cannot be interpreted without first taking into account the particular sample of text used and the selection of the variation units as well as the choice of the forms of text. The taxonomical grouping therefore does not immediately yield the major text type divisions, even if, for some well chosen samples, the two do happen to coincide.

Taxonomy does, however, have its value, especially in so far as it requires a very rigorous presentation of the facts; and it seems to raise new questions about the history of the text. Along with Dom Quentin, Duplacy sees in the manuscripts only different 'forms' of the text and refuses the notion of 'errors'. But at the same time, he moves away from Colwell by not using the generally accepted ideas about the manuscript tradition as a foundation for his work: for him, it is a matter of checking these ideas rather than making use of them. On the selection of text forms he says: 'it is better not to include in the initial sample too many text forms which can be supposed to be ''contaminated'' ' (Duplacy 1979, p. 26). The problem is that it is not known *a priori* which forms are 'contaminated'. What the rule led to in practice, in several analyses of the Catholic Epistles (Amphoux 1981b), was that the manuscripts selected were some uncials of the ninth century which were good representatives of the most common text type found among the uncials, and all the other available forms of the text which differed from the common text type. Certain of these were already familiar, such as the uncials S.01, A.02, B.03, C.04; others were less so, and some of them, such as minuscule 2138, took on considerable significance.

Thus, in just the same way that the variation units could not all be treated as equivalent, but only certain ones could be used for classifying the forms of the text, Duplacy demonstrated that so also the text forms had to undergo a process of selection and that it was not always the most well-known ones which could be used. This is a far cry from the dubious kind of construction of family trees of fifty or so years ago. The goals are more modest but also more realistic, and are better suited to the information available. With Colwell, the points of comparison are more clearly defined; with Duplacy, it is the choice of initial forms of the text to be compared which is refined. With the help of statisticians and the use of computers, involved calculations can be tested. But computerised taxonomy is only a starting point; it is the task of the philologist to interpret the first stable classification which is obtained and to see what further analyses might be done. When these were carried out for 1 Peter, Duplacy, who until then had doubted the existence of a 'Western' text, was prepared to recognise that there was such a text for the Catholic Epistles, which was attested by one of the taxonomic groups (Duplacy 1981, p. 171). In an unpublished thesis (1981b, pp. 248–52), C.-B. Amphoux distinguished a total of four text types for these Epistles, two of which made up one taxonomic group, being very close with respect to their variants. It is results such as these, even though they are still somewhat limited, which suggest that the method of text classification has now reached a point where it can present the questions that concern the history of the New Testament text in new terms. More recently still, Amphoux (1988b) has developed the idea of an 'index of variation' which enables more exact calculations to be made for the purpose of classifying different forms of a text. The role of interpretation in formulating conclusions about the history of the text is thereby significantly diminished. (See also K. Aland 1987.)

THE RESULTS OF EXTERNAL CRITICISM

In the process of all the different studies and analyses of the manuscript tradition, various kinds of information have emerged which have given rise to ideas about the history of the text, some of them more lasting than others. But all analysis of texts is bound by certain rules which it would be good to state at this point. It is customary to distinguish between two types of documents: those which constitute the 'direct' tradition and those which constitute the 'indirect' tradition.

The direct tradition

By this is meant, for the New Testament, the Greek manuscripts as a whole: papyri, uncials, minuscules and lectionaries.

The papyri

These have a value all of their own: because they include the oldest copies of the text, they have attracted special attention. And yet the literary papyri have not been welcomed with the same enthusiasm, for, generally speaking, their text is not particularly good – in fact it is often poorer than that of the medieval manuscripts. A papyrus of Plato, for example, written hardly a hundred years after the philosopher's death, may be full of mistakes. It is not hard to understand the reason, for the papyri as a rule come from private copies or cheap editions which were not made with the same care or skill as the later copies on parchment.

In the case of the New Testament, the copying of the papyri in the first three centuries, at least, appears to have been carried out by rather amateur scribes who introduced all manner of corruptions, from involuntary mistakes to deliberate alterations. After that, the New Testament papryi are probably typical of the copies of the text that would have been in the possession of ordinary individual Christians, or Christian communities in Egypt, until the seventh century.

The papyri contain some early variants, but they belong to a variety of types of text; only the type which predominates among the Greek minuscules is not found very often. Consequently, there are papyri which are in general agreement with the text of the great parchment uncials (see p. 108), which also has its origin in Egypt. There are others with a text more like that of Codex Bezae, Codex Claromontanus (P^{46} for example), the Old Latin or Old Syriac versions, and so on. Others still, though fewer in number (P^{72} has already been mentioned in this respect), resemble the witnesses to the Caesarean text in some of their readings. This preliminary classification of the papyri, taking them on their own, especially the earliest ones, is not without its importance for the history of the text. But it should be noted that it is not easy to date a papyrus with any precision, especially if it is a fragment. A wise expert would normally leave a certain margin for error, and account must be taken of that.

The uncials, minuscules and lectionaries

When external criticsm is applied to the other parts of the direct tradition, it enables the preliminary classification to be carried further. It might well be extremely rare that the precise relationship between two codices can be determined exactly (this does, however, happen in the case of the Pauline Epistles where it is clear that Codex Sangermanensis is a copy of Codex Claromontanus D.06, which is why it is known as D.^{abs}, from 'Abschrift' meaning 'copy'); it is nevertheless possible to use external criticism to sort out the manuscripts into groups and sub-groups. The first step is to note the characteristics of each witness: its age, its probable origin, its general appearance, the care taken by the scribe or scribes in their copying, and any later corrections. The second step is to consider the form of the text itself and, using the divergent readings as a point of comparison, to try to discern the principles on which the text is based. In the case of the lectionaries, and the minuscules where the liturgical readings are marked, the particular selection of the passages can provide further clues to relationships. The manuscripts can thus be classified in families, not according to genealogical affinities but according to types of text, each of which can be described in terms of its individual characteristics. One type, for instance, will be full of additions, whereas another will prefer brevity; one will be concerned with grammatical accuracy, another with the smoothest readings. And careful scrutiny will uncover many more tendencies besides. External criticism is never used, though, to pronounce an opinion on the quality of the variants. Its function is simply to enable a clear picture of them to be obtained and the distinguishing features of each group to be highlighted.

In this way, a broad sort of classification is obtained which, as will be seen, the indirect tradition will confirm and make more specific. The large majority of manuscripts can be divided into four main text types: Egyptian, Syro-Byzantine, 'Western' and Caesarean (see pp. 98–110), leaving aside the sub-groups such as the Ferrar group or the Lake group which belong to the Caesarean type (see pp. 103–5). The labels used to designate the groups are conventional rather than accurate descriptions, especially the term 'Western' which refers to a type of text which is scarcely homogeneous and includes not only Western but also Eastern material, from Greek papyri and uncials to some versions and very early quotations. External criticism can also help at times to pinpoint the best representatives of the earliest text of a family type, how that text evolved and to what influences it was subject, all of which are matters of considerable interest.

To go much beyond this – to decide, for example, by means of external criticism alone the original reading for this or that variant – would be to encounter serious problems. There would be the risk of being guided by the number, the age and the general character of the witnesses; the risk is more harmful and the danger more common than might be thought, in view of what has been seen to be the inadequacy of these criteria. It is better to acknowledge, in theory and in practice, that the results of external criticism are of limited value only.

The indirect tradition (the versions and the quotations)

The versions

The importance of the versions needs to be emphasised. It is true that not one of them stands as a perfect rendering of the Greek original and, like the Greek manuscripts, their value depends in the main on the quality of the text they present. That said, however, some of the versions are of the highest importance. As will be seen, some of them are older than the earliest Greek manuscripts (see pp. 101–3). They thus throw light on the most obscure period of the textual tradition (second to third century). Unlike the manuscripts, the text which they present can be fairly easily situated, in place if not always in time. They may show, for example, that a certain variant was around at a certain time, in a certain local church. Furthermore, an agreement between early versions may be an indication of a text which pre-dates that of the oldest recensions. The older these versions are and the more their variant readings agree, the nearer they are likely to be to the original. In other words, they provide precious information about the history of the text.

The difficulty, however, is that they are not always easy to examine. First, how is the authentic text of a version to be identified? There are only critical editions of a few New Testament versions. As far as the earliest of the versions is concerned, the information available is too slight and too confused to provide a sure text – with the recent exception of the Old Latin. It needs to be borne in mind that each one of the text types has, over the centuries, undergone changes, either involuntary or deliberate and of greater or lesser significance, even if they are nothing more than corrections in accordance with another Greek tradition or another version. How can the primitive form of the text be reached through this tangled history of contamination and alteration?

A second difficulty concerns how to find the text underlying a version. Even if the authentic text of the version is ascertained, there is still no guarantee that it will yield the original which the translator worked from. A version is not necessarily a straight translation into another language, but too often constitutes, in itself, a revision, involving a comparison and choice of divergent readings. And even a pure translation leaves room for plenty of conjecture. At times, the translator is happy to take liberties with his text, caring more for elegance or for cleverness than for faithfulness. At other times, he misreads his manuscript or is unable to translate the subtleties of the Greek, his good will being greater than his skill. Whatever the case, the reading which the translator had before his eyes remains uncertain.

A third and final difficulty is how to determine the relationship between this problematic text and the original. In order to give a confident answer to this question, it would be necessary to know the historical circumstances surrounding the writing of the version. Where and when was it written? What were its models? According to which principles was it copied? How did it come to be part of the textual tradition? For the earlier versions especially, all these questions are ill-defined.

To sum up, the authority of a version varies according to the degree to which it possesses the three following qualities, which correspond, point for point, to the three difficulties just mentioned: purity in transmission, fidelity of translation and early and close connection with the early text. The textual critic must ensure that the versions which come closest to this ideal are given due consideration when it comes to determining the original text.

The quotations

The importance of the quotations is just as great, not least because of their number. Even the earliest Church Fathers frequently quoted from the New Testament: Justin more than 300 times, Irenaeus more than 1,800, Clement of Alexandria around 2,400, and Tertullian more than 7,000. Altogether, *Biblica patristica* (see p. 46) gives more than 17,000 New Testament references for this early period (vol. I); for the second and third centuries (vols. II and III), there are more than 45,000 references to the New Testament, around 33,000 of them from Origen. Of course, the value of a quotation depends on the quality of the text it is taken from, but, even so, the quotations from the Church Fathers of the first three centuries make it possible, just as for the early versions, to retrieve a text which dates from before the oldest document of the direct tradition. They can even do better than that, in so far as they also enable a Greek text type or a version to be situated in both time and place. Because they usually belong to a tradition which is independent of that of the extant manuscripts, they can act as a very valuable tool with which to check the latter. The more precise nature of their date and place of origin also contributes to the defining of the major text types within the textual tradition. All in all, they throw a great deal of light on the history of the text.

Unfortunately, when he comes to use the quotations, the critic is confronted with the same difficulties as arose with the versions, but to an even greater extent. The first difficulty is: do we have the authentic text of the quotation? To answer this question, a critical edition should be used, if there is one. All too often, the scribes harmonised the Patristic quotations according to the text which was in use within their own restricted circle. More than anything else, it is the 'lemmata', that is extracts from passages quoted in the commentaries prior to the exegesis, which appear to have been subject to correction. The commentary sometimes appears to be using a different text from that given in the lemma. Critical editions are not always able to show these problems, for some authors are only known from translations or, as in the case of Marcion, from quotations made by their opponents, and the text used may well have been modified several times. Tatian's Diatessaron presents a particular problem in that it is never known which Gospel he is using, with the result that his text can only contribute to a study of a given variation unit if it is clear which Gospel each one of the variants comes from. A separate difficulty concerns the quotations drawn especially from the exegetical catenae. These are collections of comments made by different ecclesiastical authors on difficult passages of Scripture and must be treated with a great deal of caution because the quotations may be, for example, paraphrases or conflated readings (see Devreesse 1928; Sloane 1967). When it comes to texts which have very little manuscript support, the utmost reserve must be exercised. For example, there are very few copies of Origen's commentary on John and none from before the thirteenth century. As evidence of the similarity between Origen's Alexandrian text and that of the earliest uncial manuscripts, it would therefore be foolish to appeal to that part of the commentary which, although written in Alexandria, was copied at a later date when the Byzantine text predominated, for it is likely to have been contaminated. Prudence is called for at all times.

Another difficulty arises, once the authenticity of the quotation has been decided, as to whether it is literal or not. It is a well-known fact that the ancient writers, being more interested in the meaning than in the wording of a passage, quoted freely, summarising passages to draw out what was of interest to them. The scarcity of Bibles and the absence of Scriptural concordances also meant that they were often quoting from memory, especially in the case of shorter passages. This explains the many texts alluded to only approximately, in a form in which they never actually existed in the manuscripts. When, however, the quotation is long or is repeated in the same words or is followed by a commentary, the chances of its being accurate are greater, especially if the author happens to make a point of insisting on a certain form of the text, rejecting, for example, a particular variant reading. Probability becomes certainty if the variant cited is actually found in some other early document, either a manuscript or a version. A final word of warning: when a quotation is cited partially, nothing should ever be deduced about the missing part before making quite sure that, given the circumstances in which the author was writing, he could have been expected to provide a complete quotation.

One last difficulty: supposing that the text of a quotation is authentic and that it is a literal quotation, does it represent the original text? Generally speaking, when a writer quotes the New Testament he tends to use the text current in his milieu, but, as has been seen for the manuscripts and the versions, it is difficult to determine the quality of this text, especially for the first three centuries, because so little is known about its history. As long as that remains to be settled, it is best to look twice before relying on a quotation, particularly if it is an isolated one without any link with the other witnesses of the direct or indirect tradition.

These various difficulties demonstrate just how delicate the task is. If there is to be any hope of success, the only quotations to be relied upon are those which are authentic, literal and related to the purest form of the text. These are fundamental rules but ones which are neglected only too often.

To sum up this section on external criticism, it may be concluded that, while external criticism is powerless to determine the primitive form of the New Testament text, yet it does nevertheless have its use. It enables the different groups of the textual tradition to be identified, using a method of classifying the different forms of a text which has been carefully thought out and is quite independent of any notion of genealogical relationships. Although it is not able to trace their history, it can nevertheless distinguish fairly clearly the main text types together with their characteristic features.

INTERNAL CRITICISM

The third stage of textual criticism is very different from the second. It consists in weighing up the intrinsic value of the variants according to the text and its context. The exegete has, by this stage, already been able to eliminate certain textual corruptions (if the editor has not done so before him) by means of verbal criticism, which is, after all, only a limited and negative form of internal criticism. After that, the application of external criticism has given him the information allowing him to define the characteristics of several groups of witnesses and to have some idea of the quality of their readings. The task before him now is to set out in parallel columns all the variants which he has classified, so as to be able to evaluate them and thus make a final choice.

INSUFFICIENT CRITERIA

As early as 1711 (III), G. von Mästricht drew up, in his edition of the Greek New Testament, some forty-three rules which were supposed to lead to the finding of the best variant. These rules are a mixture of external and internal criticism, and are partly good, partly bad. Bengel (see p. 140) examined them in the preface to his *Gnomon* (1742) and reduced them to twenty-seven. Griesbach (see pp. 141 – 2) only retains fifteen of them in the introduction to his second edition of the New Testament (1796). Some of them have been left in the manuals, probably to exercise the students' memory or perhaps as a testimony to the prudence of the true critics who, rather cautious about the value of their own instinctive judgement, always prefer the safe, old rules. Two of these rules, are given here by way of example and because, despite their limitations, they may be helpful sometimes.

The shorter reading is preferable to the longer one: 'brevior lectio probabilior'

The usual tendency of scribes, especially when they are looking for a chance to make some kind of revision, is to expand the text. They happily add explanations which make the difficult places clearer; they freely insert any words which they find in the margins or above the lines into the body of the text; they carefully complete abbreviated quotations from the Old Testament; they add any detail which helps a reading to be more in harmony with parallel passages. In short, their aim is to make the text fuller and more easily understandable.

The problem with the rule as it is stated above, however, is that there are too many exceptions. To start with, there are those short readings which arise when the scribe omits a word or part of a sentence because he is distracted. This happens frequently in Codex Sinaiticus (S.01), for example. Then there are those short readings which are entirely intentional, at places where a reviser wanted to smooth out a difficulty (see S.01 in Mt 23:35); he leaves out the problematic words, and so the matter is resolved. Finally, and worst of all, there are short readings which are due to the inherent features of one of the recensions. This could be the case with the Alexandrian recension, especially for Acts (see pp. 107 – 9). Besides, it must be remembered that the writers of the New Testament were Oriental and therefore more inclined to be wordy than concise (see the interesting study by P. Head, 1990).

Consequently, a reading's brevity is not always proof that it is original. There are many short readings which are shortened readings just as there are many long readings which have never been lengthened. There are even variants which at first sight look like conflated readings but which may well be original. This becomes obvious from a consideration of certain instances: in the text of Mark, for example, an element from Matthew's Gospel is sometimes found together with an element from Luke's Gospel (see Mk 8:34a = Mt 16:24 + Lk 9:23a) without there being any trace of a variant reading to cast doubt on the originality of the verse in the text of Mark.

The more difficult reading is to be preferred to the simpler one: 'difficilior lectio potior'

It is not hard to see why this should be the case. Scribes were inclined to modify anything that seemed to them difficult or faulty. So it is only natural to attribute to them those variants which result in a smoother or more correct text. There is no doubt that the New Testament scribes often indulged in this kind of alteration, thereby getting rid of barbarisms, solecisms, irregular constructions and even mere Hebraisms or rare expressions. They show a marked tendency to harmonise conflicting passages so as to avoid any jarring disagreement. They are not afraid to soften terms which seem offensive and to change the meaning under the guise of clarity. The cleverer a scribe thinks he is, the more he is inclined to modify his text.

That does not mean that the most difficult reading is necessarily the authentic one. In the case of accidental errors, for example, this principle is not valid. Even the most experienced scribe may make slips, sometimes producing readings which are very obscure, if not unintelligible, but which are anything but original. Again, some variants find their way into the text because of a scribe's carelessness, for instance grammatical mistakes or faulty quotations which it would be ridiculous to claim as original. Worse still, there are some difficult or puzzling readings which are quite simply the product of deliberate correction of the text. A scribe may, for example, misunderstand the meaning of a passage or not see the relevance of the context, and, in a sincere attempt to make it clearer, end up making it more obscure.

It should by now be obvious why all the other rules of internal criticism are not examined here, even though they are sometimes put forward as guiding principles. They either guide wrongly or not at all. But there is one which is better than any of the others and which will be explained now.

THE THREAD OF ARIADNE

This allusion to mythology must be excused: textual criticism is indeed something of a labyrinth, and to find one's way about in it rigid rules are not of much use. Something more flexible, like Ariadne's thread, is needed to act as a guide. The thread in this case is made up of two strands, closely intertwined but always able to be separated when necessary.

Determining the 'source-variant'

The task of the critic, as he examines the text, is to choose the variant which best explains the existence of all the others and which cannot itself be explained by the others. This principle first finds expression in Griesbach (see p. 141) and since then has been canonised, so to speak, by Tischendorf (see pp. 147 – 9) who called it 'omnium regularum principium' (the chief of all rules). In practice, it is a matter of collating or comparing all the variants so as to distinguish the earliest form, on which all the others depend. This is the essential role of internal criticism.

The more variants there are, of course, the more it becomes necessary to break down the work into stages. The comparative method first of all singles out the poorer forms, which arise from the usual kind of scribal slips or from the all too common revisers' presuppositions. The next step is to apply what is known about the palaeographic, or even human, conditions affecting the transmission of the text, in order to eliminate the intermediary variants, which have some apparent value but which are clearly secondary since they can be explained by another reading. As this is done, it will sometimes happen that one variant will stand out above the rest, and this is the one which may be declared original if, when all the information surrounding the text has been examined, it becomes clear that it is not dependent on any of the other variants. It does not matter whether it is a long or a short reading, a difficult or an easy one. What is important is that it stands out as the origin of the other variants.

In a way, the work of the textual critic is like that of a geologist who seeks to reconstruct the history of a section of the earth's crust, taking its present state as a starting point. Of course, any comparison will be inexact, and this one is no less inexact than any other, but it does help to give some idea of the fundamental role played by internal criticism in the task of the exegete as he works backwards to reconstruct the history of the text. Using his knowledge of the causes of textual corruption, he proceeds step by step from the poorer, modified forms of the text until he reaches the earliest form which explains all the others.

In actual fact, this otherwise excellent rule is not always easy to apply. There are, for example, cases where two variants could both be the result of faulty reading or where a choice has to be made between two readings which both apear to be the outcome of harmonisation. It can even happen, particularly in the case of the Gospels, that the readings of a variation unit can be divided between two 'source-variants', each with equally early attestation (one of them is usually a 'Western' reading when this happens), and apparently independent of each other. Determining the original form in these cases is a delicate business, and the critic who has too much confidence in his own personal preferences is in the greatest danger of making a mistake. A solution to the problem has to be sought elsewhere; that is to say, the analysis of the intrinsic worth of the variants has to go beyond the text of the variants itself.

The use of literary criticism

It is the context of the variants which has next to be taken into account, that is, the writing in which they are situated. The critic must select the variant which best fits with the general tendencies of the author. All the elements which make up the writer's usual practice have to be considered: his vocabulary, his language, his style and his way of using quotations and of putting his text together. Sometimes, it is the rhythm of a text which is important, or the various devices of 'oral style' (Jousse 1925) which made memorising a didactic passage easier in a society of oral culture and which are possibly better preserved in one reading than in another. Attention has to be paid to the ideas of an author and, as it were, his temperament. It would be wrong to neglect the author's purpose in writing and the historical conditions under which he wrote. These are all things which may be difficult to establish but which can throw a great deal of light on the critic's search for the best reading. The point is that the revisers, bent on making corrections, had little time for thinking about the original conditions of the text. Their aim was rather to bring the text up to date so that it would remain relevant to their own generation. The variants that arose from that kind of intention must necessarily be distinguished from those which are more in line with the facts of literary history.

There is another point which is of special relevance to the textual criticism of the Synoptic Gospels. Their close interrelationship is a familiar fact. It is assumed that Luke, for example, used the Gospel of Mark, or at the very least that both authors have a common source which is closest to Mark's Gospel. Consequently, the critical apparatus of the one is very much tied in with the variants of the other, and the exegete, faced with a decision about the variants of a parallel passage, must be careful to take account of the certain, and even the probable, links between these Gospels (see Elliott 1989b).

Internal criticism is by no means, therefore, as is too often supposed, merely a matter of sentiment. When it is carried out as it should be, it appeals to objective reasons which are strong enough to give backing to serious judgement. In the work of Duplacy, the importance of internal criticism is so great that the two parts which have been described here are quite distinct: on the one hand, there is the search for the 'source-variant', closely linked to historical considerations and including verbal criticism; on the other hand, there is internal criticism proper, that is the literary and linguistic analysis which go hand in hand with each other.

This search for the 'source-variant' is generally seen as part of internal criticism, but that is only partially true. While it is true that it will take into account the contents of the variants of a passage, determining the source-variant should and can only be done within the framework and in the light of history. If anachronisms are to be avoided, then the search must focus, in the main, on the period of history immediately preceding that of the earliest attestation of the different variants. Furthermore, it is only of value in so far as it draws on information concerning the historical circumstances surrounding the text, circumstances which could have given rise to variations. (Duplacy 1981, p. 77)

CONJECTURAL EMENDATION

This refers to those variants which are not attested by any of the documents but which are put forward by the critics in certain difficult passages. J. Duplacy has this to say about them: 'The supreme victory of internal criticism is, of course, conjectural emendation, especially when it is the original text itself which is emended' (Duplacy 1959, p. 38).

Conjectural emendation is not uncommon in the field of classical philology. Because of the small number of copies, the text which has been handed down, with or without variants, is sometimes incomprehensible, and so it has to be restored using conjecture, not, however, without the help of palaeography. There have naturally been some abuses alongside the good emendations, and a large number of unfounded hypotheses could be cited. It is the same with the text of Scripture. As early as 1772, W. Bowyer, in his *Conjectures on the New Testament collected from various authors*, gives a great many tenuous and even puerile corrections. For example, Bentley, writing earlier in the century (see below, p. 139), suggests that πορνεία 'fornication' be replaced by πορκεία 'pork', where the things forbidden to Gentiles are mentioned in Ac 15:20. And the hypotheses have not ceased to grow and flourish ever since.

And yet this does not mean that conjectural emendation must be ruled out in establishing the text of the New Testament. It is true that, for the New Testament, there are so many documents, from such an early date and of such variety, that there is a very good chance that the original reading has not been lost. Nevertheless, it must be borne in mind that in the very early period, in the second century for example, when the form of the text is not easy to determine, corruptions of the text were possible. Moreover, it is worth remembering that some particular manuscript variant that is widely attested may well be nothing more than a conjectural emendation made by an inexpert reviser, and consequently carries less weight than the hypothesis of a modern philologist. And so conjectural emendations cannot be rejected out of hand.

In practice, wisdom and restraint are called for in using them. No such restoration of the text can be proposed before it has been examined with extreme care and without there being, either in the contents or in the form of the text, some clear indication that alteration has taken place. Most of the conjectural emendations would never have been made if this first elementary rule had been observed. Apart from this basic rule, the critical principles explained above should also be respected. Any conjecture should be firmly based on the witness of the other variants which seem to depend on it, as well as on a study of the corruptions inherent to the transmission of the text and of the author's usual practice. There are two good examples in the commentaries by Lagrange (Mark, 1929; John, 1925a): in Mk 1:2, the dual quotation by Isaiah and Malachi prefaced with a reference to Isaiah alone is deemed to be an interpolation, and in Jn 19:29, the word 'hyssop' ὕσσωπος is corrected to ὑσσός 'javelin', since the stem of a hyssop branch would not be strong enough to take the weight of a wet sponge. As a general rule, a conjectural emendation will command a more favourable response the more closely it adheres to the text. Finally, it would be sensible to confine conjectural emendations, even the best of them, to the critical apparatus of the editions of the Greek New Testament, until such time as new discoveries provide evidence for them.

CONCLUSION: THE ECLECTIC METHOD

This would seem to be the best description to give of the particular method of textual criticism of the New Testament. Eclecticism implies no watertight division between the various disciplines: verbal criticism, external criticism and internal criticism, all have their role to play and they complement each other. Understood in this way, the eclectic method seeks to follow a middle path between the main systems which continue to hold sway in the editing of Classical and medieval texts. On the one hand, there was the German school of Lachmann in which – even in its revival by Dom Quentin – external criticism received the lion's share because of the overwhelming insistence on the construction of family trees. On the other hand, there was the French school whose founders had lost all confidence in external criticism. 'It has to be recognised with the old humanists, that we have only one tool at our disposal: taste' (Bédier 1928, p. 356). 'Each case must be considered separately and a solution found ... for reasons independent of the manuscripts ... The editor's choice is, of necessity, arbitrary' (Martin – de Budé 1927, Preface, p. xx). The most successful method in the field of New Testament criticism uses the best from both these schools.

Verbal criticism results in not much more than a preliminary sorting out of the obvious or possible mistakes. It is only of limited use for the student who is working from the critical editions because the apparatus in these is selective and because the more obvious mistakes have already been eliminated. Verbal criticism really comes into its own when the actual manuscripts are read directly.

External criticism constitutes the first main stage of the eclectic method. The French school is right to reject any kind of mechanical procedure which is supposed to lead to the original form, or at least the archetype, of the extant copies. Applying external criticism in that way would only result in disappointment. For, while it is true that the construction of the 'stemma codicum' represented a move forward from the old system of dividing the witnesses into good and bad in the manner of the Last Judgement, definite progress has nevertheless been made since that, especially by Colwell and Duplacy. More precisely defined groups can now be established by selecting variation units and especially forms of a text – a selection made easier by the use of computers. These groups can be interpreted from a historical point of view without the necessity of a complete genealogical reconstruction – something which always has to be treated with caution. A rather simplistic formalism is thus avoided and the history of the text, as will be seen, is accorded its rightful place. External criticism is insufficient of itself to establish the original text. But it performs a useful task in allowing several early text forms to emerge and a separation between early and late variants to be made. It thus prepares the way for internal criticism.

Internal criticism must have the last word. That is not to say that the respective value of the witnesses is of no interest. It is precisely on that point that the eclectic method draws on the work of the German school. For it is through the findings of external criticism that the character of the great recensions of the third and fourth centuries is beginning to be recognised; this is important in evaluating the quality of a variant which is proper to one or another of these overall revisions. Again, because of external criticism, several types of text are beginning to be identified which pre-date the major recensions and one of which (in the Gospels and Acts) could even date from before any recension at all; this also is of great value for determining the quality of a reading. But it cannot be said too often that internal criticism in many cases is powerless. It can demonstrate that a certain reading is a correction but it may be the correction of an error. It can establish that another variant is an addition but it could be simply that an omitted word is reinstated. It is therefore always necessary to bring into the discussion the distinctive nature of the manuscript group or the single manuscript in which the variant is found. The less that is known of this, the stronger must be the arguments of internal criticism to enable a decision to be made.

In practice, every discussion about the variants has two parts to it. The first is given over to external criticism; at this point the divergent readings are classified, initially according to the types of text which are more or less independent of the great recensions and, subsequently, according to the great recensions themselves. This breaks down the work into smaller parts and, as it were, stakes out the path to be followed, without, however, removing the obstacles. It may thus become apparent that a certain local and very early type is preserved in versions which can be suspected of having undergone harmonising modifications; or again, that a certain recension is not clear or is not well represented in its early stages. So it is frequently not possible to come to definite conclusions at this point. But for each variant, note will be made of its age, and the diversity and quality of its attestation, before moving on to applying internal criticism.

Here, the task becomes slower and more delicate. For each particular instance of a variant reading, the variants have to be compared one by one in the search for the source-variant. Where there are only two divergent readings, the question is, which one is the origin of the other. It is often difficult to decide, for the text and the context provide contradictory evidence. Where the number of variants is greater than two, it is best first of all to put on one side those which are very obviously the result of redactional processes, such as conflated or harmonising readings – the more so if they belong to manuscripts where this kind of thing happens often. Only two or three variants will be retained from among which a choice has to be made as before. But before any decision is taken, the results of internal criticism should be set alongside the results of external criticism; in other words, for each reading, its intrinsic value should be assessed together with the value of the documents which attest it. And, even then, the final decision must be taken with a certain amount of caution. K. Lachmann (Prolegomena; see 1831 – (III), Preface, p. xxxiii) used to have a system of annotation to indicate the degree of certitude or probability of each variant: certain, almost certain, probable, doubtful, uncertain, null. One of the Greek editions in use today (UBS) has taken up this system; the problem is that, even when a variant is in the highest category, this does not constitute a guarantee of its representing the original text; what then of those in the other categories? In the case of the UBS Greek New Testament, the degree of certainty accorded to them is, as much as anything, an indication of the presuppositions concerning the history of the text shared by the five members of the editing committee (see Metzger 1975, Preface, pp. xv – xxiv).

Essentially, the method to be followed in New Testament textual criticism depends on the history of the variants. In every case, the critic attempts to get beyond the less pure forms to the form which is closest to the original. In the process, as actual examples are worked through, a general idea is acquired of the value of the different types of text and, simultaneously, of the history of the text. It is this history which helps the exegete at each stage of his investigations. It is of such importance that it needs a chapter of its own, for in fact it governs the whole of textual criticism.

3

The history of the written text

THE PERIOD OF RELATIVE FREEDOM (to AD 313)

The history of the text during this period is as important as it is difficult
to reconstruct. The ecclesiastical writers give very few clues. The
historian finds himself like someone trying to do a jigsaw puzzle which
has most of the pieces missing and some of the rest damaged. He has
to settle for a rough outline, much of it guesswork. With admirable good
sense, most authors skim lightly over this period of the text, but, as long
as the use of hypothesis is acknowledged as legitimate, there is no need
to follow their example. Bearing that in mind, the reader is asked to
forgive the numerous question marks in the pages which follow; there
could doubtless be many more still.

COMPOSING A TEXT AND COMMITTING IT TO WRITING

When a piece of prose is produced today, its composition and its setting
down in written form tend to be one and the same act. It starts off as
a rough draft; then it becomes an autograph manuscript, that is, one
written by the author himself; this, in turn, is used to produce the proofs
of a book which is finally published in a (first) edition. At each stage,
everything revolves around the written text. The same cannot be said
of societies whose culture is an oral one – societies such as that which
gave birth to the New Testament. The composition, or the initial
creation, of a literary work, has to be distinguished from the writing
down of the text, an act which has the effect of determining the exact
words which will be reproduced when the text is subsequently copied.
Between the two stages, many changes are likely to occur, generally
filling out the text and always bringing it up to date. Even after the work
has been committed to writing, other alterations sometimes occur in
an effort to adapt it to a new situation: this produces what is known as
a recension, and is the point at which one enters the domain of textual
criticism. It is understandable why, in circumstances such as these,

the autograph manuscript of the author should have had less importance than it would have today, for it represents only one stage in the development of the work which is neither the first stage nor even, at times, that which is the most frequently reproduced by the manuscript copies of the work. As Jousse (1925) says: 'The great problems of mankind are distorted, from the outset, when they are considered from the angle of the written word'. With respect to the New Testament, it is inevitable that most importance is accorded to the authors of the written text. But that does not mean that their works did not originate in the way which was customary for their time (see Achtemeier 1990).

THE AUTOGRAPHS

Of the autographs of the New Testament, nothing is known precisely, other than that, if they existed, they soon disappeared. The early Apologists who sometimes discuss the contents of the biblical text never refer to the originals. Tertullian, at the end of the second century, appears to make an allusion to them (*De praescriptione haereticorum*, 36) when he appeals to the churches which still possess the presidential seats of the Apostles and 'their authentic letters', but it may well be yet another instance of the fiery Apologist succumbing to rhetoric; or else his words are to be understood as meaning either the canonical books as opposed to the apocryphal ones or, possibly, documents written in the original language rather than in translation. But, whatever may be decided about Tertullian's allusion, the numerous, similar traditions which flourished in the Middle Ages are nothing more than pious legends, as one example will suffice to demonstrate: the so-called original manuscript of Mark's Gospel which Venice once so proudly claimed to possess turned out to be nothing more than a fragment of a Vulgate type of Latin codex.

It is not really surprising that the New Testament manuscripts should have been lost so quickly. In all probability, they were written on the usual material of the time, namely fragile papyrus. A single sheet would have been sufficient for some of the shorter Epistles. Some of the other books would have needed quite long scrolls (about nine metres for the Gospel of Matthew). In either case, the material would not have been tough enough to stand up to much handling.

The New Testament has very little to say on the subject. There are a few passing allusions to scrolls (Rv 6:14; Hb 10:7), and occasional mention of writing materials: the papyrus leaf (2 Jn 12), the pen (3 Jn 13) and black ink (2 Cor 3:3), but that is all. When Paul speaks of his parchments (2 Tm 4:13), he is more likely to be referring to a copy of some Old Testament books than to a copy of the Gospels, or to his own letters.

Concerning the actual redaction of the New Testament autographs, the information is almost as scanty. The secular writers of the period made use, even for their letters, of the services of redactors: scribes, secretaries or shorthand writers (see Roller 1933). It is not known to what extent the biblical writers used them. What can be said is that Paul employed secretaries and that sometimes, by way of signature, he was content simply to add a few words in his own hand (e.g. Rm 16:22; 1 Cor 16:21). The scribe, who was probably a careful amateur, would have written with small or medium-sized cursive letters (see Gal 6:11, where Paul mentions, by way of contrast, the large letters with which he writes). As for the books by the other authors, they could equally well have been written using everyday means, for want of financial resources, or they could have been given more than the ususal care, in view of their destination and the importance of their contents. In either case, they would resemble other documents of the time in that there would be no accentuation, no punctuation and no separation of words.

BEFORE THE RECENSIONS

The first copies made from the autographs have not been preserved either: the fragment P^{52} (see p. 7) is all that remains of the New Testament from before AD 150. And the rare quotations from before Marcion do not yield much information. But the books of the New Testament were known by the middle of the second century, especially in Rome where they were soon to be translated into Latin (see pp. 101 – 2). Copies flourished despite persecution. The text was a living text, for ordinary people. It was learnt by heart and quoted freely, interpreted as best one could. According to the information that is known about the period between AD 150 and AD 200, the actual New Testament text existed in a wide variety of forms with predominantly 'Western' variants, so called because they were first noticed in the Latin or Greek – Latin manuscripts (see pp. 26 – 30), the most typical 'Western' representative being Codex Bezae. What explanation can be given for the great diversity in form, greater than any later diversity, of a text which had been fixed in writing for several decades?

A brief word first about the involuntary variants. It is not difficult to see how they arose. Copies of the text made on fragile papyrus must easily have become damaged and the missing parts then left out of subsequent copies. Copying was often made more difficult by the poor quality of writing in the model worked from, or simply by the system of lettering in use at the time. But above all, the part played by the scribes themselves must not be forgotten; if even professional scribes were guilty of making many mistakes (Strabo XIII, 1, 54), what of the amateur scribes, ordinary individuals copying the Scriptures for their own use? There was the whole range of involuntary mistakes (see pp. 53 – 7) just waiting for their chance to intervene; the door was wide open to divergent readings.

Another cause of variants was the all too common disregard for literal accuracy.

Many times St Jerome points out that the Christians of the first centuries, including the Apostles and the Evangelists, in quoting the Old Testament, did not regard the letter of the sacred writings with the same superstition as was beginning to characterise the Jewish attitude. They realised that the letter only had value through the meaning and that 'the Book was made for man not man for the Book'. (Durand 1911, vol. 126, p. 311)

This way of viewing the text of the Scriptures is already apparent in the rare occurrences of New Testament quotations in the writings of the early ecclesiastical authors, the Apostolic Fathers and the Apologists. Not only do they quote from memory, in an approximate fashion, but they also often use allusions rather than precise quotations. It seems clear that what they saw in the text was a deeper meaning which could not be affected by any kind of textual alterations.

This brings us to the intentional variants, the importance of which has already been mentioned (see pp. 57 – 61). Some of them are the work of scribes who, following the literary custom of the time, took certain liberties with the document they were copying: corrections of spelling, grammar or style. Sometimes they had little choice, as when, faced with such things as words between the lines, marginal notes, difficult words or divergences in the models they were using, they were unsure as to what the text should be. Their intentions may have been laudable, but the results were not generally very successful.

But all these variants amount to little compared with the more significant variants which separate, in particular, the 'Western' text from the rest of the manuscript tradition. In the Gospel of Luke and the Book of Acts, the differences are so great that the theory has been advanced that the author himself may have made two editions of his work (Jean Leclerc, in a letter written in Latin in 1684 to Richard Simon, expresses his misgivings about this theory; other scholars later argued in support of its validity: see, notably, Blass 1895, pp. 30 – 2). The most that can be said for certain is that the main variants were already in existence between AD 150 and AD 200 and that the documents available do not permit of any affirmation to be made concerning the state of the text in use before that date. In other words, with regard to the pre-recensional text, one can do little more than suggest hypotheses and opt for the one which accounts for the greatest number of facts.

The smaller number of witnesses to the 'Western' variants has led to a favouring of the other form of text as a starting hypothesis. It is that text which has been in popular use, and has been taken as a basis for translations and commentaries, since the time of the major Vulgate editions (see pp. 116 – 19), even if these latter do not belong, in the finer detail, to the same textual tradition. It has thus happened, almost as a matter of course, that the 'Western' text has been put aside as being a product of the fringes of Christianity. The lack of unity amongst the witnesses to the 'Western' text has further created the image of a loose collection of mixed variants, which have been studied in isolation from each other. No study carried out so far, however, has succeeded in demonstrating clearly the origin of these variants. On the contrary, the theories advanced have been highly questionable, not least the connection which has been supposed between the 'Western' text and a theological tendency either for or against the Jews (see chiefly Epp 1966 and Klijn 1966; also Barrett 1979 and pp. 168 – 9 below). As for the relationship between the variants of the 'Western' tradition and those of the more widely accepted tradition, no explanation has yet been found.

It is tempting, in the circumstances, to follow the cautious approach of Jean Duplacy, who conceded that in many instances there is no answer to the question of the priority of one form of the text or another (Duplacy 1973, p. 128). But that dilemma is, in fact, a reason to consider the alternative possibility to the priority of the usual text, that is the possibility of the priority of the 'Western' text. Duplacy never actually formulated it in so many words, but his work, over a period of more than ten years, of creating a list of Patristic quotations and studying in depth specific variation units, and also of researching the history of the text before AD 200, all had as its main aim the confirmation – or the rejection – of this second hypothesis. And it tended to be consistently supported and strengthened by the results of his work.

The hypothesis of the priority of the 'Western' text means that, with all its diversity of variants, it is assumed to represent the text as it was before any recension. The collection of smaller variants, which may include changes that the tradition as a whole has undergone, is left on one side. What are taken into account on this hypothesis are the more important variants, together with some of the minor ones, which are viewed as being the remains of a pre-recensional text form – the oldest to be handed down and, as far as can be seen at present, the closest to the first written text of the New Testament. This hypothesis needs to be expanded to be defensible, for three kinds of problem surround it: first, the stylistic variation found in the 'Western' text; secondly, the obscurity of the meaning of certain variants; and thirdly, the unknown factors concerning the exact circumstances which caused this pre-recensional text to be discarded and the first recensions to be produced.

The 'Western' variants often contain a repetition of words which is not found in the other text types. At first sight, this looks like an unintentional slip which crept into a text which did not have the repetition, and remained there for a certain length of time. But another avenue of exploration, one suggested in particular by Marcel Jousse (1925), is opened up if one sees these repetitions as one of several characteristics of 'oral style', that is a particular set of rhetorical devices which are used for teaching purposes in societies with an oral culture (see Alexander 1990 and the bibliography cited there). Part of the main difference between the 'Western' variants and the others can be accounted for by bearing in mind the difference between, on the one hand, oral style developed to aid the memorising of the spoken text, and, on the other, written style with its more careful attention to accuracy, elegance, clarity and concision. Klijn makes precisely this observation when he posits the co-existence of two textual traditions, one oral, one written (Klijn 1969, pp. 66 – 70).

At first sight, the apparent meaning of a number of 'Western' variants poses difficulties. There is, for example, the parable of the two sons (Mt 21:28 – 32) where, in the 'Western' text, the chief priests seem to give the answer that the will of the Father is accomplished by the son who says 'yes' but who does not go to the vineyard after all. Or the last meal of Jesus in Luke (22:15 – 20) which finishes with the bread. Or the saying found only in Codex Bezae in Lk 6:5, which appears to attribute to Jesus a condemnation in the name of the law. When these readings are given further thought, however, it becomes clear that they carry a meaning which is profoundly evangelical, as long as they are read carefully, with due weight given to the full significance of each word, a procedure not unlike Philo's method of exegesis. In his book *La Trame et la chaîne* (1983, p. 517), J. Cazeaux makes a distinction between the surface features of 'grammar' and 'rhetoric' (such things as word-order, choice of vocabulary or use of conjunctions) and the more subtle aspects of 'dialectic' and 'philosophy': the first he compares to tools which strip off the outer appearance of words and bring to light the inner meanings which are hidden behind the ordinary meaning. They are used to reveal a secret code, only accessible to the learned or initiated. If the 'Western' text is seen from this perspective, it becomes less of a product of a certain theology than of a certain system of meaning. The message of the text is to be found not so much in the individual words as in the rhetorical construction of each story and of the arrangement of the episodes. But this sophisticated kind of coded writing is not suitable for general circulation. For wider distribution, the text had to be adapted to the mentality of the people who were going to receive it, it had to be revised and changed so as to make it acceptable to an audience who were not expecting to have to look for hidden meaning. There was not just one such revision but several, to judge by the variety of texts which existed in the period AD 150 – AD 200, and they seem to have been made in a groping fashion, in progressive stages. Throughout, however, in its underlying exegesis, the revised text was careful to preserve the original meaning for the new recipients.

The wide stylistic gap between the two main New Testament text types, the 'Western' on the one hand and all the other types on the other hand, cannot have arisen by chance. Rather it is indicative of a cultural gap between two periods, separated from each other by a marked split which must have occurred prior to the time of Marcion. C.-B. Amphoux (unpublished article) views the pre-recensional text of the Gospels and Acts as witnessing to an edition made around AD 120 in Asia Minor and connected with Polycarp and Papias. In the troubled period which followed, under the rule of the Emperor Hadrian, one event stands out from among the others because of the upheaval which ensued: the disappearance of the Messianic kingdom of Bar-Kokhba in AD 135, when it was wiped out by the Roman army after four years of existence. The consequences suffered by Judaism are well known: the official religion abandoned all hope of a political Messiah and turned its attention to a largely legalistic interpretation of Scripture. The new literature which emerged caused the writings of previous generations to be reworked, subjecting them to thorough revision. This was the period of the treatises of the Mishnah. Christianity seems to have been less affected by the event since, for the Christians, Bar-Kokhba was nothing more than an impostor. They were not involved in his defence and they do not appear to have been troubled by the Romans. And yet the intensity of polemical debate between Jews and Christians reached such a peak after AD 135 that a complete cultural split would appear to have been inevitable. Is it possible that, in these circumstances, the Christians revised their Scriptures, too, and brought them up to date? Such a thing is plausible. Indeed, in AD 178 the secular writer Celsus stated in a polemic against the Christians:

Some of the believers ... have changed the original text of the Gospels three or four times or even more, with the intention of thus being able to destroy the arguments of their critics.　　　(quoted in Origen, *Contra Celsum*; *SC* 132, 2, 27)

Origen does not deny the existence of such changes, rather he seeks to attenuate their importance, saying that they were made by Marcion, Valentinus and Lucanus, a disciple of Marcion. In another place, he acknowledges something more of their importance:

It is an obvious fact today that there is much diversity among the manuscripts, due either to the carelessness of the scribes, or to the perverse audacity of some people in correcting the text, or again to the fact that there are those who add or delete as they please, setting themselves up as correctors.

　　　　　(*In Matthaeum* XV, 14, *PG* 13, col. 1293)

This gives grounds for considering the 'Western' text, or at least some of the 'Western' witnesses, to be pre-recensional. For – and this is another difficulty – the 'Western' text is very diverse; there are in fact several text-types within it. Most of the witnesses, in Syriac or Latin, attest a revised form of text belonging to the following period, after Bar-Kokhba (AD 135 – 200; see p. 98). There is no witness to the pre-recensional form of the text for the Epistles or Revelation. For the Gospels and Acts, the main witnesses are Codex Bezae (Greek – Latin), Codex Glazier (Coptic, Acts 1 – 15) and the readings in the margins of the Harclean version of Acts (Syriac); to a lesser extent, there are also a Syro-Palestinian fragment of Acts (see p. 36), and notably P[48] (a leaf of Acts, from the end of the third century, with the same readings as D.05 for two short passages); Justin and Irenaeus also use a text of the Gospels and Acts of the same type as Codex Bezae. And that is about all.

P^{66} (John, certain readings), S.01 (for Jn 1 – 7 in part), E.08 (Acts), W.032 (for Mk 1:1 – 5 and 30 only) and 0171 (a fragment of Luke 22) all represent other text types which probably date from the first recensions; likewise the texts used by Clement of Alexandria, Origen, Tertullian and Cyprian. Of course, in the texts of the witnesses of this next period, in the 'Western' ones as well as in the Caesarean ones and in some of the later versions, there are readings from the pre-recensional text which have been preserved to some extent. As for the Epistles, the earliest witnesses available are from the period of the first recensions of the Gosples, that is after AD 135. It is there-fore not possible to reconstitute with certainty the earliest text, even though there is no doubt about its having existed in written form from a very early date, without a preparatory oral stage.

This, at least, is the hypothesis which makes the best sense of the diversity of variants which date back to the second century. Other explanations have been put forward and are discussed in chapter 4. Between AD 135 and AD 200, the pre-recensional form of the text was reworked, but it did not disappear altogether, for its main witnesses were copied at the end of the fourth century or the beginning of the fifth. In AD 616, near Alexandria, Thomas of Harkel used one of them from amongst others for his version of Acts; in 1072, in Constantinople, one of the secretaries of the Emperor Michael Doukas made a copy of Acts and the Epistles using an old manuscript with a number of early variants, albeit not the most important ones; and, today, about twenty other Greek manuscripts have been recognised as being related to the one which he used and which was copied up to the sixteenth century (see p. 23 on min. 2138). From the limited access that we have to the pre-recensional text, it appears that it was full of theological significance, not intended to be read for its moral or historical value. In order to make this text available to modern readers, it would be rather impractical to use it in place of the text usually used in Greek editions or translations, but it could be referred to much more frequently in commentaries on the text. This would enable the first-century cultural background of the New Testament writings to become more apparent, often providing fresh and important information.

THE FIRST RECENSIONS[1]

[In an article not yet published, C.-B. Amphoux (forthcoming 1991) suggests the following chronology for the first forms of the text of the Gospels: first, an edition would have been made in Smyrna towards AD 120 by Polycarp and Papias. This would be the pre-recensional text of Codex Bezae. Then, between AD 138 and AD 172 each Gospel would have been revised in Rome by the various schools: Luke and perhaps Mark by the school of Marcion, John by the school of Valentinus and Matthew by the school of Justin (probably the work of Tatian). Following these revisions, a new edition would have been made in Alexandria by Pantaenus, the founder of the Alexandrian school, towards AD 175; this would be the origin of the text type of P^{75} and B.03 in particular. Soon afterwards, the first versions began to be made (Latin, Syriac and Coptic), integrating different elements, in differing proportions, from the edition of Smyrna and the edition of Alexandria. The same would be true of the revisions of the Greek text which took place at that time, especially in Palestine, attested by various manuscripts. If this suggested schema is ever confirmed, there would need to be a re-organisation of the paragraphs which follow here concerning the first, great recensions – for the Gospels at least, and perhaps for the New Testament overall. The chronological outline which is described by Amphoux remains in line with the thought of Vaganay, whose basic preference was always for the 'Western' text rather than the Alexandrian text; but it is also close to the theory of Westcott and Hort (see p. 150) who see in B.03 especially a very early form of the text, if not the earliest. It should also be noted that P^{52} is possibly a witness to a Gospel tradition contemporary with the edition of Smyrna though different from it.]

In the period following AD 135, the recensions proliferated with a resultant textual diversity which reached a peak before the year 200. The first versions in Syriac or Latin often respected the pre-recensional text, and the Church Fathers up to the beginning of the fifth century quote from it. But alongside them, there appeared a more radical revision of the original text, probably made in Palestine. It has not been transmitted as a unified text but its first witnesses, in particular P^{46} (around AD 200) and Clement of Alexandria, show that it existed in the second century. Finally, the first Coptic versions made in the third century, especially those in Sahidic, attest a recensional form of text

---

[1] The paragraph within square brackets was written by the reviser for the English translation.

which indicates a relationship with that of the second century. Two authors occupy a place of particular importance in the recensional activity, Marcion and Tatian.

Marcion

Marcion was the son of a bishop of Sinope in Pontus and travelled to Rome in about the year 138. It was not long before he was making known his dogmatic views and by AD 144 he had been excluded from the Christian community. In his book *Antitheses* (which has been lost), for example, he set in opposition the Law and the Gospel, the righteous God and the compassionate God. And yet he remained essentially a Biblicist. In his understanding, Jesus came to bring an absolutely new era of salvation, which involved repudiating the Old Testament. He believed that the Apostles were not always successful in shaking off the fetters of the old system and that consequently most of their writings are tainted. Only the Gospel of Luke (the *Evangelion*) and Paul's letters (the *Apostolicon*) are deemed sufficiently sound to be used, and even these undergo a thorough revision. From Luke's Gospel, Marcion removes the stories of the nativity, and from the Epistles he takes out the Pastoral Epistles and Hebrews. Any further assimilation of God the Father (of Jesus) to the God of the Old Testament is systematically erased. These, broadly speaking, are the features which characterise the Marcionite recension of the New Testament (see p. 47). It was translated into Latin at an early date to serve the needs of his dissident church.

Strange as it may seem, the readings written into Marcion's text were reproduced by later ecclesiastical scribes on more than one occasion. Traces of them are found almost everywhere, in the Old Latin versions, in the Old Syriac versions and in Codex Vaticanus, e.g. Rm 1:16. Not all of these variants are of a tendentious nature: a great many, for example, are harmonisations in passages where Luke's text is slightly different from Matthew's or Mark's; nor are such readings necessarily the work of Marcion. Rather they represent variants of the text he inherited, though he may well have made some changes to them.

All things considered, Marcion's text, in so far as we know it, represents an intermediary stage between the primitive text and the first recensions. His text is actually closer to the latter, which suggests that he had something to do with the later revisions, especially as Marcion was one who rejected any kind of symbolic exegesis. It is difficult, nevertheless, to be specific about the extent of his influence, which some believe was particularly strong on the Old Latin versions. Dom De Bruyne, an expert in this field, wrote: 'For some years now, I have come to suspect that our Latin text is nothing but the Marcionite *Apostolicon* corrected and completed. As for the Gospels, several Marcionite alterations have crept into (or have remained in) our early Latin manuscripts' (De Bruyne 1921, p. 14. For an opposing view, see Fischer 1972, p. 26, nn. 73 – 4; pp. 30f., n. 88; pp. 44f.). According to Metzger 1977 (p. 328), there existed a Latin version of Marcion's New Testament alongside the other versions. Marcion's version was probably closer to the 'European' type (that of the majority of manuscripts) than the 'African' type. In our own opinion, a Marcionite reading may, in certain cases, give the early text. As long as there is no point of doctrine involved, Marcion is a good representative of the text in use in Rome at his time. Moreover, if the variant is not a harmonisation and if it is supported by other witnesses, it has a chance of being an excellent reading, even if Tertullian does not agree with it. In any case, Marcion's text deserves careful study.

Tatian

Tatian was of Assyrian origin but lived in Rome where he was a disciple of Justin. Having become leader of the school on the death of his master, he broke with the Roman church towards AD 172 on account of his leanings towards Encratism, and went back to his own country.

He wrote several works, amongst them a Gospel harmony – that is a narrative in which the texts of the four Gospels are ingeniously woven together to present one continuous story. He gave it the title 'Diatessaron' (see pp. 31 – 2), meaning 'through four' (Gospels) or, more probably, an allusion to the four-note chord typical in ancient musical harmony. It is likely that he composed it in Greek, no doubt in Rome, and that he translated it into Syriac on his return to the Middle East. A number of critics believe that there also existed at this early date a harmony in Latin which could have had some influence on his work or which might simply have been a translation of Tatian's harmony. At any rate, the Diatessaron was a great success in the Syriac-speaking churches, where it remained the official Gospel until the fifth century.

Did its influence extend any further? In particular, did it affect the early text forms of the Gospels where harmonising corrections are clearly visible? Without a doubt, there are numerous points of contact between Tatian's harmony, on the one hand, and the Old Latin, the Old Syriac and certain Greek manuscripts on the other. Because of that, H. von Soden would have had the Diatessaron be 'the unique source of all the important alterations made to the Gospel text' (see p. 157). His opinion did not attract any following; nevertheless, the obsession with seeing Tatianisms everywhere has lasted to this day. And yet harmonising variants were around before Tatian – in Marcion, or the Gospel according to Peter, for example, or in authors who were not under Tatian's influence (Irenaeus and Clement of Alexandria). Furthermore, the Diatessaron is not necessarily the first harmony which was attempted; it is also possible that harmonising variants initially came into the text during the work of the very first recensions before any Diatessaron was made at all. If the harmony of Tatian is often in agreement with certain readings from early forms of the text, it is perhaps because, quite simply, both these early forms and Tatian's harmony are witnesses to the primitive text. Just as Marcion presented a text which was an intermediary between the primitive text and that of the recensions, so, as far as one can judge, did Tatian; but his text was generally closer to the primitive text than to the recensions.

In practice, one cannot be too wary of Tatianisms when they present merely a tendentious reading or a harmonising variant. But, if they do not, they must not be rejected *a priori*. Although Tatian proves himself to be something of a sophist and a virtuoso in his arrangements of the texts, he may still be a faithful witness to the Roman tradition of the middle of the second century.

The Old Latin versions (see pp. 27 – 31)

For a long time, all the pre-Vulgate Latin versions were grouped under the title 'Itala' or 'Italic', in accordance with a rather obscure passage in Augustine (*De doctrina christiana* II, 15, 22). Nowadays, the name rightly preferred is simply the Old Latin versions. For some books, such as the Acts of the Apostles, there is only one early version. But for the other books, such as the Gospels, it is usual to recognise several text types representing different translations. Attempts have even been made to localise these translations, using quotations made by the early ecclesiastical writers. This has been successful for the African Latin text (indicated by **K** in *Vetus Latina*; see p. 29). It is possible to have quite a good idea of the text known to Cyprian in Carthage, around the year 250. Otherwise, though, the history of the Old Latin versions is not very clear. *Vetus Latina* sees in Tertullian's quotations (including those attributed to Marcion) a type, for Paul's letters, which precedes **K** (indicated by **X**, Frede, *Vetus Latina* vol. 125) and further discerns two other main text types, both European and dating from before the Vulgate (indicated by **D** and **I**). For the Catholic Epistles (Thiele, *Vetus Latina* vol. 126), a Spanish type emerges (indicated by **S**) which was around in Spain by at the latest AD 370, that is before the quarrels between Priscillian and the Church.

It seems legitimate to date the first Latin versions to around the middle of the second century, but as to the identity of the authors, the exact date and the place of composition (Africa, Rome, Northern Italy, Gaul or Spain), that remains largely unknown. And there are further questions which are equally difficult to answer. How were these early versions made? All at once, or bit by bit as it was needed? What prompted the translations? Is there any reason to think that a Latin Diatessaron or a Marcionite Bible in Latin preceded them? What influences did they come under once they were made, either from each other or from outside? There are, as yet, no answers to these questions.

But the importance of the Old Latin versions should not be underestimated. Despite translation errors, harmonisations and all manner of corrections, and even though there is a wide diversity of form, they have certain characteristics in common which make them interesting from a textual critic's point of view. They are all written in a rough, popular style with a 'powerful element of creation and verbal adaptation which had repercussions on the whole of Christian literature' (De Labriolle 1920, Introduction, 1). They display a desire to be faithful to their model which produces a somewhat slavish translation, but also one which is valuable, in its literalness, by virtue of reconstituting the model. They are based on a text which was not only early but, what is more, was distributed quite widely; for a few rather curious readings crop up in the Old Syriac, in the Coptic, in Irenaeus and in Clement of Alexandria, as well as in several Greek manuscripts. All things considered, as long as they are used with due care, the Old Latin versions, and especially the African type, can be very useful in helping to establish the contents of the pre-recensional text which is closest to the original from all points of view.

The Old Syriac versions (see pp. 31–6)

The history of these is difficult to reconstruct in the absence of any information handed down by tradition. The best that can be done here is to summarise the view shared by most critics concerning the text of the Gospels. The two manuscripts, sy^s and sy^c, both influenced by the Diatessaron to some extent, represent, despite their differences, a single version which existed before the Peshitta but which is now lost. On all other points, there is total disagreement. Have the Tatianisms come from the translators or the later revisers? In what way, if any, are the two manuscripts dependent on each other? When should the Old Syriac version of the Gospels be dated? Is it right to place it before Tatian or should it be seen as dating from as late as the beginning of the fourth century? These are all questions which continue to be disputed.

In view of the quality of its variants and the short form of its text, this version could well have been made towards the middle of the second century, from a mainly pre-recensional text in Antioch. It would have been written for the needs of a limited community within which it remained because of the popularity of the Diatessaron outside it. This would be true only of the original form of the version, and it should not be overlooked that later forms were considerably modified, especially sy^c. Its chief interest lies in certain characteristic readings which are in agreement with other early witnesses from such diverse places as Rome, Carthage and Alexandria. All in all, in the manuscripts of this version there are, despite many patches of extraneous material, more than a few pre-recensional variants which are one more proof of the extent to which the primitive text was known.

As for the Old Syriac version of Acts and the Pauline Epistles, which is only known now by quotations (see p. 33), it would appear to bear the same marks of an early age. It is not possible to determine its exact date, and it is not a unified text, but it is still fair to say that it probably attests, albeit in a revised form at times, one of the forms of the Greek text current in the second century.

The Palestinian or Caesarean recension

This recension is traditionally attributed to Pamphilus, well known as a disciple of Pierius while living at Alexandria and afterwards as master of the school at Caesarea in Palestine. He was a fervent admirer of Origen, who was a reminder to him of both Alexandria and Caesarea. He was particularly interested in the writings of Scripture and worked on a number of copies. He died a martyr's death towards AD 309 (Eusebius, *Historia ecclesiastica* VI, 32, 3; VII, 32, 25–6; VIII, 13, 6; *De martyribus Palestinae* V, 2; VII, 4–6; IX, 2–3).

Unfortunately, there is little information on his recension of the

New Testament. Origen speaks of having shrunk from such a task (*In Matthaeum* XV, 14, 3); but he did leave some copies of parts of the Bible which he no doubt sometimes corrected with his own hand, and which were held in great esteem for a long time in Caesarea along with those of Pierius (Jerome, *In Matthaeum* 24, 36; *In epistolam ad Galatas* 3, 1). Is it possible that Pamphilus worked on these manuscripts, with the additional help perhaps of the text used by his master in his homilies and commentaries? The conjecture seems legitimate especially if, in addition to Jerome's vague comments (see p. 107), the discovery in the twenties of a new type of text is considered. It was Lake and Blake (see p. 159) who threw light on this type, which is related in some way to Origen's Palestinian text and to that of Eusebius, a disciple of Pamphilus.

The witnesses to this recension were first of all identified for the Gospels. There are only a few of them: Θ.038, W.032 (for Mk 5:31–16:8 only), 0188, 28, 565, 700 and the Families 1 and 13 including the Evangeliary *l*547; the lectionary fragment *l*1604 (Greek–Sahidic, fourth century) according to Hedley 1934 (p. 39); and, finally, the versions sy[pal], arm (in part), and geo (the Old Georgian). The difficulty is that most of these witnesses are contaminated by the Byzantine type and are far from being in agreement amongst themselves. On the other hand, they present a fair number of agreements with P[45] which dates from before Origen and thus also before Pamphilus. The specific contribution of the latter is thus probably limited and the Caesarean recension could come, to a large extent, from work carried out in the second century, perhaps in Palestine and used by the first recensions in Egypt (whence the closeness in form between the Caesarean and Egyptian text types, so striking that the two types are sometimes confused). These recensions would have been known to Origen and would have subsequently been reworked in a variety of ways. Duplacy makes the comment: 'One must envisage the possibility that the "Caesarean" text type could be the result of a proto-Alexandrian influence on a Palestinian pre-recensional text' (Duplacy 1959, p. 93).

Outside the Gospels, a text displaying similar characteristics is to be found. G. Zuntz (1953, pp. 151f.) sees it for the Pauline Epistles in P[46] and 1739, in particular, and describes it as 'Caesarean', considering it to be proto-Alexandrian. In fact, it is as close to B.03 as it is to Origen. We would also suggest classifying some of the bilingual Greek–Latin manuscripts supposed to have a 'Western' text in this category: D.06, F.010, G.012. For the Catholic Epistles, M. Carder (1969) sees this type in some Greek minuscules, especially 1243; C.-B. Amphoux and

B. Outtier (1984) would see it rather in 1739 (and about ten other minuscules amongst which is 1243), especially in the variants it shares with C.04, P[72] and the witnesses to the Old Georgian version. In all these studies, the Caesarean type emerges as slightly different from the Egyptian type and probably anterior to it: it could be one of the very first forms of the text of this recension. Whether or not that is so, the importance of this text type is too great to be ignored.

The Old Coptic versions (see pp. 36–9)

From the dates of some manuscripts, it is possible to ascertain that there existed Coptic versions as early as the third century, and from Athanasius (*Vita Antonii*, 2) that there was at least one around AD 275. But nothing at all is known about their origin, and it is doubtful whether all the various early fragments, even all those in Sahidic, represent a single translation. Internal criticism indicates that some of the Coptic translations represent a Greek text from before the third century. The most remarkable witness in this respect is Codex Glazier which is a translation of a form of the text of Acts as little revised as that of Codex Bezae. For the Gospel of Mark, there probably existed two Sahidic versions, one of which follows a Caesarean type of text (M 569), and the other an Egyptian type (Codex P Palau; see Bouvarel-Boud'hors 1986). Elsewhere, the variants attest a substratum which is a mixture of the type of the great uncials (S.01, B.03, etc.) and pre-recensional type readings which are also found in the Old Latin and Old Syriac manuscripts, and in Codex Bezae, etc. The order of some of the books is interesting: John–Matthew–Mark–Luke in certain Sahidic documents, Luke before Mark in Codex Barcelona (fifth century), Hebrews after 2 Corinthians, and so on. Some of the versions could come from a Greek text which is no longer extant but which was known to Clement of Alexandria, for example. They represent, so to speak, variant witnesses which have survived the later alterations made from the great Alexandrian recension which will be discussed below (p. 107). True, this is yet another hypothesis, but it is excusable in view of the strange medley of the Old Coptic versions.

Thus, between the years 150 and 250, the text of the first recensions acquired a host of new readings. They were a mixture of accidental carelessness, deliberate scribal corrections, involuntary mistakes, a translator's conscious departure from literalness, a reviser's more systematic alterations, and not least contamination caused by harmonising to an extent which varied in strength from place to place. All these things contributed to diversification of the text, to giving it, if one may so put it, a little of the local colour of each country. Furthermore, this new text itself sometimes exerted an influence, especially in the bilingual manuscripts, on the transmission of the Greek text, and so continually added to the tangle of alterations. So much did this happen that towards the end of this period, there no longer existed truly local texts, each belonging to its own area, but instead profoundly different types of the same text. The major task of textual criticism is precisely the restoration of these different types. So far, the work of classifying the documents has yielded very uneven results, and most of the research has not yet been put to use. Once it has been further developed so that the types of text used at Rome, in Egypt, in Palestine and in Syria can be reconstituted, as well as that of Cyprian in Carthage, for example, then a good deal of light should be thrown on the whole of the history of the text in this period.

Was the New Testament translated into any other languages before AD 300? It is difficult to be certain, for there remains no documentary evidence. It is plausible that a translation was made in Persia, where Christianity enjoyed great popularity as early as the second century. Elsewhere, it was not until the fourth and fifth centuries that an alphabet was even created; and when it was, it was with the express purpose of translating the Bible. Were there, prior to the writing down of the New Testament in these countries, oral translations? That is a question that cannot be answered with a clear 'yes' or 'no'. There are versions in many languages other than the ones which have already been examined which have preserved early pre-recensional variants. It would be difficult to account for the continuing existence of these variants after the great Greek recensions, without there being some kind of early traditions firmly established in the languages in which they are found.

THE GREAT RECENSIONS

The next recensions of the Greek text, the first of which we know anything, date from the start of the second half of the third century to about AD 313. Around AD 390 Jerome, in the preface to his translation of Chronicles (*PL* 28, col. 1324), makes an interesting remark. He distinguishes, for the Septuagint, three kinds of manuscripts: those of Hesychius which are the principal ones in Egypt, those of Lucian which are used from Constantinople to Antioch and those of Origen, made available for popular use in Palestine by Pamphilus and Eusebius. This classification is in all probability also valid for the New Testament. Six years earlier (in about AD 384) in a letter to Pope Damasus where he sets out the principles behind his translation of the Gospels (*PL* 29, col. 527), Jerome complains of the bad recensions of Hesychius and Lucian as opposed to the older, excellent manuscripts which he used. Now at this time he had not yet gone to Egypt, and the local recension of Hesychius may have been less well known to him. As for Lucian's, like all things new, it was strongly criticised at Constantinople, from where he had just returned. On the other hand, he was full of admiration for the critical work of Origen. At just the right moment, again at Constantinople, he had come across certain famous manuscripts which he presumably took to be the legacy of the great doctor, Eusebius, the very manuscripts which Constantine himself had ordered from Eusebius in Caesaraea for the churches in the capital (see p. 111). Would that not be the type of text he preferred, although he did not actually name it? Later on, after his journey to Egypt and his exegetical discussions with Didymus (AD 386), he shows less disapproval of the other two texts. It is to his credit that, in such circumstances, he should change his mind. Such, in brief, is what seems to us to be the best explanation of what is known traditionally to be Jerome's preference for Origen's text.

The Egyptian or Alexandrian recension (H, for Hesychius to whom it is attributed)

The author is not known for certain although he may have been the Egyptian Bishop Hesychius, martyred around AD 311 in Alexandria under Maximinus (Eusebius, *Historia ecclesiastica* VIII, 13, 7). The work itself is difficult to disentangle for three reasons. First, it seems to have taken a large part of its inspiration from much earlier recensions: it would certainly be foolish to see it all as original work. As early as AD 200, P^{66} attests certain of the readings of this recension, and several years later P^{75} also attests most of the ones in Luke and John. Secondly, the recension may have been carried out only in stages: some books appear to have remained in their early form longer than others, for example Mark's Gospel in P^{45} (third century) and W.032 (fifth century). Finally, it was later subjected to further alterations, sometimes being embellished, sometimes being pruned (for texts too suffer reversals of fortune). It is to be expected, therefore, that the opinion of so careful a critic as Kenyon (1901) on the main representative of this Alexandrian recension, Codex Vaticanus B.03, should be that it reflects, not the primitive text in almost its original state, but rather the work of a skilful reviser using the best authorities available.

The general principles of this revision are not as obscure as the state of the text itself, but are still not very clear. They were probably not very different from the principles followed at the same time and in the same place to establish the texts of secular writers, such as Homer. The earliest manuscript was taken as the base and then compared with the other manuscripts; any details deemed useless were obliterated, especially if they were absent from some copies, being considered the work of scribes who were fond of filling out the text; finally, any spelling corrections and grammatical corrections thought necessary were made. These are, broadly speaking, the characteristics of the Hesychian recension: it has as its goal to make the text old, short and correct. But 'old' does not necessarily mean 'earliest', and this recension may be based on texts of the second century. What is more serious is that the desire to keep the text short has led to a number of deliberate omissions, especially in Acts but also probably in the Gospels, as in Lk 22:43–4 (see Duplacy 1981). And, in any case, even in its best representatives, it is not exempt from additions, harmonisations, or exegetical corrections. Yet, in spite of all these faults, it is a valuable recension marked by its high literary quality if not by its faithfulness. Since the time of K. Lachmann (see pp. 146–7), who was the first to take it as the basis for his edition of the New Testament, it is the one which has been used by most Western editors of the text.

Its representatives are relatively few and most of them are only partial witnesses. These are the main ones: P^{66} (in part), P^{74}, P^{75} (most of it), $P^{64.67}$ and P^4 (in the tiny fragments of them which exist – they are possibly all from the same codex); B.03 (most of it: some variants, in the Catholic Epistles for example, could be Caesarean), S.01 (except Jn 1–7 which has a 'Western' text), A.02 (except for the Gospels which are of the Syro-Byzantine type), C.04 (in part, the other variants being probably Caesarean), W.032 (for Jn 5:12–end and Lk 1:1–8:12). Mention may also be made of I.016, T.029, H.015, Z.035, L.019, Ψ.044, M.021, Δ.037, 059, 060, 070; of the minuscules: 6, 33, 81, 104, 326, 579, 892, 1175, 1241; for the lectionaries, Hedley gives the following list (quoted by Duplacy 1970): several early fragments from the fifth to the seventh centuries: *l*1043, *l*1354, *l*1276, *l*1353, and also *l*1602 from the eighth century, but only for Matthew and Mark (Luke and John have another type of text); of the versions: sa (not always, nor in all the manuscripts), bo, and vg (in part); finally, of the Fathers, the most noticeable are Athanasius, Didymus and Cyril of Alexandria.

The Syro-Byzantine or Antiochene recension (K, for 'Koine' or the common edition)

This recension is attributed with a fair degree of confidence to Lucian of Antioch, famous because of his exegetical knowledge and for his death as a martyr around AD 312 at Nicomedia, under Maximinus (Eusebius, *Historia ecclesiastica* VIII, 13, 2 and IX, 6, 3). It is not so easy to determine the original form of the recension, especially as continual alterations caused it to deteriorate in quality. It also became increasingly widespread so that quite quickly it developed into the Byzantine type which itself produced the 'received' text (see p. 126).

Broadly speaking, what characterises this recension is the desire for elegance, ease of comprehension and completeness. It tends to put most of its effort into attaining literary correctness: better balanced sentences, better chosen words: a text, in short, for people of letters. It further displays a studious preoccupation with clarity, for it tries in every way possible to explain difficult passages. Finally, it aims to lose nothing of the sacred text, by freely amalgamating the different readings of a passage. The result is a kind of 'plenior' text, one which is longer but also full of major faults. That does not make it entirely without value. Here and there, in one witness or another, there are a fair number of readings known to the Syrian communities of the first centuries. So there are some valuable elements in this mixture; they simply need to be decanted.

The vast majority of manuscripts belong to this recension. The main representatives are: A.02 (only for the Gospels), W.032 (only for Matthew and Luke 8:13 – end). Mention may also be made of: Ω.045; V.031, S.028; E.07, F.09, G.011, H.013, K.017, Π.041, K.018 (most of it), L.020 and, to a lesser extent, P.024, Q.026, R.027 and Γ.036; the mass of the minuscules and most of the lectionaries; the versions syᵖ and goth; and finally the quotations of certain Fathers like John Chrysostom or Titus of Bostra (Luke).

THE 'WESTERN' TEXT

This survey of the history of the text in the first period up to around AD 300 would not be complete without another brief look at the question of the so-called 'Western' text. This geographical label goes back to the eighteenth century; it is not an accurate one but it has become the conventional term, so that it makes sense still to use it as long as it is written in inverted commas. The variants of the 'Western' text are numerous and generally very early; they have held the attention of many generations of scholars, but in so doing have prevented them from noticing a rather important point: this text is not a type of text, rather it contains several types. Indeed, under the term 'Western' are grouped witnesses which are acknowledged to be heterogeneous. Whilst they have some variants in common, there are at least two types which are Latin, and one which is Syriac; and for the Gospels, Codex Bezae is the sole, constant representative of yet another type. It has been said of this text that it is old and universal. It is old, but in varying degrees: one of the types is pre-recensional, the others bear witness to the first recensions made at the time of the first versions. And it is also universal, for it gathers together the oldest text types, those from which all the others directly or indirectly descend.

The 'Western' text has been made into a branch on its own in the textual tradition. But the most important division of the textual tradition actually cuts right through the 'Western' text, and not between it and the others. It is a cultural division and separates two periods in time rather than two geographical areas, since it occurs around AD 135, a time when the pressure of events demanded that the writings which had been collected be revised and brought up to date. The text which was gradually left behind is still attested by Codex Bezae and some others. The first revisions were cautious, so that their representatives still come under the heading of 'Western'; the Latin version, in use in Africa until around AD 250, is largely pre-recensional. Parallel to those tentative revisions, even before the year 200, more radical revisions were taking place. Their representatives are classified under other types of text; whilst being more clearly distinguishable from each other, they nevertheless were made for the same purpose, that is to adapt to the current age works that had been written before AD 135 in a cultural context whose language was no longer meaningful. The transformation seeks to preserve the message intact. The urgency of the task makes it seem disorderly, in the initial stages at least; and the role of the great recensions is to tidy things up, to give a functional homogeneity to the whole, either by the quality of its written language or else by its adaptability to a new oral purpose, that of liturgical readings.

This has been a summary, in broad outline, of the history of the text in the first period. It is a history which calls for admiration because of the Christians' zeal to spread their sacred books, but it is a history which is also confused, with only general facts available and with the important names and even the major events largely unknown. And yet, for all that, it is a history which is of great value, as long as we know how to derive benefit from it and not to hold on to any illusions. Duplacy expressed the matter well: 'History is not composed of possibilities, but neither is it composed without considering them'.

THE PERIOD OF LIMITED CONTROL
(AD 313 – around AD 850)

During the earlier period, the New Testament text experienced an increasing diversity, in spite of occasional attempts on the part of more or less official revisers of the text to slow the process down. Throughout the first centuries, the overall situation of Christianity was such that more control than that was hardly possible. Quite apart from the last persecution under Diocletian in AD 303, when the books were seized and thrown into the flames on the orders of the Emperor (Eusebius, *Historia ecclesiastica* VIII, 2, 4), the difficulties within the Church and the necessity of spreading the Christian writings kept the authorities in charge too busy for them to keep a check on secondary matters. When, with the arrival of Constantine, the Church recovered a state of peace, this could not help but have some influence on the transmission of the text of Scripture.

IMPROVEMENTS IN THE PRESENTATION OF THE MANUSCRIPTS

One of the results was that copies of the New Testament became more numerous and more carefully produced. Parchment began to take over from papyrus for the manufacture of biblical manuscripts. In AD 331, Emperor Constantine gave an order to his friend Eusebius for fifty Bibles, which were to be both easily legible and portable, for use in the churches of his new capital city. He specified that they were to be written by professional calligraphers and in codices of fine parchment (Eusebius, *De vita Constantini* IV, 36f.). Similarly, the damaged papyrus scrolls that formed the libraries of Origen and Pamphilus at Caesarea were transcribed onto codices of parchment under the Bishops Acacius (AD 338–65) and Euzoius (AD 376–9) (Jerome, *Epistola ad Marcellam* XXXIV, 1). The use of this new material not only caused manuscripts

111

written on scrolls to disappear, but also brought about certain changes in the writing. The characters became more definite and less squashed together as the 'biblical' uncial type of writing developed, a type which was borrowed from the literary papyri. As a rule, copies of the Bible were made by professional scribes. J. Duplacy (1965) estimates that the total number of New Testament Greek manuscripts produced in the fourth century was between 1,500 and 2,000, allowing for an average of four to five copies made by each diocese during this period (there were around 400 dioceses towards AD 400).

The editors began to imitate, in certain respects, the scholarly editions made by the Classical philologists of the time. There most probably existed already some kind of divisions in the text (see Clement of Alexandria, *Stromateis* VII, 14, 84; Tertullian, *Ad uxorem* II, 2), but now systems of chapters or shorter sections gradually developed. Nestle's edition (see p. 153) indicates some of them in the inside margin. According to J. Gribomont (1957), Basil of Caesarea seems to have had the idea in AD 360 of introducing a new system, 'unknown elsewhere', as a system for referring to the biblical text in his *Regulae morales*; in the end, he decided to quote the text in full himself, no doubt because the divisions were not yet properly fixed (see Duplacy 1980, pp. 81–2). Emphasis was laid on the signs used to indicate the various kinds of division: a dash or a blank space at the end of paragraphs, the first letter written as a capital or standing before the beginning of the line. Another change which became more common was that titles or summaries were placed at the beginning of books to indicate their contents. Sometimes, at the beginning of a work, the aim and subject matter were summarised. Notes at the start and at the end of a work, the inscriptions and subscriptions (see p. 9), became more developed; the length of a work was often shown at the end of the book by giving the number of stichoi. All these improvements are of interest.

For the Gospels, Eusebius introduced a system of 'sections' and 'canons' which was to be very useful. His intention was to bring out the similarities between the four Gospels. This he did by dividing the text of each Gospel into a certain number of sections (Matthew 355, Mark 233, Luke 342, John 232), thought for a long time to be the work of Ammonius. Then he drew up a table of ten canons:

1   sections common to the four Gospels;
2–4 sections common to Matthew–Mark–Luke, to Matthew–Luke–John and to Matthew–Mark–John;

5 – 9 sections common to Matthew – Luke, Matthew – Mark, Matthew –
      John, Luke – Mark and to Luke – John;
10   sections peculiar to each Gospel.

In the margin were written the number of the section and underneath
the number of the canon. In order to find the parallel passages of a
Gospel, all that was necessary was to consult the table of canons and
to read the concordance set out beside the number of each section.

In the fourth century also, so it seems, Euthalius brought out a new
edition of Acts, the Pauline Epistles and the Catholic Epistles. Not much
is known about the man himself except that he was a deacon of an
Eastern church. His work has been so much revised that it is difficult
to see just what the original looked like. What seems probable is that
there was a prologue at the head of each of the three sections; the text
was divided into chapters which were themselves divided into smaller
sections; there were marks to indicate the beginning and the end of
passages read at the services; there was a list of the contents of the
chapters and of their subdivisions, and another list of Scriptural and
secular quotations; finally, most importantly, the text was written not
in lines of equal length but in lines which corresponded to the meaning
(see p. 9), which made it easier to read in public. Some manuscripts
such as Codex Bezae or Claromontanus (D.05 and D.06) also used this
system of sense lines. The Euthalian apparatus has been reproduced
by Migne (*PG* 85, cols. 619 – 790) but the critical edition of his work is
that by A. Vardanian 1930; see also Birdsall 1984; Willard 1971; Zuntz
1945).

The reading of the New Testament in Christian meetings had other
effects on the presentation of the text. To make it easier to find the right
passage of Scripture that was to be read on a particular day, there were
at first simply two tables of readings placed at the beginning of the
manuscript, one for every day of the year starting from Easter (the
synaxarion), the other for the saints' days starting in September (the
menologion). All that was then needed was to turn to the passage indicated
to find the exact liturgical section which was marked by rubrics in the
margin. Very quickly, however, more practical books came to be made,
namely the lectionaries proper (see pp. 24 – 5).

Besides this, the decoration of the manuscripts tended to become
more ornate, a trend harshly criticised by Jerome (*Epistola* XXII, 32)
as pomposity and pride. Sometimes, the parchment was covered with
some substance to make it whiter, sometimes it was dyed purple. Letters

in gold and silver were often used to make the text stand out, and occasionally elaborate illustrations were inserted. Some of these de luxe manuscripts were produced during Justinian's brilliant rule (AD 527–65), for instance N.022, O.023, Σ.042, Φ.043 and 080, all of which appear to have been made in the same place. The manuscripts had come a long way from the poverty of the papyri.

EFFORTS MADE TO UNIFY THE TEXT

When the ecclesiastical authorities first started to take action with regard to the text, it was initially by keeping a more watchful eye on heretical interpretations. The Patristic writers, for example, frequently accused the Arians and the Nestorians of falsifying Scripture (Didymus, *De trinitate* II, 11; Ambrose, *De spiritu sancto* II, 6, etc.). In fact, what happened on more than one occasion was that the Apologists mistook what was in reality a very early variant for a recent corruption instead. A clear instance is in Hebrews 2:9, where χωρίς in place of χάριτι was believed by Oecumenius to be a Nestorian falsification but is actually already present in Origen and Ambrose. The control of the text was, in any case, anything but strict; there were still some well-intentioned scribes or correctors who, without having any official status, continued to introduce into the manuscripts new variants, which were sometimes very favourably received.

Nevertheless, on the whole, greater importance than before was attached to the quality of the text to be copied. Good exemplars were treasured as valuable models for scribes to copy. The high esteem in which Origen's manuscripts were held has already been pointed out (see p. 107); Jerome referred to them as 'exemplaria Adamantii' and freely appealed to their authority. Sometimes, a scribe even took the trouble to say which copies he had collated in order to determine his text. At times, it was 'the exact exemplars from the library of Eusebius and Pamphilus at Caesarea' (Euthalius); at others, it was the Bible of 'the great and divine Basil' (George Syncellus); or else it was simply the commentaries of the Church Fathers. No doubt mistakes were made on occasion about the value of a model, but what can be said, at the very least, is that an effort was made to adhere to the texts reckoned to be the best.

It was the major recensions which commanded the most respect in the Greek-speaking East, but they were not used exclusively. In Egypt, the pre-recensional text was still copied at this time: 0171 (fragments of Matthew and Luke), W.032 (for Mark 1 – 5), S.01 (for John 1 – 7). In the other languages, things are less clear: the old text was copied into Coptic (Codex Glazier), into Latin and Syriac with corrections (it[a.b.] sy[s.c.]); a Greek manuscript of the old type which was kept at the Monastery of Enaton near Alexandria was used as late as the beginning of the seventh century as one of the models for a new Syriac version (sy[h]) with marginal readings of the highest interest (sy[hmg]).

But the greatest obstacle to the unity of the textual tradition lay principally in the revisions of the great recensions themselves. Not one of them resisted this need for change, this law of every living thing. True, the new revisions were not always very sweeping. Sometimes, it was just a matter of bringing back old readings which had been rejected by the previous revisers, carrying to excess the principles which had guided the first recension. The texts of the different recensions began to influence each other and there were further variants which arose simply in the process of copying. And so the work of unifying the text was soon going to have to be done all over again.

Some examples will demonstrate the problems. First, from the Alexandrian recension: B.03 is doubtless its oldest representative, on the whole, but in the Catholic Epistles it has some Caesarean, even pre-recensional, variants; S.01 has retained many readings which are supported particularly by Caesarean witnesses (the manuscript was corrected, perhaps even copied, at Caesarea); C.04 contains an appreciable number of early variants (along with Ψ.044 in Mark and Acts) and it has a definite Caesarean type of test in the Catholic Epistles; W.032 has a text which is anything but homogeneous, in places following the Syro-Byzantine recension; L.019, a later manuscript (eighth century) is full of so-called grammatical and stylistic improvements.

The triumph of the Syro-Byzantine recension was not without its setbacks. The quotations of the Church writers in the fourth century reveal a text which is slightly different from the one we have today. It may be that the revision made by Lucian was subject to alteration early on, either through the reintroduction of readings which had been rejected or through influences from the Caesarean tradition. This makes it difficult to say which are the purest representatives of this type, A.02 (for the Gospels) or the eighth- to ninth-century uncials (such as E.07, V.031 or Ω.045). All that is certain is that this type of text spread very rapidly throughout the Greek-speaking world when John Chrysostom and other Syrians had occupied the patriarchal see at Constantinople.

Before taking over almost exclusively, in the form of the Byzantine type (see p. 126), the Syro-Byzantine text already began to make its influence felt on the other text types. Instances of that have been seen in some of the Alexandrian manuscripts mentioned above; the same happened in Θ.038, which is the best representative of the Caesarean recension of the Gospels at this time and which was badly affected by the Syro-Byzantine text.

From this all too rapid survey, it can be seen that the diversification of texts continued from the fourth to the ninth centuries in spite of all efforts to prevent it. The great recensions channelled, as it were, the streams of the manuscript tradition but they were far from obtaining the unification of the text; and to make things worse, they widened the gap between the texts in use and the original.

THE GREAT VULGATES

In the other parts of the Empire, however, where Latin, Syriac or Coptic were spoken, as Christianity began to prevail the need was felt to bring some kind of unity to the biblical versions by appealing to the authority of the Greek text ('Graeca auctoritas'). To this end, revisions were made of the early versions which sometimes displayed great diversity (according to Jerome, in Latin there were 'almost as many text forms as manuscripts'). An attempt was made to replace them with a uniform text which, as time went by, was to be recognised as the official translation and the one in common use (vulgate).

The Latin Vulgate (cf. pp. 30–1)

At the end of the fourth century, the Latin recensions were more numerous than satisfactory. Anyone who wanted to understand the text properly had to be prepared to undertake a revision of it. Thus Augustine revised the Gospels and the Pauline Epistles for his own use (see the studies made by Dom de Bruyne, indicated on p. 50). But the revision which had lasting success was that of Jerome, a work which needs to be discussed in two parts: the Gospels and the rest of the New Testament.

There is no problem with the origin of the new edition of the Gospels. On his return to Rome (AD 382), Jerome was given the task by Pope Damasus of putting an end to the disorder of the Latin translations. No-one could have been more fitted to the job. In AD 383–4, the great scholar presented his work, with an explanatory preface dedicated to the Pope in which he said that he had simply revised the current Latin text in accordance with ancient Greek manuscripts; in order not to disturb established custom, 'I have used my pen with some restraint and while I have corrected only such passages as seemed to convey a different meaning, I have allowed the rest to remain as they are' (*Epistola ad Damasum, praefatio in quattuor evangelia*, translation from *A select library of Nicene and Post-Nicene Fathers of the Christian Church*, eds. P. Schaff and H. Wace, 2nd series, vol. VI, p. 488).

Unfortunately, he does not say which Greek or Latin manuscripts he used. Modern scholars have tried to discover which they were, but the likelihood of there having been several types used makes any attempts at reconstructing his witnesses all the more fragile (see for example Vogels 1928). In order to reconstruct Jerome's edition, it would be necessary to have more information about the manuscript tradition of his time. Old Latin texts and early witnesses to the great Greek recensions are at present too few for us to be able to do anything but wait until the situation changes.

Overall, even though Jerome's revision is far from perfect, it undeniably marks a step forward. It is faithful without being slavish; it clears away a good many parasitic readings; it avoids a colloquial style without becoming too literary. From a text-critical point of view, it is of some importance. In so far as its sources can be discerned – both the Greek and the Latin ones – it enables the critic to get back beyond the fourth century and to reach the Latin tradition which generally gave way to Alexandrian type readings when there was any question of meaning involved.

As far as the other books of the New Testament are concerned (Acts, the Pauline Epistles, the Catholic Epistles, Revelation), the origin of the Vulgate is very uncertain. It is doubtful whether it should be attributed to Jerome. In the opinion of J. Gribomont (1960, p. 48), Jerome abandoned the project of revising the whole of the New Testament once he had finished the Gospels. Dom de Bruyne (1915) believes that a comparison of the text of quotations with that of the Vulgate indicates that for the Pauline Epistles the Vulgate is the work of Pelagius, but his findings are contested. Whoever the author is, the fact is that the work of the revision was carried out in a rather superficial manner and was based on very different principles from those followed in the case of the Gospels. However, what this means is that this part of the Vulgate remains sufficiently related to the Old Latin text for it to make a significant contribution to New Testament textual criticism.

Despite strong initial opposition, the new translation was gradually accepted, without there being any Council decree, in all the churches of the West – albeit with a certain predictable caution in Rome. But the greatest victories bring with them disappointments. More than one reviser of an Old Latin manuscript got tired of his work of bringing it into line with the new version and left the end of the old text unchanged. The Old Latin took, as it were, a kind of revenge by infiltrating the new text in the form of unfortunate corrections. The Vulgate was copied so frequently, in any case, that it was inevitable that it should be corrupted by negligent or careless scribes, so much so that revision was soon called for. Mention need only be made of the attempt of Cassiodorus in the sixth century; or, at the end of the eighth century, under the influence of Charlemagne, the work of Alcuin, Abbot of Saint-Martin of Tours, and Theodulf, Bishop of Orleans. Many times, later on, the work had to be done again. Such was the price of the success of the Vulgate, as it began to be called.

The Syriac Vulgate (see p. 34)

Towards the beginning of the fifth century took place the writing of the Syriac Vulgate or the Peshitta. The origin of the name 'Peshitta' meaning 'simple' or 'common' is a matter of debate. In general, it is a revision of the Old Syriac version to bring it into line with the Antiochene recension. Despite a good many mistakes and too much freedom in the translation, the Peshitta is of interest from two points of view: first, as a witness to Lucian's text; secondly, because of the numerous readings from the Old Syriac which were no doubt preserved for reasons of piety. According to F. C. Burkitt (1904) (III)), it could well be the work of Rabbula, Bishop of Edessa from AD 411 to 435. In the first place, it is never quoted before the first half of the fifth century, and, in addition, in one of his canons Rabbula ordered that 'in all the churches a copy of the separate Gospels be kept and read', and it is known from his biographer that 'he translated the New Testament from Greek into Syriac'. But, according to A. Vööbus 1954 (pp. 90–9), the text quoted by Rabbula is so different from that of the Peshitta that it is difficult to think of him as the author of this version, which, besides, lacks homogeneity and is more likely to be the work of several authors. In any case, the Syriac Vulgate must have been created between the death of Ephraem (AD 373), who still used the Diatessaron, and the Council of Ephesus (AD 431), after which time the Nestorians would have rejected this version (see Metzger 1977, p. 48). It was, in fact, received very favourably to the extent that it has remained the official version of all Syrian Christians, whatever their church affiliation. Unlike the Latin Vulgate, it managed to hold its own with relative ease and, despite divisions in the church, to remain unaffected by major variants.

The Coptic Vulgate (see p. 38)

It is even more difficult to determine the origin of the Coptic Vulgate in the Bohairic dialect. Tradition provides no clues and internal criticism allows only conjectures to be made. The first thing to note is that there existed at least one other version in Bohairic, that of Bodmer Papyrus III, for John's Gospel. Compared with that version, and those in other dialects, the Vulgate seems more recent: R. Kasser (1965) places its origin between AD 500 and 650, that is in the period preceding the Arab conquest. One thing is certain, that it is closely related to the main witnesses of the Alexandrian recension, B.03 and S.01 in particular, although it appears to have undergone in some passages the influence of previous Coptic versions, especially the Sahidic ones. And so, when all is said and done, it should perhaps be viewed, if not as a revision of the Old Coptic version based on the Alexandrian recension, at least as an attempt at a more literal translation with occasional glimpses available of the old popular versions. It very quickly became accepted and has hardly been altered at all. For the purposes of textual criticism, it is of lesser interest than the other Vulgates: its main contribution is to confirm in general, along with some of the later papyri (P^{74}, seventh century), the stability of the Alexandrian recension after the fourth century.

THE NEW VERSIONS

During this period, the number of variants in the New Testament text increased as the continuing spread of Christianity created the need for new versions to be made: versions in new languages, in new dialects, for new communities.

Versions in new languages

Gothic

The Goths were no doubt introduced to Christianity as early as the third century, when they settled in Moesia. But, according to the historian Socrates, it was Ulfilas, of Cappadocian descent and Arian bishop of the Goths (died AD 383), who translated most of the biblical books into his native language, inventing, for the purpose, a Gothic alphabet. On the New Testament side, this version has been examined by G.W.S. Friedrichsen (1926; 1939). It seems to be a fairly literal translation of an Antiochene text, but it also contains certain 'Western' variants (see Gryson 1990, p.67). These are usually attributed to alterations made to the translation from Latin versions in use in the north of Italy at the time when the Goths arrived there. If there is any truth in this explanation, which is yet to be proved, the importance of this version for textual criticism would be limited.

Armenian

The Armenians also invented an alphabet at the end of the fourth century in order to translate the Bible. A fairly reliable tradition (though perhaps tainted with legend) has it that they also received the Christian faith before the Council of Nicaea. As for the first Armenian version, their own historians date it to the beginning of the fifth century (before AD 414), in the days of the Patriarch Sahak. This version is no longer available in manuscript form but it can be traced in the quotations and identified, according to L. Leloir (1966), as close to the Old Syriac version, or, according to S. Lyonnet (1950), to the Diatessaron. The model of this first version is generally considered to be of Caesarean origin, either Greek, or Syriac, which would explain the high number of Syriacisms in the Armenian text. Was the original Armenian version thought to have been carried out too hastily? Possibly, for it was revised by AD 450 using Greek manuscripts with a Byzantine text, and a second version produced, which is that of the extant manuscripts. The text is improved but there are still many Caesarean variants, especially in Acts and the Pauline Epistles (see Lyonnet in Lagrange 1935, pp. 459 and 527–8), but also in the other books. The Armenian version plays an important part in the textual criticism of the New Testament because it is one of the few witnesses to the Caesarean recension.

Georgian

The Georgians in Caucasia seem to have written down their language at an earlier date (see Metzger 1977, p. 184). They were also evangelised at an early date, towards the beginning of the fourth century. There are two traditions concerning this event, one from Armenia and the other from Greece, and, naturally enough, the first has the missionaries come from Armenia, the other from Constantinople. No less naturally, they each claim that the Georgian version was made from a text in their own respective language. What seems to be the most probable story is as follows. There are, in the manuscript tradition, at least two early Georgian versions, known as the 'Adysh type' (geo^1) and the 'pre-Vulgate type' (geo^2). The former seems to be based on an Armenian model, and could be a translation made around AD 450 from the first Armenian version, which has been lost; the latter would then be a revision of this version using Greek witnesses of a Caesarean type (see Birdsall 1988). That there were special links between Georgia and Palestine at that time is confirmed by the Old Georgian lectionary which is one of the best witnesses to the Jerusalem liturgical readings at the beginning of the fifth century. (The Armenian lectionary in its oldest part is also a very valuable witness.) It is from this point of view that the Old Georgian versions are of interest. Not only do they suggest evidence for a first Armenian version which has been lost, but, moreover, they are among the best witnesses to the Caesarean text.

Arabic

The Arabs, that is primarily the inhabitants of present-day Jordan and the south of Palestine, received Christianity probably as early as the first or second century. And yet, as Devreesse says (1942, p. 113), 'at the beginning of the fourth century, the majority of the population remained untouched by the spread of the Gospel ... After Constantine, Christianity gains ground, albeit slowly.' The question of the Arabic versions of the New Testament is still largely uncharted territory (see pp. 42 – 3). According to tradition, the first Arabic translation of the Gospels dates back to the seventh century and was based on a Syriac model. But at this time or in the following century, other translations may have been made based on Greek, and Coptic or Latin, manuscripts. For the purposes of textual criticism, it is the versions which attest an early recension which are of the most interest. At the present stage of knowledge, it is not possible to affirm more than that there are some witnesses of a version of the Gospels, probably made from the Greek, which preserve some early readings in particular of a Caesarean type. Certain Arabic versions thus made a positive contribution to knowledge of the New Testament text before AD 200: that in itself is sufficient to justify further study of them.

Ethiopic

In Ethiopia, Christianity made inroads in the fourth century. The date of the first version is more difficult to ascertain: the fifth to the sixth century is sometimes stated, but without much evidence (see Metzger 1977, p. 223). Unfortunately, most of the Ethiopic manuscripts are late (see p. 43), written after alterations had been made, especially from Arabic manuscripts. How far they resemble the first versions is therefore uncertain, but there are a few clues which show that in the Ge'ez dialect in particular there are some features of the first recensions, even of the pre-recensional text. The distinction which Zotenberg (1877) makes between the 'early' or 'primitive' version and the 'corrected' version (e.g. Zot. 32 or 42 on the one hand, and 35 or 41 on the other) is to be taken seriously. But, as things stand at present, it is not possible to consider the 'early' Ethiopic version as a witness to a fixed text type.

A version in a new dialect

Little is known for certain about the origins of the Palestinian Syriac version (see p. 35). Some scholars link it to the religious political policies of Justinian and Heraclius (sixth to seventh centuries): that is, the Bible would have been translated into the language of the Jews and the Samaritans of Palestine, who had been converted, by force if not of their own accord. The relatively late date of this version (although Lagrange places it at the beginning of the fifth century; see Lagrange 1925b) accounts for the large number of Byzantine type variants. At the same time, however, it displays certain affinities with Origen's Caesarean text and, for an isolated fragment of Acts (see p. 36), with Codex Bezae. In spite of its fragmentary state, it is thus of some importance for textual criticism as a source of information about the text before AD 200, but certainly not as the most faithful record of the words of Jesus, as has been claimed.

Versions for new communities

Following the great controversial Christological debates, the Mono-physites set about making new versions in Syriac. Towards AD 508, Philoxenus, Bishop of Mabbûg (Hierapolis) gave his chorepiscopus, Polycarp, the task of making a more literal and more complete trans-lation of the Greek manuscripts than was the Peshitta. Brock has shown (see pp. 34 – 5) that this translation survived more especially in the form of quotations, and that it was not devoid of theological emphases. About a century later, towards AD 616, Thomas of Harkel (Heracleia, near Mabbûg), who had been deposed as Bishop of Mabbûg and had taken refuge in the Monastery at Enaton near Alexandria, revised this trans-lation with a less theological and more philological concern than Philoxenus, according to Brock. There is a large collection of manuscripts of his work which is known variously as the 'Philoxenian' or the 'Harclean' version. It displays two noteworthy characteristics: first, the diacritical signs in the text, obeli and asterisks, the meaning of which continues to be a subject of debate among scholars; secondly, the marginalia referring to variants in the Greek or Syriac manuscripts which were collated for his translation. The interesting point, as far as the Greek manuscripts are concerned, is that they do not all belong to the Alexandrian recension: one of those used for the Gospels turns out to have a Caesarean type of text, and that used for Acts has a distinctly 'Western' text. Furthermore, the 'old Syriac manuscript' which is men-tioned on more than one occasion must have been very similar to the Sinaitic Syriac manuscript (sy^s). All in all, the text as well as the marginal notes of the Harclean version represent one of the main sources of information concerning the New Testament text before AD 200.

THE PERIOD OF STANDARDISATION
(AD 850 – the sixteenth century)

Already in the preceding period, serious attempts to reduce the number of different forms of the text and to establish a more settled text were being made. In this last period, the need for a fixed text was felt even more keenly. From the ninth century, when the books of the Bible began to be reproduced in great numbers, until recent times, there was a predominant tendency to create a uniform text or, as one might say, to implant a sort of ecclesiastical text for the Greek as well as for each version. The causes of this may have been various: political influences, the defence of the status quo, the absence of critical preoccupations or the growing strength of a new oral tradition, created by the memorisation of biblical passages through the constant hearing or reading of them in slightly varying forms according to the text followed. Whatever the cause, the fact cannot be denied. Nor was this characteristic tendency to establish a fixed text in any way overshadowed by the concurrent changes taking place in the way the manuscripts were written.

THE PRESENTATION OF THE MANUSCRIPTS

In a general way, efforts were made to make the reading of the text easier. For this purpose, new chapter divisions were introduced: our modern divisions were created by Stephen Langton, Chancellor of the University of Paris and Archbishop of Canterbury (died 1228). The inscriptions and the subscriptions of the manuscripts (see p. 9) were amplified, and, in addition, new historical information was supplied: a list of the twelve Apostles and the seventy disciples, stories of Paul's journeys, remarks concerning the lives of the Apostles and the New Testament writers. Sometimes 'scholia', or notes of a more or less learned nature, were also inserted into the margins.

It was also during this period that there flourished in the East the exegetical 'catenae', a literary genre which had its beginnings in the previous period (around the sixth century). This is the name used to designate the collections of fragments of commentaries on passages of Scripture. Two main types can be distinguished on the basis of external features. Sometimes the Scriptural text takes up the centre of the page, with the commentary placed around it on three or four sides: these are known as 'marginal catenae'. In other instances, the Scriptural text and the extracts from the commentaries follow on from each other: these are the 'long-lined catenae'. Most of the time, neither sort reveals any kind of doctrinal preoccupation. Their purpose is simply to present as complete a collection as possible, in compact form, of selected passages. The authors of these collections are generally unknown, there being just a few names associated with them, such as Nicetas of Heraclea in the eleventh to the twelfth century. The reason that these catenae are so interesting is that, whether in Greek, Syriac, Armenian or Arabic, they have preserved such a large part of the tradition of Scriptural exegesis, even though it is frequently difficult to know who is responsible for the fragments quoted. For the purposes of textual criticism, they are of far less importance because, in general, they all reproduce the same type of text: the Byzantine type. Occasionally, though, some early variants are preserved, as in the catenae of Andreas on Acts, which were the inspiration for the commentaries of Oecumenius and Theophylact.

A further curious change which occurred during this period was the transition from uncial to minuscule writing. This change of alphabet (whether from one language to another or from one system of characters to another) is known as transliteration (see Dain 1975, pp. 124 – 33). For some time the uncial continued to be used, especially in the transcription of lectionaries. But, at the same time, the growing demand for new copies meant that the amount of parchment needed for each one had to be reduced. It was for that reason that, first, palimpsests were increasingly used as a makeshift solution (see p. 9), and, secondly, the uncial script was abandoned, as its large characters, which were generally separated from each other, took up too much room. The minuscule took over: it took up less space and was also quicker to write; as a bonus, its joined-up letters made it easier to read. In Byzantium, the transliteration of the Greek manuscripts went hand in hand with a major work of philological revision. Minuscule 1739, which is an important witness to the text of Acts and the Epistles before AD 200, bears a number of characteristic features of a transliterated manuscript. It was copied around the year 950 at the Imperial scriptorium by Ephraem, and has notes in the margin referring to Irenaeus, Clement of Alexandria, Origen, Eusebius and Basil – that is to Church Fathers of the second to the fourth centuries; it is furthermore the oldest known manuscript of a group of minuscules which have Caesarean variants.

Some de luxe copies were still being made during this period. There were dynasties of Byzantine emperors, those of Commenus (eleventh to twelfth centuries) or of Palaeologos (thirteenth to fourteenth centuries), for example, which sought to rival the splendour of the reign of Justinian. New copies of Bibles and lectionaries were made, using the finest parchment and ornately decorated, sometimes even using gold ink. Examples that may be noted are the minuscules 565, 1143 and 1394, or the lectionary *l*46. But this kind of extravagance is rather rare. Generally speaking, the size of manuscript was reduced from folio and quarto to octavo and even sexto-decimo. The parchment became thicker and in the end was replaced by paper. The increasing number of copies of the Scriptures produced could not but have a negative effect on the external presentation of the manuscripts.

THE FORM OF THE GREEK TEXT

This period saw the triumph of the Byzantine text, otherwise known as the ecclesiastical or imperial text. The name is of little importance but the fact of the predominance of this form of the text is striking. It developed from the Antiochene recension and dominated the whole of the Greek-speaking East. It also found its way into the West, with the result that there are several Greek – Latin manuscripts which have a Byzantine text opposite an Old Latin text. The collation of these manuscripts gives an impression of uniformity.

There are, however, as will be seen, a number of exceptions to the rule. And it must not be thought that this type was, so to speak, crystallised; it continued to have some kind of life and to give birth to many different varieties. But, within these groups, the underlying and original character of the Byzantine text is still present. What distinguishes one from another is the varying number of older readings which they have retained. And it is precisely this differing proportion of early variants which helps to break the monotony of the type as a whole.

As a matter of fact, the history of the Byzantine text has yet to be written. H. von Soden undertook to write it as part of his major work on the New Testament (see p. 155), but when the result is examined closely it can be seen to be full of inaccuracies, unsound in its principles and haphazard in its application of them. In a word, it needs to be rewritten; but at least the groundwork has been done. In particular, the general grouping of the manuscripts is seen more clearly. On the one hand, there are the few copies which are closely linked to the chief manuscripts of the Antiochene recension (see p. 109). Some which concern the Gospels are S.028 and V.031, related to Ω.045; F.09, G.011, H.013, related to E.07; K.017 and Π.041, related to A.02. These latter two groups have been studied by S. Lake (1936; Π.041 (VI)) and more recently by J. Geerlings and R. Champlin (1962 – 8; f¹³, E.07 (VI)). On the other hand, there is a great mass of manuscripts (more than 2,000) which constitutes a whole crowd of witnesses to a text which is both later and increasingly mixed. There would be little value in indicating the various subdivisions that some have tried to work out.

One remarkable feature of the text of this period, which von Soden pointed out, was the frequent interchange of manuscripts between the monasteries of Athos, Patmos and Sinai. So, although the Byzantine type was predominant, copies of the other recensions were still made here and there, even though they were often made to conform to the favoured text. Sometimes it was some local interest which was behind a copy, such as to preserve a traditional form of the text. Sometimes it was a taste and respect for antiquity. Sometimes it was simply good fortune as the first copy to hand was transcribed without any particular value being attached to it. Whatever the reasons behind them, the following are the chief manuscripts which depart from the Byzantine tradition.

Generally speaking, the Alexandrian recension, which had not been very widespread since the Arab conquest (seventh century), is not common. There are nonetheless the manuscripts Δ.037, 33, 892, 579 (except for Matthew) and 1241, for the Gospels, and 33, 81 and 104 for Acts and the Epistles. The Caesarean recension has more witnesses but they are almost all contaminated by a Byzantine influence. In addition to a few isolated manuscripts (28, 565, 700), there are Families 1 and 13 for the Gospels and the group 1739 for Acts and the Epistles (see pp. 22 – 4). Some other groups are so disfigured that they seem to represent the Syro-Byzantine text slightly corrected with Caesarean variants: M.021, 7^e, 1424; U.030, 1071; Λ.039, 1604. As far as the 'Western' text is concerned, there is no Greek representative of the Gospels in this later period, whereas for Acts and the Epistles there is the group 2138, which has about twenty manuscripts (see p. 23), although they, too, are all more or less contaminated by the Byzantine text. And there are some further rare copies which are of great interest because they have preserved some very early readings even down to this late date, despite the predominance of the standard text.

THE FORM OF THE VERSIONS

Outside the Greek-speaking Orient, it was the Vulgates or common texts which reigned. Nothing needs to be said about the Syriac Vulgate, for its text had become rigid. In Egypt, the Sahidic Coptic dialect which had survived longer than the other dialects slowly died (around AD 1000, according to Kasser 1965), leaving the field open to the Vulgate version in Bohairic, which, probably under the influence of the Byzantine text, underwent some alterations, such as the episode about the woman caught in adultery (Jn 7:53 – 8:11), added at a later stage. In the West, the success of Alcuin's recension (see p. 118) caused a number of alterations to be made to the Latin Vulgate. Between the tenth and the twelfth centuries several people, including Stephen

Harding, Abbot of Cîteaux (1109 – 34), made attempts to revise the text. In the thirteenth century, a new attempt was made when the University of Paris, wanting to make the teaching of theology easier, decided to choose one Latin manuscript and to make copies from that one alone. The resultant text was known as the 'Parisian text'. Unfortunately, the text chosen was not a good one and it soon needed to be corrected. The corrections were written in the margins or in books made especially for the purpose and known as 'correctoires'. All tastes were catered for, and the Parisian text remained dominant until the sixteenth century.

During this later period, isolated versions were revised and new Vulgate editions published, and translations were made of the New Testament into some new languages. These versions are of little interest for textual criticism because, on the whole, they were made either from the Byzantine Greek type of text, or else from the Latin, Syriac or Coptic Vulgates. The only possible interest lies in the scattered traces of the Old Latin text which can still be found. A brief mention of the main translations is therefore all that is necessary. In the East, Cyril and Methodius invented a new alphabet (probably the Glagolitic, older than the Cyrillic) to translate the Bible into Slavonic (around AD 865). A little later, the Old Georgian versions underwent three revisions based on the Byzantine text and known as the Athonite revisions: that of Euthymius in AD 980 for the Gospels, that of George in AD 1030 for the whole of the New Testament and finally that of Ephraem in AD 1080 for Acts and the Epistles (see Outtier 1988 (V), p. 173). The first 'corrected' version in Ethiopic (see p. 122) should be dated a little later still. New versions in Arabic were undertaken, both in the West and in the East. Finally, the earliest Persian versions known today date from this period. In the West, the first versions appeared in the local languages of ordinary people: Romance languages, Anglo-Saxon, Bohemian.

To summarise, from the time of the autographs to the sixteenth century the text of the New Testament moved further and further away from its original form. So much, at least, is clear. Of course, the revisers constantly tried to stabilise the text and steer it away from all the influences which were impinging on it. They were sometimes successful in achieving a certain stability of the text, but unfortunately in its least pure form. With the invention of printing and the resurgence of textual criticism, the situation improved. At first, the mistakes of the former period were repeated, but, little by little, the printed text has tended to recapture the better forms of the manuscripts. It took fifteen centuries for the text of the manuscripts to be corrupted; may it take less time for the printed text to be purified!

4

The history and the future of the printed text

At the present time, the number of editions of the Greek New Testament is estimated to be more than one thousand. But it is not as difficult as might be thought to trace their history, for there are major works along the way whose dates act as landmarks. There are four main periods. First of all, there is the period of the haphazard formation of what was later called the 'textus receptus' and of its enthronement, which was as swift as it was unwise. Then followed the reign of the 'textus receptus', which was long though not particularly splendid, and during which time the true precursors of textual criticism strengthened their attacks against it, without, however, daring to free themselves of its control. Its downfall came in the third period, with the triumph of methods which were scientific, even though still tainted with individualism. The final period has seen the creation of some major projects, which have been greatly helped by the organisation of research in teams, and at the same time by the arrival of computer technology. The realisation of a major critical edition is still, however, a hope which belongs to the future.

THE RISE OF THE 'TEXTUS RECEPTUS' (1514–1633)

There was no Greek New Testament among the incunabula, and even sixty years after the invention of printing only a few fragments of it had been edited: the Magnificat and the Benedictus, the Prologue to John's Gospel and its early chapters (1:1 – 6:58), the Lord's Prayer and the Annunciation of the Angel. In the West, people were not very well acquainted with Greek. What interested the scholars were the works of secular literature which had recently been made available to them. As for the Bible, they already had it in Latin.

THE COMPLUTENSIAN POLYGLOT (1514)

The honour of having undertaken the 'editio princeps' of the New Testament in Greek goes to Francisco Ximenes de Cisneros (1437 – 1517), the Cardinal Archbishop of Toledo. It forms the fifth of six folio volumes of a polyglot Bible known as the 'Complutensis' because it was prepared and printed at Alcalá (*Complutum* in Latin). Ximenes first conceived the idea for his work in 1502 and was assisted by a great many men of letters and theologians, among them Lopez de Stunica. The printing of the New Testament was completed on 10 January 1514 and that of the other volumes in 1517. But its publication was not authorised by Pope Leo X until 22 March 1520 when the manuscripts which had been lent by the Vatican had been returned.

The text of the New Testament is set out in a rather curious way. There are two columns on each page: the one on the left is wider and has the Greek text, while the one on the right has the Vulgate text. A system of sigla allows a very close correspondence to be maintained between the lines and even the words of the two texts. Of the marginal notes, only a rare few are of interest for textual criticism. The whole is printed with a great deal of care.

In the preface, which is in Latin, the editor says that he has consulted 'the most ancient and correct models ..., so ancient and correct that if they are not fully trusted no others, it seems, deserve to be'. It would be naive, of course, to take this claim literally. While it is true that not all the manuscripts used at Alcalá for the New Testament have been identified, nonetheless it is clear that they were recent and totally unconnected with the famous Codex Vaticanus. That does not mean, however, that it is not a work which is both scholarly and conscientious; and it is to be regretted that this 'editio princeps' did not exert more influence over later editions. Although commendable in many ways, it was unfortunately prevented from being more widely distributed by a combination of adverse circumstances: the limited number of copies, its high price, the lack of publicity and the delay in publication.

THE FIVE EDITIONS BY ERASMUS (1516–35)

Public favour was accorded to a much less careful work. At the suggestion of Frobenius, a printer at Basle, Erasmus of Rotterdam (1467 – 1536) agreed to edit the Greek New Testament. The main concern was to bring it out ahead of the Alcalá edition, and so printing was begun in a hurry and finished in less than six months. The new work came out on 1 March 1516, dedicated to Pope Leo X. It was a small folio, relatively easy to handle, with the Greek text and an elegant Latin translation made by Erasmus himself in two parallel columns, and additional copious exegetical notes at the end of the volume.

Published before the Complutensian Polyglot, it was highly acclaimed. The author, moreover, knew how to sing his own praises. He had used, he said, many manuscripts, both Greek and Latin, and not just any sort but the oldest and the most correct. He had carefully collated them and had used them, in short to correct the New Testament and so bring it back 'ad Graecam veritatem, ad Graecae originis fidem'. These are the claims of a self-satisfied humanist, claims which he freely re-iterates in the title, in the end-piece and in the dedicatory epistle to Leo X.

In reality, Erasmus' edition is one of the poorer editions, and it has been compared, not without some truth, to the work of a schoolboy. It is now known how he went about his work. In order to get it finished as quickly as possible, he gave the printers three manuscripts which he had to hand, namely codex 2^e (Gospels), 2^{ap} (Acts and the Epistles) and 1^r (Revelation); and he simply used a few other manuscripts (1^{eap}, 4^{ap}, 7^p) to make some slight alterations to the text. But all these manuscripts are of a late date (none is from before the tenth century), and, with the exception of 1^{eap} which is from Family 1 but scarcely used in any case, they are all of the Byzantine type of text, unquestionably the least good.

Furthermore, to make matters worse our learned humanist, either from vanity or haste, was rather slapdash in his use of his texts. The only manuscript which he had for Revelation was damaged at the end (22:16 – 21). But that posed no problem for him; he simply filled in the missing part by translating the Vulgate back into Greek. The job was done badly, and Erasmus did not take the trouble to improve on it subsequently; that alone is sufficient to act as a warning against exploits of this kind. 'As for the Fathers whose testimonies he enumerates,' writes Berger (1879, p. 58) 'we may smile at the thought of Erasmus, no doubt in too much of a hurry as he read, making Theophylact, the Archbishop of the Bulgarians, a new author called Vulgarius.' To crown it all, there were numerous grammatical mistakes and printer's errors; on all counts, the edition was sadly wanting. By some irony of fate, however, it was this careless piece of work which was to meet with success and become, as will be seen (p. 133 below), one of the elements which made up the 'textus receptus'.

Erasmus himself made four new editions of his work and each one was printed several times. But no real improvement was ever made to the text. Although in the second edition (1519) the author proclaimed that he had made a careful revision of the original work, nevertheless the only corrections were to put right the worst printing errors and to introduce some good, and also some bad, readings; so that, on the whole, the end product was not much of an improvement.

And yet, as is well known, Luther used this text for his translation into German (1521). Erasmus' third edition contains the verse about the three witnesses (1 John 5:7–8), which was inserted on the basis of the reading of a sixteenth-century manuscript (minuscule 61). In the fourth edition (1527), the Vulgate found a place, and at last use was made, albeit very sparingly, of the Complutensian Polyglot. It has been said that Erasmus had neither sufficient love for the truth nor sufficient humility to profit from this latter text – a judgement which may sound harsh, but it is a fair one. The fifth and last edition (1535) did nothing to change this state of affairs.

THE EDITIONS OF SIMON DE COLINES (1534) AND ROBERT ESTIENNE (1546–51)

Robert Estienne (1503–59), the famous royal printer, first of all worked under the direction of Simon de Colines, his mother's second husband. The latter made an edition of the Greek New Testament in octavo (1534) which has a text that was remarkable for its time and certainly better than anything which had been published so far. The author took Erasmus' third edition as a basis for his work, but made many modifications using the Complutensian Polyglot and, above all, referred to the manuscripts themselves (minuscules 119 and 120, twelfth century, kept in Paris) to introduce new readings which modern scholars recognise as excellent. It was like a forerunner of critical editions, based on the collation of manuscripts. It is a pity that for a long time others did not follow the way opened up by Simon de Colines.

Not even Robert Estienne followed it, despite appearances to the contrary. His first edition published in Paris (1546) is in small, elegant volumes in 16mo. In the preface ('O mirificam ...', which gave the work its name) he praises the generosity of François I and repeats the inevitable refrain about the antiquity of the manuscripts which he has used ('codices ... ipsa vetustatis specie paene adorandos'). Almost adorable! Nothing less. The second edition (1549) was very similar to

the first, but the third (1550), a folio edition, became famous as the
'Regia' (Royal edition). For the first time, the Greek text was accompanied by a critical apparatus laid out in the inside margins. There, the
author gave the variant readings of the Bible of Ximenes and fifteen
manuscripts, amongst which were two uncials, D.05 and L.019, which
his son, Henri Estienne, had collated for him. Finally, in the last edition,
which was published in Geneva (1551), the Greek text was set out
between the Vulgate and Erasmus' translation, with the three texts
divided into smaller sections so as to be more easily compared. This is
the origin of our present-day verses.

But there was basically no progress. There would be no point in
drawing attention to the verse divisions of the text: one has only to look
at a chapter of the New Testament to see how little thought went into
the work. And it is a known fact that it was done 'inter equitandum',
during a journey between Paris and Lyons, in other words without due
care. As for the text itself, it was established according to the same
principles and without any major changes in all four editions. It rests,
for the most part, on the fifth edition of Erasmus and on the Complutensian Polyglot. Despite what he says, the author made very inadequate
use of the variants in the manuscripts and the collations were inaccurate
in any case. The task was no doubt beyond his capability. As Berger
writes (1879, p. 130): 'It has been noticed that in the great Royal edition,
as the work progresses so his hand grows tired and his courage droops,
so that, with only a very few exceptions, all the corrections which
Estienne made to the text of Erasmus are to be found in the historical
books of the New Testament, whereas the Epistles and Revelation stand
just about in the same form as in the edition of the critic of Rotterdam
[Erasmus]'. What that amounts to is that as time went on Robert
Estienne leant more and more on the authority of the printed text instead
of on the real value of the manuscripts. He turned his back, in other
words, on the right critical method.

He also set a very bad example, for editors after him increasingly
preferred to use the printed editions in place of the manuscripts (cf. the
Polyglot editions of Antwerp and Paris, pp. 142–3).

THE EDITIONS OF THÉODORE DE BÈZE

Even though he had in his possession some documents of great value
for textual criticism, Théodore de Bèze (Beza, 1519–1605) did not
improve on the established trend. From 1565 onwards he published nine

editions of the Greek New Testament, four of them folios and all of them very similar to each other. It is known that, for the purposes of determining the text, H. Estienne had made available to him the collations which he had prepared for his father and had also given him the variants of ten new manuscripts and of the chief previous editions. Beza was himself in possession of two famous manuscripts, D.05 and D.06, the former of which continues to bear his name. He was also able to use the Syriac Peshitta, of which the first edition had come out in 1555 (see p. 135), and the Latin translation by Tremellius in 1569; and, lastly, for the Gospels at least, there was available an edition of the Arabic version, with a Latin translation of 1591 (see p. 136).

On the whole, he made poor use of these documents. His text is essentially the same as the fourth edition of R. Estienne, with just some occasional elements borrowed from Erasmus or the Complutensian Polyglot, and very few contributions of his own. He was, by inclination, much more of a theologian than a textual critic. When he presented the famous Codex Bezae to the University of Cambridge he declined to publish it, 'so as to offend nobody'. He removed from his Greek text a number of variants which he had included in his *Annotationes* or in his Latin version. Later on, he even withdrew some good readings which he had introduced into this Latin text right from the start. He appears, in fact, to have understood very little about the importance of a correct text. And yet, despite these shortcomings, he exerted a great deal of influence, and the closeness of several of the later editions to the text of Estienne is due to their use of that of Beza. Such was the case with those responsible for the famous Authorised Version which was published in London in 1611 and which has been held in honour for so long by the Church of England. The value of a work is by no means always equal to its reputation.

THE ELZEVIRS AND THE ENTHRONEMENT OF THE 'TEXTUS RECEPTUS' (1633)

Beza's text was to appear yet again in the notorious 'textus receptus'. The origin of this name is no mystery. In 1624, Bonaventure Elzevir together with his brother's son, Abraham, published in Leiden a Greek New Testament 'according to the royal editions and others that are numbered among the best'. The work met with some degree of success. In order to encourage its sale the editors made some exaggerated claims. 'It has been accepted by everyone'; so reads the preface to the second edition (1633). And a little farther on: 'here is a text which is received by all, in which we give nothing changed or corrupted'. A bookseller's advertisement or 'blurb': that is the real origin of the 'textus receptus', the commonly received text.

The truth of the matter is that it was a text which was determined without any scientific basis. It simply reproduced the first edition of Beza (1565), corrected here and there from the 1580 edition. Or, to go back further, it was essentially nothing other than the text which was current in the churches of the East in the fifteenth century, many copies of which had been brought to Europe by refugee Greeks after the fall of Constantinople (1453). Nevertheless, the Elzevirs' edition, well printed, of convenient size (24°) and moderately priced, quickly gained public favour. Seven editions were published with very little difference between them – an indication of the success achieved by this mediocre 'received text'. The response of the modern scholar is: 'textus receptus sed non recipiendus' (a text which has been received but which can be no longer received).

In brief, during this first period most of the editions were seemingly prepared without much care. The chief concern was to get things done as quickly as possible, working from the preconceived notion that any text, so long as it was Greek, was better than the Latin Vulgate. And so, for quite some time, the work produced was shoddy and the attempts of such rare scholars as Stunica or Sirlet to slow down this unthinking rush of enthusiasm are to be applauded.

THE FIRST EDITIONS OF THE EARLY VERSIONS

Copies of the early versions which did not really fare any better than the Greek text began to be printed in the sixteenth century. Brief mention is made here of the most important ones.

The first printed edition of the New Testament in Ethiopic came out in Rome in 1548–9 (two quarto volumes), thanks to the efforts of three Ethiopian monks who had fled to Rome bringing with them some manuscripts, and who adopted the collective name of Petrus Ethyops. The quality of the text, and of the edition too, is very poor (see Metzger 1977, p. 229). For the Syriac, the first printed edition of the Peshitta was the work of J. A. Widmanstetter, carried out in Vienna in 1555. A new edition was made in Geneva in 1569, with the Syriac text printed in Hebrew characters with the vocalisation, and accompanied by a Latin translation by the editor, I. Tremellius (Metzger 1977, pp. 52–3).

The first Arabic edition was published in Leiden in 1616 by Thomas Erpenius. An edition of the Gospels had already been brought out by G. B. Raimundi (Rome, 1590), and a Latin translation made of it by A. Sionita in 1591, with a second edition in 1619 and a third in 1774 (Metzger 1977, p. 265). The other Oriental languages were not edited before the late seventeenth century (see pp. 142 – 3).

As for the Latin versions, the first printed editions used the Parisian text (see p. 128), which was a very poor one. And the situation was made worse by the new translations of the Bible brought out by both Catholics and Protestants around the same time. The Council of Trent (session 4, 8 April 1546) commissioned 'the most correct possible' edition of Jerome's version to be made and to be adhered to. The work was not carried out until a later date (1590) by Sixtus V. Even with the corrections made to it by Clement VIII (1592), it is not perfect, nor does it claim to be. But thanks to the high standard of Jerome's work and of his successors (see pp. 116 – 17), the Clementine Vulgate (Vg^{cl}) undoubtedly offers the best text edited in the sixteenth century. Consequently, the systematic opposition to the text of the Latin Vulgate, simply on the grounds that it was the Church's official text, inevitably led to the most regrettable deviations. To be involved in intrigues for the love of Greek is not always an innocent pastime.

THE REIGN OF THE 'TEXTUS RECEPTUS' (1633 – 1831)

The great editions of the Greek New Testament which were published during this period were very similar in England to Estienne's third edition and, on the Continent, to the Elzevirs' second edition. This was the text also adopted by the Bible societies, Canstein's Bibelanstalt from 1710 onwards and the British and Foreign Bible Society from 1810 to 1904. And so everywhere the 'textus receptus' was in power, but that is not to say that scientific research stopped completely. Variant readings continued to be collected as research was carried out in libraries, as manuscripts were collated and as lists were made of the divergent readings – all of them ways of making a rich collection of critical material. Efforts were then made to bring some kind of order to all this material, as different families or groups of manuscripts were distinguished from each other, and as the versions and the quotations were classified separately. Very little of this immense undertaking was seen in the printed texts. The editors went no further than to put the results either in the Prolegomena or in the notes of their editions. This was a way to escape, although not always successfully, from attacks and even prosecution. But whatever the reason for the 'textus receptus' thus continuing to be printed, it gradually came to be viewed with less and less esteem.

THE FIRST SIGNS OF MISTRUST

In 1657 the fifth volume of Walton's Polyglot was published in London, containing the New Testament in six languages: Greek and Latin; Syriac, Persian, Arabic and Ethiopic, with Latin translations. The Greek text was that of Estienne's Royal edition (1550) with changes in only three passages. But at the bottom of the pages were many variants from Codex Alexandrinus (A.02). And in volume VI, in addition to these variants, a new collation of fifteen manuscripts, two of them uncials, was inserted. Finally, in the Prolegomena of volume I, there were several pages on 'the variants in the Scriptures', an essay which is somewhat elementary and open to question, but which marks the beginnings of textual criticism.

The Greek New Testament of Etienne de Courcelles was published in Amsterdam in 1658 and it reproduced more or less exactly the 'textus receptus'. However, the text of 1 Jn 5:7–8 was put between brackets and, more than that, at the end of the book there was a new collection of variants which the author took care to specify might be sometimes better than the readings of the text itself. He even went so far as to draw attention to several conjectures and to recommend them on the grounds that they could be correct.

In his work *Catena graecorum patrum in evangelium secundum Marcum*, published in Rome in 1673, P. Possinus gave posthumously the collations which the Cretan scholar J. M. Caryophilus had prepared for a new edition of the Antwerp Polyglot (see pp. 142–3). Although they are not always strictly accurate, they nevertheless are of some interest because they refer to twenty-two manuscripts of which several, notably Codex Vaticanus (B.03), belong to the Vatican library.

Two years later, J. Fell's Greek New Testament was published anonymously in Oxford. The text is none other than that of the Elzevir edition, but the critical apparatus is of more importance. The author claimed to have used more than one hundred manuscripts and early versions, but in fact he borrowed a large number of variants from the editions of Estienne and Walton, as well as from other previous collections (in particular the variants of Codex Vaticanus). There was, however, a new element, namely the readings peculiar to the Bohairic and Gothic versions and also those of eighteen manuscripts belonging, in the main, to the Bodleian Library. With this edition, then, compared with that of E. de Courcelles, a real step forward was taken.

Richard Simon was responsible for neither an edition nor a collection of variants; but an important landmark was nonetheless created in the history of textual criticism by his work on the text, the versions and New Testament commentators. In his four books (1689, 1690, 1693, 1695), there are some very provocative views expressed on the value of the Vulgate, the nature of variants in heretical works and the importance of internal criticism for the examination of divergent readings. It is unfortunate that this famous Oratorian priest should have confused rather too often questions purely of textual criticism and problems more related to the New Testament canon.

THE FIRST ATTEMPTS AT INDEPENDENCE

The attempt at independence made by John Mill (1645 – 1707) was a somewhat timid one but the great edition which he published in Oxford in 1707 and which had cost him more than thirty years in preparation caused no less of an uproar for that. He reproduced the text of Estienne's 1550 edition but not before he had made corrections to it in thirty-one places. Furthermore, in his very scholarly Prolegomena he gave a kind of history of textual criticism and acknowledged that there were many other divergent readings which deserved to have been put in the text. But what created the greatest stir was the critical apparatus which, in this edition, often took up two thirds of the page. He had collected almost thirty thousand variants from a great number of manuscripts, including eight uncials and some very important minuscules. He also allowed ample room for the quotations of the Fathers and for the early versions, especially the Old Latin and the Vulgate. This monument of erudition was violently disparaged. At least Mill was spared having to read the unjust attacks for he died the same year that his work was published.

The work by N. Toinard, *Evangeliorum harmonia graeco-latina* (1707) which came out the same year provoked much less reaction. And yet this Catholic writer showed himself to be more daring than Mill. He himself declared in his Prolegomena that he had altered Estienne's text according to two very early manuscripts from the Vatican and also the Latin Vulgate where it agreed with these manuscripts. In this Gospel harmony the text was thus beginning to depart clearly from the 'textus receptus', and it was furthermore the first Greek edition to recognise the critical authority of the Vulgate.

To correct the text from the manuscripts was likewise the goal which E. Wells set for himself in his great edition of the Greek New Testament published in ten parts in Oxford between 1709 and 1719. Its main interest lies in the new readings which find a place in the text. For the most part, Wells took them from Mill's vast collection, but he exercised such skill in selecting them that many of his variants have been adopted by modern editors.

R. Bentley (1662 – 1742) was bold enough to suggest that the 'textus receptus' be abandoned altogether. In his famous *Proposals for Printing a Critical Edition of the New Testament* (1720) he outlined a plan of the work which needed to be done. He proposed to edit the text which was current in the fourth century using only the earliest Greek and Latin manuscripts. It was essentially a matter of doing what Toinard had done but on a larger scale. He even gave the last chapter of Revelation as an example, departing in more than forty places from Estienne's text which he said had 'unfortunately become the Protestants' Pope'. There was a tremendous outcry and Bentley was fiercely attacked and suspended from teaching for a time. Not being a man to allow himself to be intimidated, he set about collecting together the materials for his work; but, as he grew older, either for the sake of peace or because of the difficulties of the task, he finally gave up. His *Proposals*, however, continued to exert a profound influence.

Indeed, the Greek New Testament with an English translation published by the Presbyterian W. Mace (London 1729) under the cloak of anonymity continued the opposition against the 'textus receptus'. In departing from it, the editor displayed no scruples but a great deal of discrimination, for many of his readings have been maintained in the text established by recent editors. It is true that his independence was not always very thorough as his justification of the conjecture at Gal 4:25 illustrates: 'There is no manuscript so old as common sense'. He was strongly attacked. Overall, his work, which is dependent on Mill's variants, marked some steps forward.

The edition of E. Harwood (London 1776) was an even greater departure from the usual printed text. The author used Codex Bezae for the Gospels and Acts, and Codex Claromontanus for the Epistles of Paul, turning to Codex Alexandrinus where there were lacunae in the other two. This preference for the early manuscripts rather than the recent editions denotes a certain acuteness of judgement in this theologian, but even he did not have a scientific method for selecting the variants. Such a method, however, had already been prepared several years earlier by the initiators of textual criticism in Germany.

THE FIRST SERIOUS ATTACKS

So far, the adversaries of the 'textus receptus' had shown more erudition than critical judgement. Some limited their work to collecting variant readings, others made an attempt to decide on the right reading but relied on their intuition or on the early age of the manuscript. Nowhere was there a real system.

With J. A. Bengel the situation changed. The edition which he published in Tübingen in 1734 appears, at first sight, to be overly modest. Even though he added new variants to Mill's apparatus he almost always retained, except in Revelation, the received text. His occasional corrections were deliberately cautious so as to reassure the more fearful of his readers. Indeed, he admitted no reading into his text which had not already appeared in a previous edition, whatever the weight of the manuscript authority behind it. But in the margin he set out a scale of values for the variants, with five grades: original readings, readings better than the printed text, readings equally good, less good and finally no good at all. In doing this, he let the reader understand that the text should not be adhered to blindly: that in the first two groups of variants there were things of great value. Not only that, but in the 'apparatus criticus' at the end of the work he gave a scientific explanation for his gradings of variants. He grouped the manuscripts into families according to the readings which they supported (see p. 65): the Asiatic family from Constantinople or the surrounding district, containing the largest number of manuscripts, but all recent ones; and the African family, subdivided into the Alexandrian tribe and the Latin tribe, with a smaller number of manuscripts, which were older and better than the previous group. This classification may be contestable in its details, but all honour is due to Bengel for devising the principle, and indeed that was his chief accomplishment. Thanks to him, witnesses began to be weighed and no longer simply counted.

His rival J. J. Wettstein (1693–1754), despite the fame which he achieved, made a much lesser contribution to textual criticism. He remained rather in the line of the great men of learning of the previous period, though he carried on the fight with more energy and more persistence. As early as 1713, he published a treatise on the variants of the New Testament and travelled throughout Europe for the purpose of collating manuscripts. Suspected of heresy, he was driven out of Basle and forced to take refuge in Amsterdam. It was there, in 1751 – 2, that he published his famous edition of the Greek New Testament (reprinted Graz, 1962). In the Prolegomena, which he had already published in 1730 without indicating the identity of the author, his main aim was to reply to the attacks of his adversaries. As for the text, it was none other than the Elzevir text but it was accompanied by quite a considerable critical apparatus which was fuller than it seemed, for an ingenious system of sigla enabled him to keep it compact. For the first time, the uncials were designated by letters, the minuscules by numbers. And furthermore, so that there could be no doubt as to the feelings of the author, he indicated, between the text and the apparatus, the readings which he deemed to be the best. One final innovation was the space given at the bottom of the page, and sometimes even spread over half a page, to many texts from Classical, Jewish or Christian writers that offered a parallel to New Testament passages. This was the most original part of his work and one which is still consulted today.

J. S. Semler (1725 – 91) continued in the tradition of Bengel, developing it further. He did not edit the New Testament, but his writings on textual criticism, with deliberately neutral titles (1764 – 7), are worth drawing attention to. He was the first to see that the Greek manuscripts, even the earliest ones, were recensions. After some hesitation he finally discerned three main recensions for the Gospels: the Alexandrian, the Eastern (Antioch and Constantinople) and the Western ones (see p. 65). He also realised that each one could contain variants from an earlier tradition. With Semler the different readings of the New Testament text became the object of historical study.

It is, however, his disciple J. J. Griesbach (1745 – 1812) who deserves to be considered as the true precursor of textual criticism. In addition to his commentaries and various biblical studies, he published three editions of the Greek New Testament: the first in Halle from 1774 to 1777; the second, amplified and amended, in Halle and London, 1796 – 1806; the third, which represents his final thoughts, in Leipzig, 1803 – 7 (see Metzger 1968, p. 121). Taken as a whole, Griesbach's work is the one which crowns all the previous work of Bengel, Wettstein and Semler. From the latter, Griesbach borrowed the theory of the three recensions, the Alexandrian, Western and Byzantine. His particular contribution was to distinguish more clearly between the witnesses to each of the three groups, noticing, for example, that the Gospel text of Codex Alexandrinus belonged to the Byzantine family (see p. 109). For his critical apparatus, he drew on Wettstein's work, adding to it the results of his own research. He paid special attention to the quotations of ecclesiastical writers and the early versions. Finally, from Bengel, he borrowed the idea of classifying variants according to their value; but there again he added an original touch, for it was not just agreement between the main families of manuscripts which determined his choice, but rather the intrinsic worth of the readings. Hence he had little time for the Byzantine recension, which often found itself on its own and of less good quality. In practice, it is true, he was not very strict with the 'textus receptus', which he retained for the most part. But nevertheless his theory had the effect of destroying the confidence with which this text, of a relatively late date, had hitherto been regarded.

Consequently, he came in for some vigorous attacks from all sides. In their editions of the New Testament, the Protestant C. F. Matthaei (1744–1811) and the Catholic A. Scholz (1794–1852), both of them men of learning, but short-sighted in their critical work, undertook an apologetic of the Byzantine text on the basis that the majority of manuscripts attested it. From a historian's point of view, they merely serve to underline the merits of Griesbach. Of more interest is another contemporary Catholic, J. L. Hug (1765–1846), who was not afraid to go down the newly opened road and even to widen it in quite a remarkable way in his *Einleitung in die Schriften des Neuen Testaments* (1808, 1847⁴). He first of all distinguished what he called the 'common edition', that is the common primitive text which, being uncontrolled, gave rise to forms of the text which were less and less pure, and identified it as the 'Western' family. This 'common edition' underwent three recensions in the middle of the third century: that of Origen in Palestine, that of Hesychius in Egypt and that of Lucian in Syria. This hypothesis is of course open to criticism: the recension attributed to Origen is a mistake and Hug's distribution of the documents among the families is far from accurate. Nevertheless, his idea, although it has been paid scarcely any attention, was very clear-sighted. Its only fault lay in its being over-simplified.

THE DEVELOPMENT OF THE EDITIONS OF THE EARLY VERSIONS

After the Complutensian Polyglot (see p. 130) there were three other polyglots which mark a point in the history of multi-lingual editions, if not in the history of the printed text itself. The Antwerp Polyglot, also known as the 'Royal' Polyglot, printed by Plantin (1568 – 72), belongs to the preceding period. The New Testament is printed in four columns, with the Peshitta on the left and then its Latin translation (by G. Lefèvre de la Boderie), next the Vulgate and finally the Greek. At the bottom of the four columns the Syriac is reprinted in Hebrew characters and vocalised (as in the 1569 edition, see p. 135). There is nothing original about the printed texts: the Vulgate and the Greek follow the Complutensian Bible with a few borrowings for the latter from Estienne's 1550 edition. The Paris Polyglot edited by Le Jay (1628 – 1645) reproduces the Antwerp Polyglot for the New Testament, replacing the Hebrew characters of the Syriac with an Arabic version and a Latin translation which uses a new manuscript (see Metzger 1977, p. 266); but it stays very close to the 1591 edition (see p. 136). Finally, the London Polyglot, or 'Biblia Polyglotta', edited by B. Walton (1654 – 7) takes up the text of the previous ones but introduces two new versions, Ethiopic and, for the Gospels, Persian (see p. 45). The Greek is of a little more critical interest; the Ethiopic repeats the edition of 1548 (see p. 135) but with fresh mistakes, and a Latin translation is provided; the Persian is based on a manuscript dated 1341 which contains a version of the Peshitta.

The versions in ancient languages which were not yet included in the polyglots also received some attention. The first printed edition of the Bible in Armenian was produced by an Armenian bishop, A. D. Oskan (Amsterdam, 1666), followed shortly (1668) by an edition of the New Testament alone, also by Oskan. The editor used a thirteenth-century manuscript which he corrected in places according to the Latin Vulgate. The edition was published by Zohrab in Venice (New Testament, 1789); the whole Bible (1805), using a fourteenth century manuscript and a few others (not specified), with the variants printed at the bottom of the page, was a slight improvement, remains the basic edition of the Armenian version in use today and will continue to be until such time as further work is done. For the Georgian, an edition of the Gospels came out in Tbilisi in 1709; the first edition of the whole Bible was published in Moscow (1742 – 3). They are both editions of the common Georgian version or Vulgate which was the result of the Athonite recensions (eleventh century, see p. 128). According to L. Leloir, the Moscow Bible 'is the first successful outcome of the attempts at a critical edition of the Georgian Bible which were begun in the seventeenth century by M. Orbeli and his son, S. Orbeliani' ('Bible' (Articles) 1960 (VII), col. 832). The Coptic and Gothic versions are mentioned by R. Simon, and certain variants were already included in the edition by J. Fell (1675; see pp. 137–8 above). But the first printed edition of the New Testament in Coptic is that of D. Wilkins (Oxford, 1716): it is an edition of the common Bohairic version or Vulgate with a Latin translation. The editor shows no critical concern: although he has used about twenty manuscripts, he mentions none of their variant readings, only some places of difference with the Greek or with other versions. This edition nevertheless was the one used as a base for the ones which followed until Horner's edition was published (1898 onwards).

It was not until the middle of the eighteenth century that there was any interest on the part of scholars in an edition of a non-Vulgate type of text in any of the translation languages. The first radical departure from the Byzantine Greek text was made by E. Harwood (1776, see p. 139). On the side of the Latin text, R. Simon drew attention, as early as 1690 (see p. 138) to the existence of early versions; and J. Mill mentions in the critical apparatus to his monumental edition (1707) certain Old Latin variants. The first edition of the Old Latin Bible was made by the Maurist father Pierre Sabatier (Rheims, 1743 and Paris, 1751[2]; repr. Munich, 1976). It was a remarkable work of criticism. The editor took account of the variants in the manuscripts he used (some of which have been lost and are known only through him) and also in the fragments and the quotations of the Fathers. It was only the discovery of new manuscripts which made it worthwhile to make a 'new Sabatier' in the twentieth century, a task currently underway at the Vetus Latina Institut in Beuron. Thus, thanks to Sabatier's edition, the Latin translation is the one for which the most critical work has been done. But that is not to neglect the edition of the Harclean Syriac published by J. White in Oxford, first the Gospels (1778) and then Acts and the Epistles (1779–1803). In the title White mentions, albeit mistakenly, the 'Philoxenian' version (see p. 34). The edition was based on two manuscripts, in other words not critically: it does, however, reproduce the numerous diacritical signs (obeli and asterisks) and also the marginal readings which confer on this version such a great value for textual criticism. No more recent edition of the Harclean version has yet been published (other than for Revelation: A. Vööbus, *The Apocalypse in the Harklean version*, 1978).

In summary, it may be said that in this second period there was no real progress in the editing of the Greek text of the New Testament. But at the same time, the collections of variants, their methodical classification in manuscript families, the critical hypotheses concerning these documents, the appearance of editions of non-Vulgate early versions – all these things acted as the best possible preparation for the period which was to follow. In the struggle which had started between the partisans of the 'textus receptus' on the one hand and, on the other, the scholars convinced of the superior worth of the early manuscripts, the latter were bound to emerge victorious. They have sometimes been reproached for their lack of boldness in editing the text, but they are not to be blamed for that, for public opinion was not ready. They would never have found a publisher prepared to publish a critical text, nor would they have had a public to support it. They were, however, frequently wrong in one important matter, that is in the way they asked questions of textual criticism, mixing them with problems of dogma which were completely out of place. In addition, their violent and disrespectful manner must have often alienated many minds. What is worth noting is that it was Bengel, the most moderate among them, who was responsible for the greatest progress. In any case, the reign of the 'textus receptus' was coming to an end. The foundation had been laid for its replacement.

THE FALL OF THE 'TEXTUS RECEPTUS' (1831–1934)

Already towards the end of the preceding period, New Testament textual criticism, instead of being a simple catalogue of manuscripts, was becoming a scientific study. The division of the manuscripts into different groups was not only a means of bringing some clarity to the general confusion of the documents, it was also the first step towards constructing a history of the manuscript tradition. It was a step which did not really lead to tangible results since it stopped at merely amending in places the 'textus receptus', for there was a reluctance to replace it with an earlier and better text. Nevertheless, it was a step which was of great significance, for it was subsequently taken up on a wider basis and with the additional contribution of new discoveries.

Indeed, during this third period, all the authors whose names are of any importance in the history of textual criticism moved beyond replacing the 'textus receptus', as they went on to reconstruct the history of the manuscript text using a more scientific classification of the variants. That reconstruction was a goal which they all shared, although they differed greatly in their theories about the history of the text.

Their common concern was to establish a text as close as possible to the original with the help of critical principles. By the end of the nineteenth century the famous 'neutral' text of Westcott and Hort was believed to be this text, so much so that it almost became revered as a new 'textus receptus'. In the first three decades of the twentieth century, patient research caused the 'neutral' text to lose ground; it was no longer received with the same spontaneous enthusiasm as before and good readings were often found elsewhere. Thus, this period saw the fall of the 'textus receptus' and the victory of the critical text. But the actual picture of events is rather confused and only some sketchy details of the most important people will be given here.

THE TWO EDITIONS OF K. LACHMANN (1831–50)

It was to be a philologist and not a theologian who made the first real break with the 'textus receptus'. For, indeed, the honour fell to K. Lachmann (1793–1851), professor of classical languages in Berlin. Briefly, he accomplished the goal of Bentley: to establish the text of the New Testament on the basis of the earliest Greek manuscripts and those of the Vulgate without paying attention to the printed editions. In the first edition of the New Testament which he brought out (1831) he made reference to his article ('Rechenschaft über seine Ausgabe des Neuen Testaments') in *Theologische Studien und Kritiken* (1830, pp. 817–45) for an exposition of the critical principles he had followed. To have the theoretical discussion in a separate article was an error in method that he made good in the second edition (1842–50), which included detailed Prolegomena, the Vulgate text and an indication of the sources of the readings preferred by him.

Lachmann did not set himself ambitious goals, which is to his credit. He did not aim to find the original reading nor even the earliest, but only to determine which, out of all the early readings, was the one most widespread in the fourth century. His intention was thus to present an intermediary text, one which could be used as a starting point for further research. His method was strict. He first of all took the text which was in use in the early Eastern churches at the time of Jerome, and, where the usage was not uniform, that is where he came across divergent readings, he chose the text which was in agreement with the more authoritative documents from Africa and Italy. If no agreement was possible he put the uncertain words in brackets and the variants in the margin. The only exception to this procedure was with respect to the 'textus receptus' whose readings were all relegated to the end of the work.

Lachmann's edition represented a great innovation and the work was often discussed in the most unfair manner. That is not to say that it was free from error or that it was complete. The critical apparatus was mediocre: there were faulty or doubtful collations, the Syriac and Coptic versions were neglected and the quotations from the Church Fathers were inadequate. The text was established on a very narrow basis, sometimes on only one or two manuscripts, such as Codex Alexandrinus. His method was also too rigid. As a Classical linguist, he forgot that in the New Testament, much more than in Classical literature, there are many deliberate variants, and he therefore paid too little regard to internal criticism. But Lachmann was nevertheless a noteworthy pioneer. His courageous rejection of the 'textus receptus', the importance he gave to the earliest witnesses and especially to the Vulgate and his use of critical methods in establishing the New Testament text are all ample reasons for his name to be remembered.

THE EIGHT EDITIONS OF C. TISCHENDORF (1841–72)

The name of C. Tischendorf (1815–74) is one of the most renowned in the history of New Testament textual criticism, and justifiably so. It can fairly be said that he dedicated his whole life to this study. At an early age he travelled throughout Europe and the East in a search for new manuscripts. He was particularly fortunate, and of the uncials alone he found twenty, amongst them the famous Codex Sinaiticus which he carefully edited. He also published for the first time eighteen manuscripts of great value such as Codex Vaticanus, Codex Ephraemi rescriptus, Codex Claromontaus. And he was the first to collate the variants from twenty-three other uncials.

What contributed greatly to his renown were his eight editions of the New Testament, most of which have been reprinted many times. In the first three (1841–2), he departed only slightly from Lachmann's text, and in the next four he seemed to be taking backward steps in moving closer and closer towards the 'textus receptus'. But in the last, the *Editio octava maior* (1869–72), he radically changed his perspective and closely followed Codex Sinaiticus, which he had discovered and edited in the meantime (1859–62). The critical apparatus of the eighth edition, the edition which is meant when one speaks of Tischendorf's New Testament, is still indispensable today for New Testament textual criticism.

With respect to the Patristic quotations especially, nothing so complete had been published previously.

In point of fact, the text itself was not so important. Tischendorf had essentially no firm principles from which to work. He was an enthusiastic and fortunate explorer, an active and vigilant editor, an ardent collector of variants, but he did not have a critical mind, in the true sense of critical. Generally speaking, he continued in the tradition established by Lachmann, giving preference to the earliest Greek texts but he paid only scant attention to their classification into families. He appeared indeed to mistrust any theory about the history of the text, preferring to rely on his own judgement to decide between several early variants. He was unfortunately always influenced by the last manuscript he happened to have studied. Everyone acknowledges, for example, that in his last edition he set too much store by Codex Sinaiticus. Besides, he did not have time to write his own Prolegomena. This was left to one of his disciples, C. R. Gregory, who published his Prolegomena, a superb work of textual criticism, as an appendix to the *Editio octava maior* (vol. III, 1884; re-edited and enlarged, 1894).

Caspar René Gregory also continued the work of compiling a list of the New Testament manuscripts, giving a brief description of each one. The result is a work of fundamental importance: *Textkritik des Neuen Testamentes* in three volumes (1900–9). The first deals with the Greek manuscripts, adopting the nomenclature used by Tischendorf which goes back to Wettstein. The second volume contains the earlier manuscripts of the various early versions. Finally, the third contains additions to the other two volumes and adopts a new system of numbering the Greek manuscripts which consists entirely of figures and which is still in use today. There were two people who took over the work from Gregory, E. von Dobschütz and K. Aland (see p. 10). In just one century, the number of manuscripts has doubled. For the manuscripts of the versions, except for the Latin, there is still no successor to Gregory; the situation at present is that each editor uses his own signs or somebody else's, thus causing a certain amount of confusion.

In conclusion, it may be said that Tischendorf did not really contribute to the improvement in method of New Testament textual criticism. He simply introduced an element of flexibility into the method of his predecessors in allowing more room for internal criticism. Honour is due to him rather for the discovery and the edition of new witnesses to the text. He was, above all, a man of learning and, so to speak, a man of the variants. It was Gregory who was to be the man of the documents. There are, it is true, many errors in the lists they compiled, even though great care was taken. On the whole, they represent a monument which is neither bold in its design nor balanced in its proportions, but it is at least solid in its foundations.

THE NEW TESTAMENT OF B. F. WESTCOTT AND F. J. A. HORT (1881)

Before talking about these two names, mention should be made, even if only briefly, of a contemporary of Tischendorf, the English scholar S. P. Tregelles (1813 – 75). His edition of the New Testament (1857 – 79, London) is in no way to be preferred to that of his German rival. But at least he followed the path of Lachmann, and with a richer and more ordered critical apparatus. He would no doubt have done better if he had been acquainted with Codex Sinaiticus and the new collations of Codex Vaticanus before determining the text of the Gospels. He was of a more discerning mind than Tischendorf and displayed a better judgement in his appreciation of the variants presented by the early versions and Patristic quotations. In fact, credit is really due to him for leading his fellow countrymen away from the 'textus receptus', just as Lachmann had done on the Continent.

Much more important is the work of the two Cambridge scholars, B. F. Westcott (1825 – 1901) and F. J. A. Hort (1828 – 92). They worked together for nearly thirty years before publishing *The New Testament in the original Greek* in two volumes (London, 1881). The first contains the text, but without a critical apparatus; there are some variants in the margins, and at the end a brief description of the method follows. The second volume, which was the work of Hort, is made up of two parts: an introduction to New Testament textual criticism in which the new elements of the text are justified from history; and an appendix comprising a very detailed commentary on a great many variants which, though they were of some interest, had been rejected. In all, it is a work of criticism rather than of erudition. The materials which Mill had accumulated had prepared the way for Bengel; in the same way, the successful research of Tischendorf had prepared the way for Westcott and Hort and, in a sense, had determined the contents of their work.

The system adopted by these two scholars is based on a detailed examination of the variants, and their theory is as follows. In numerous New Testament passages there are three main forms of a reading: two of them short, and one long where the two short ones have been combined, for example in Mk 9:38. These longer or conflated readings must be later than the others, for they are generally not present in the earlier writers but only in the ecclesiastical authors after the fourth century. The manuscripts in which they are found constitute the Syrian type that originated, it would seem, at Antioch in Syria. To be precise, these manuscripts appear to date from the recension made of the New Testament by Lucian of Antioch towards the end of the third century. This late text was subsequently taken to Byzantium from where it spread to all of the Orient as the official Vulgate text of the Greek Church. It is characterised by a concern to correct the style, to explain obscure details, to smooth out difficulties, to combine variants and to harmonise parallel passages. It is inevitably the least good text, even though it has the greatest number of witnesses, and it is the ancestor of the 'textus receptus'.

Having put this first type of text on one side, Westcott and Hort then distinguish three other earlier texts which they call 'pre-Syrian'. First of all, there is the 'neutral' type, so called because it manifests no particular tendency. It is basically the primitive text, preserved by good fortune in at least a relatively pure state, if not in its original form. Unfortunately, its representatives are rare: B.03 and S.01, but especially B.03.

There is another very early type, the 'Western' text. In short, it is a text that has been corrected. It owes its origin to scribes who, in the second century when many copies of the New Testament were being made, viewed the text which they had before them with rather too much liberty and did not hesitate to change it. At times, they completed it with interpolations, especially in Luke and Acts; at other times, they harmonised parallel passages, more particularly in the Synoptic Gospels; and at other times, they corrected or even deleted certain details which were offensive in some way. Even though the 'Western' text has many representatives, including D.05, D.06, E.08, F.010, G.012, the Old Latin and the Old Syriac versions, Irenaeus, Tertullian and Cyprian, it is basically a corrupted text.

Through corruption of another kind, the 'neutral' text gave rise in the third century to a third pre-Syrian type: the 'Alexandrian' type. It was inevitable that the Greek of the New Testament should appear too colloquial to the scholars of Alexandria. They consequently attempted, on several occasions, to restore it to the Classical language by making grammatical and literary corrections. The result was really a degenerate Egyptian form of the 'neutral' text as it is found, though not in its pure state, in such manuscripts as C.04 or L.019. It is a sort of scholastic revision which is of little importance.

The foregoing paragraphs represent the theory of Westcott and Hort. The rules they followed, in practice, in order to determine the original text of the New Testament can be summarised thus:

1. Any reading not found in the 'neutral', 'Alexandrian' and 'Western' texts is to be rejected as 'Syrian';
2. Any reading of the 'Western' or the 'Alexandrian' texts is not to be accepted if it has no support in the 'neutral' text;
3. Furthermore, the passages of the 'neutral' text which are absent from the 'Western' text (= 'Western non-interpolations': the editors are not brave enough to call them 'additions made by the pure text') should also be rejected as doubtful.

What it amounts to is that the manuscripts to be trusted are the main representatives of the 'neutral' text, especially Codex Vaticanus. The resultant text is a short and critically expurgated one.

This brief survey shows something of the originality of the system. More than anything, the chief aim of Westcott and Hort was to develop the method of textual criticism. They were not specialists in palae-ography nor in comparative linguistics. They did not publish nor even discover any new manuscripts. They played a more modest role but at the same time a more important one: they succeeded in bringing out the value of the mass of documents collected by Tischendorf. Never before had anyone attached so much importance to classification into families, to the characteristic features of the individual groups and to the relationships between manuscripts. And on many points, especially on the value of the 'textus receptus', their opinion was subsequently upheld. There were certainly, as will be seen, many weak parts to their work, not least the title: *The New Testament in the original Greek*; there are fewer illusions nowadays, or rather the illusions have changed. And yet, despite the shortcomings, the work of Westcott and Hort deserves to be the landmark that it has become in the history of textual criticism.

THE BATTLE OVER WESTCOTT AND HORT'S WORK

In 1881, at the same time as Westcott and Hort's edition was brought out, two other volumes were published in Oxford which were to cause some stir: the Revised English Version, intended to replace the 1611 Authorized Version, and the Greek text that was the basis of the Revised Version. On the whole, the editors kept close to the text of the Westcott and Hort, who had generously passed on to them the results obtained during the course of their work. For the New Testament alone, this 'revised' text differed in more than 5,000 places from the 'textus receptus'.

An uproar was caused among Anglican churchmen. There were even scholars, such as F. H. Scrivener, J. W. Burgon and E. Miller, who became involved in the violent campaign against the Westcott – Hort text. Their arguments were summarised in Scrivener's main work, *A plain introduction to the criticism of the New Testament* (1894[4]), vol. III, pp. 274 – 312. In France, Abbé P. Martin had the unhappy idea of joining in the fight for the defence of the 'textus receptus'. Reasons of a dogmatic nature were put forward first of all. It was not possible that Providence should have allowed the true text of the New Testament to have been lost for nearly fifteen centuries. People talked as if the 'textus receptus' were the traditional text throughout the whole Church. So-called critical motives were then put forward: the mass of manuscripts which bear witness to this text; its early age as established by the supposed testimony of ancient ecclesiastical writers; its character, certified as original despite conflated readings; and, besides all that, the tendency of the 'neutral' text, which was claimed to be semi-Arian, thus causing it to be excluded from public use and thereby protected from the ravages of time.

To tell the truth, the partisans of the 'textus receptus' were generally at their strongest when they took the offensive. They argued that the Westcott – Hort text could not be taken as traditional either, for it represented only a limited region, namely Egypt; it had none of the older ecclesiastical authors among its witnesses; it bore clear marks of revision. But these attacks in no way established the primitive character of the 'Syrian' text, and it was this argument which quickly came to settle the debate, against the 'textus receptus'. Subsequently, from time to time, there were some obscure pleas raised in its favour. Today, it seems that this notorious text is now dead, it is to be hoped for ever.

In the midst of this bitter debate, Westcott – Hort's text began, however, to be well respected. That is scarcely apparent from the book by R. F. Weymouth (1886) who was satisfied to adopt the readings selected by the majority of contemporary editors. On the other hand, it comes over very clearly in the work by B. Weiss (1894 – 1900) who puts all his trust in Codex Vaticanus. Not that there was anything servile in his attitude. Being a careful exegete he insisted on leaving the last word in New Testament textual criticism to the intrinsic value of the readings.

The 'neutral' text continued to dominate the editions of F. Schjøtt (1897), J. M. S. Baljon (1898) and A. Souter (1910), although each of them, especially the last two, had their own particular merits. The edition planned by C. R. Gregory (1911) would not have altered the situation in any way, for Gregory was a scholar who was in full agreement with Hort on the history of the text. Even F. G. Kenyon who, as an expert on the 'Western' text, took care to bring out the original character of certain of its elements, did not dare to go any further than that. It would be easy to add more examples. It looked as if, after Westcott and Hort, textual criticism had been laid to rest.

Two things helped particularly to spread the 'neutral' text. In 1898, Eberhard Nestle published, under the auspices of a Bible society (the Privilegierte Würtembergische Bibelanstalt), a Greek New Testament based on the editions of Tischendorf, Westcott – Hort and Weymouth (replaced by Weiss after 1901), and following the convenient principle of the majority for each reading. Furthermore, from 1904 onwards it was this 'middle' text, almost identical with the 'neutral' text, which was adopted by the British and Foreign Bible Society, so ensuring its success throughout the whole world for the next eighty years (see p. 166). Thus, by the irony of fate, Nestle, who was one of the first critics to understand the occasional merits of the 'Western' text, apparently contributed more than anyone else to the spread of the 'neutral' text and to the creation of what we might call a modern 'textus receptus', established, like the previous one, on the basis of the real or imagined authority of the principal printed editions, and not in accordance with the value of individual variants.

Shortly after the victory of the Westcott – Hort text over the 'textus receptus' quarrels sprang up with the successful allies, as so often happens in history. Westcott and Hort already suspected that there were several additions in the 'neutral' text and highlighted a number of 'Western' variants in the margin. But attention was drawn to the exclusive partiality generally shown by the Cambridge pair. To be specific, the same reproaches which Westcott and Hort brought against the 'Syrian' text were brought against the 'neutral' text. For example, when Codex Vaticanus and Codex Sinaiticus are subjected to close scrutiny, some serious objections to their text can be raised. None of their characteristic variants are found in Christian literature before the third century. Furthermore, these manuscripts too seem to contain corrections reflecting certain prejudices, and to be nothing more than the product of a scholarly revision. The campaign was carried on, especially in England, in numerous journal articles, and reached its peak in the detailed and instructive book by H.C. Hoskier, *Codex B and its allies* (1914). But quite some time earlier, J. Rendel Harris had already sounded the alarm to warn future generations against the tendency to canonise the 'neutral' text (see *Four lectures on the Western text of the New Testament*, 1894).

So, at the same time as these attacks on Westcott – Hort's 'neutral' text, critical research also focused attention on the interest of the 'Western' text. Just a few of the details and the important names will be cited here. For example: detailed studies on Codex Bezae (Harris 1891, Weiss 1897, Vogels 1926); editions of the Old Latin versions, in *Old Latin Biblical Texts* (1883 – 1911) and *Collectanea biblica latina* (vols. II, III, V, VII and IX, 1913 – 1953); the discovery and publication of new manuscripts of the Gospels (sy^s, W.032, Θ.038); the reconstitution of Family 1 and Family 13 amongst the minuscules (Lake 1902 (VI), Ferrar 1877, Harris 1893, 1900); the examination of New Testament quotations made by Irenaeus, Clement of Alexandria, Cyprian, and others: all these things showed how widely diffused were the more or less related early types of text. Some critics took advantage of this to insist on their own position: how can the 'Western' text be viewed otherwise than as a mere deformation of the authentic text, since it is the only text to be represented by the earliest witnesses?

The critics, it is true, are far from agreeing about the origin of the 'Western' text. Some maintain that it is the primitive text, at least for the writings of Luke who must himself have made a double edition of the Gospel and Acts (Blass 1895, Zahn 1916). Others say that it is a corrupted text, having been reworked in a prototype, either Latin (Harris 1894, Vogels 1926) or Syriac (Chase 1893). Others again insist that it is a mixed text in which the better readings have to be disentangled – that is, those which have an original flavour and which are also the best attested. If, on the whole, it is the 'neutral' text which is preferred, it is nevertheless recognised that on a number of points the 'Western' text will stand up to comparison with it. But studies on this subject tend to neglect the aspect of the rhythm, the oral style and in general terms the very striking literary genre of the 'Western' text (see p. 110); and so it retains its rather enigmatic quality.

This completes the survey of the many essays on textual criticism written during the thirty years following the publication of Westcott – Hort's work.

Chapter four

THE WORK OF HERMANN VON SODEN (1902–1913)

Hermann von Soden (1852–1914) deserves a section of his own in view of the extent of his work, *Die Schriften des Neuen Testaments in ihrer ältesten erreichbaren Textgestalt* (1902–13). The first part is taken up with the Prolegomena, the second part contains the text and the critical apparatus. It was prepared with the assistance of a whole team of helpers who searched the libraries of Europe and the Near East, and it entailed almost twenty years of hard work. This undertaking stands out for the breadth of its vision; it was to replace Tischendorf's scholarly apparatus and, at the same time, the critical work of Westcott and Hort. There are three innovations in von Soden's system: the notation of the documents, the theory of the history of the text, and finally the text itself.

The notation of the documents is founded on several excellent principles: to use a uniform notation for the uncials and the minuscules, to designate each manuscript with a single symbol and to choose this symbol in such a way that it would provide an indication of the age and contents of the manuscript. In practice, the result was that the author divided the witnesses into three groups: those with only the Gospels (ε = εὐαγγέλιον), those without the Gospels (α = ἀπόστολος) and those with more than the Gospels (δ = διαθήκη). Within each group, each manuscript or fragment of a manuscript was denoted by a number in Arabic figures added to the Greek letter of its group. The particular number chosen indicated, by means of a series of sigla that von Soden devised, the approximate age and the exact contents of the manuscript (see table 1). The whole system, however, has two major drawbacks. First, it is complicated and therefore rather tedious to use. But, more especially, it assumes that it is possible to fix the date of each manuscript exactly, whereas very often those responsible for cataloguing the manuscripts, as well as palaeographers, hesitate between several centuries. So it was inevitable that there should be many errors of notation, and it would not be very useful to go into more detail about the nomenclature, which has now been dropped. The table which follows may, nevertheless, be helpful so that one may occasionally consult von Soden's apparatus which is still the best source of information on the Greek manuscript tradition.

The theory of the history of the text is based on a new classification of the manuscripts. According to von Soden, there existed, within the boundaries of the third and fourth centuries, three great recensions of the New Testament. There was the recension K (see p. 109), attributed

Table 1

Century	Gosp + (Ac/Ep) + Rev	Gosp + (Ac/Ep)	Gosp	(Ac/Ep) + Rev	(Ac/Ep)	Ac–Cath	Paul	Rev
IV–	δ1–δ849		ε1–ε99 ε01–ε099	α1–α49				
X	δ50–δ899		ε1000–ε1099	α50–α99		α1000–α1019	α1020–α1069	α1070–α1099
XI	δ100–δ149	δ150–δ199	ε100–ε199 ε1100–ε1199	α100–α149	α150–α199	α1100–α1119	α1120–α1169	α1170–α1199
XII	δ200–δ249	δ250–δ299	ε200–ε299 ε1200–ε1299 ε2000…	α200–α249	α250–α299	α1200–α1219	α1220–α1269	α1270–α1299
XIII	δ300–δ349	δ350–δ399	ε300–ε399 ε1300–ε1399 ε3000…	α300–α349	α350–α399	α1300–α1319	α1320–α1369	α1370–α1399
XIV	δ400–δ449	δ450–δ499	ε400–ε499 ε1400–ε1499 ε4000…	α400–α449	α450–α499	α1400–α1419	α1420–α1469	α1470–α1499
XV	δ500–δ549	δ550–δ599	ε500–ε599 ε1500–ε1599 ε5000…	α500–α549	α550–α599	α1500–α1519	α1520–α1569	α1570–α1599
XVI XVII	δ600… δ700…		ε600–ε699 ε700–ε799	α600… α700…			α…. α1700…	

Key: Gosp = Gospels; Ac/Ep = Acts and the Epistles; Rev = Revelation; Cath = Catholic Epistles; Paul = Pauline Epistles.

to Lucian of Antioch and represented by the manuscripts of the type hitherto referred to as 'Syrian', 'Antiochene' or 'Byzantine'. It forms numerous families, offering a text which becomes increasingly altered with the passage of time; but, in its earliest form, it is independent of the other recensions and even influenced manuscripts such as Codex Sinaiticus and Codex Vaticanus. There was the recension H (see p. 107), which includes specifically the manuscripts S.01, B.03, C.04 (amongst others), the papyri, the Coptic versions and the Alexandrian Fathers such as Athanasius, Didymus and Cyril. It embraces Westcott – Hort's 'neutral' and 'Alexandrian' texts. There was, lastly, the recension I (the first letter of 'Jerusalem' in Greek), made up of the great many varieties of the 'Western' text (nine groups divided into sub-groups). It corresponds in principle to the famous manuscripts of Origen which were edited at Caesarea by Pamphilus and Eusebius. This is the best recension, but unfortunately it is no longer found in its pure state. An example is Codex Bezae, one of the main witnesses of this recension, but one which has a very contaminated text. Finally, at the base of these three recensions, there was the archetype I-H-K, which no longer exists but which it is possible to reconstitute by comparing the three revised texts, either with each other or with earlier witnesses (Old Latin or Old Syriac versions, quotations of the Fathers). There was obviously one serious problem. The primitive text, which had been preserved for a fairly long time in a relatively pure state, was corrupted in the second century by Marcion in the Pauline Epistles and, more particularly, by Tatian in the Gospels and Acts. One of the essential tasks of textual criticism consists in uncovering and eliminating these influences which had so badly and so profoundly altered the so-called 'Western' text. Only then can there be any chance of recovering the earliest form of the text.

This construction of the history of the text was no less attacked than that of Westcott – Hort. It exposed itself to even more serious criticism, the better founded of which is summarised here. First, there is the independence of the recension K: the 'Syrian' text appears rather to be an eclectic text; then, the unity of the recension I: it is, on the contrary, a ragbag of all the witnesses which could not be fitted into the other two recensions; then, the predominant influence attributed to Tatian: many harmonisations are not his doing since they are found in Marcion's writings. And many more no less shaky hypotheses could be cited. In other words, the history of the text as conceived by von Soden rests on data which are frequently very questionable.

As for the text itself and the critical apparatus, they, too, were received with serious reservations. The problem with the former is that the rules used to establish it are rather too arbitrary and mechanical. For example, when two recensions are in agreement they are generally preferred to the third, as if all the recensions were of equal value. Or again, when the three recensions band together with Tatian, preference should be given to a variant supported by early manuscripts, Church Fathers or versions as if all of Tatian's readings were to be treated with suspicion. The same old obsession is to be seen (see p. 101). What is more, numerous faults in the apparatus have been noted: omissions, wrong information and even quotations that have no documentary support. Worst of all, the text proposed by von Soden was a backward step rather than anything else. Certaintly, he avoided the false elegance and the harmonising readings of the 'textus receptus' but, at the points where he moved away from Westcott–Hort, he only too often drew closer to the 'Syrian' text. K. Lake called it 'a tragic failure' (1933, p. 78); 'to be wept over', Hoskier dramatically proclaimed. And yet, eighty years on, it still represents the most complete work on the Greek New Testament manuscripts. Duplacy has written, 'With von Soden, research passed a very important landmark ... The overall result of our own work would seem to be in line with the conclusions of von Soden' (Duplacy 1980).

It would be wrong to be unfair. Errors of detail are inevitable in a work containing thousands of references. The apparatus is difficult to use, it is true, but it is nonetheless a tool of great value for the specialist. The classification of the manuscripts into groups and sub-groups is not always justified, and the procedures used are unknown or dubious. And yet previously there had existed no such detailed examination of the minuscules, and more recent studies (see p. 164) are still not near to completion. The general theory of the history of the text is never likely to be accepted as it stands. But the extensive research of von Soden and his assistants was not in vain. It shed a brighter light on the number and the early age of the witnesses of the 'Western' text, their variety and their widespread circulation. It may well be, in any case, that von Soden was correct to see in I, H and K, in that order, the three great stages of the early history of the text. His work emphasised, especially, the unity of the whole of the Alexandrian group and its recensional nature. It could, in consequence, have barred the way once and for all to the so-called 'neutral' text which, however, still dominates the most recent editions, UBS 1983[3a] (1966– (III)), and Nestle–Aland 1979[26]

(1898 – (III)). History clearly continues to move by fits and starts, sometimes forwards, sometimes backwards.

THE GREAT NUMBER OF SPECIALIST STUDIES

The twenty years following von Soden were not marked by any one particular work. There were, on the other hand, a great many studies, often very well documented, on specific points of interest; there were also some important discoveries; and two books only (discussed below, pp. 160 – 61) which conveyed some original insights, able to stimulate research even if they did not indicate a definite direction to be followed. This was the period when the projects for the great collections of documentary information and the idea of working in teams took root; they were to flourish in the next period.

Of the weightier studies, reference must first be made to the numerous works by H. J. Vogels on the Old Latin and Old Syriac Gospels (1919, 1926b). His schools' edition of the Greek New Testament (1920 (III); 1955[4]) is praiseworthy on more than one account, as is also that of A. Merk (1933 (III); 1964[9]). On the text of Acts, mention should be made of J. H. Ropes' work in *The beginnings of Christianity* (1926 (III)), which is a mine of valuable information and a model of cautious criticism. H. Lietzmann's introduction to the textual criticism of the Pauline Epistles (1933) is worth citing, and likewise the work of K. T. Schäfer on the Latin version of the Epistle to the Hebrews (1929). Lastly, it would be unjust not to give pride of place to the monumental work by H. C. Hoskier on Revelation (1929), in which the apparatus of the variants is far superior to any of the previous collations.

In journals, there were often articles of value to do with textual criticism. The names to be remembered, amongst others, are those of M.-J. Lagrange, H. A. Sanders, J. M. Bover, F. C. Burkitt, A. Vaccari and A. Souter; and, of course, that indefatigable team of Benedictine monks working on the Vulgate and the Old Latin versions: Dom G. Morin, Dom B. Capelle, Dom D. de Bruyne, Dom A. Wilmart.

The articles of K. Lake and R. P. Blake (1923, 1928 (with S. New)) deserve a special mention. These eminent critics, deliberately limiting their work to the text of Mark, reconstituted a new family of manuscripts, the Caesarean family (see pp. 103 – 5), to which Origen's Caesarean text as well as that of Eusebius belonged. It is easy to see why this work should be so important.

Nor should we neglect two distinguished historians of early Christian literature who, from time to time, turned their attention to New Testament textual criticism: A. von Harnack and C. H. Turner. The former brought out a defence, rather too much like a commercial advertisement for our taste, of the Latin Vulgate text (von Harnack 1916a) but more important are his study on Marcion (p. 47) and many articles collected after his death (von Harnack 1931). As for C. H. Turner, he published some articles mainly of an introductory nature in the *Journal for Theological Studies* of which he was the first editor. They did not create much impression, but some, such as 'A textual commentary on Mark 1' (Turner 1927), are worthy of attention.

Concerning discoveries or noteworthy editions, there is not much to mention: about twenty new papyri, including the Chester Beatty collection (see pp. 11 – 12); a few fragments of uncials, in particular the very interesting 0171 and 0189 (fourth century); the oldest Vulgate manuscript of the Gospels (see pp. 30 – 31); John's Gospel in the sub-Achmimic dialect (see p. 38); and the Armenian version of Ephraem's commentary on Acts (Venice, 1921).

Lastly, something must be said about two very thought-provoking books. The first was by B. H. Streeter (*The four Gospels. A study of origins*, 1927). The author set out proposals for a new classification of the Gospel manuscripts. He divided them, after the disappearance of the autographs, into five main families linked to the most important sees of the Church of the time. They were what he called the local texts in current use in Alexandria, Caesarea, Antioch, Carthage, and in Italy and Gaul. The chief aim of textual criticism was precisely to reconstitute these primitive witnesses, with the help of the versions and the Patristic quotations, but also with reference to the great recensions (Hesychius, Lucian) and the later Vulgates. The artificial groups recognised by Westcott – Hort and von Soden – the 'neutral' text, the 'Western' text and the I-H-K text – at once appeared clearly as nothing more than scientific myths. The Alexandrian text was, it is true, still reckoned to be the best. But there was no longer a text which was taboo. Generally speaking, Streeter had many clear-sighted observations. Although some of his theories have to be treated with caution, he nonetheless had the rare merit of orienting people's thinking towards a truer and more living conception of the Gospel manuscript tradition.

The book by A. C. Clark, *The Acts of the Apostles* (1933 (III)), was just as original. His aim was to establish as clearly as possible the value of the long readings of the 'Western' text of Acts. Formerly, he had regarded the numerous omissions of the great uncials as accidental (see Clark 1914). He now showed that they were part of a very clear design on the part of a reviser who cared little for exact detail, especially for geographical detail. Although certain examples may be debatable, the overall result seems to be quite secure.

A final word is in order on the progress made on the editions of the versions throughout this period after Lachmann. There were still not the great critical editions that one might have hoped for but, on the whole, the ones made in this period have not yet been superseded, and they are the ones mentioned in chapter 1 of this book (see pp. 26 – 45). Only editions of the Ethiopic, the Armenian and the Harclean Syriac versions were not completed and, for those, the earlier editions continue to be used.

For once, the critics were not going round in circles. Indeed, they had spent more than three centuries just shuffling along. That, in itself, is not surprising in view of the small number of workers and the unrewarding nature of the task, besides an unhelpful state of mind which arose from two factors: 'the canonisation of the ''textus receptus'' in Protestant circles and the exclusive reliance of the Catholics on the Latin Vulgate' (Durand 1911, vol. 127, p. 325). There was, now, perceptible progress despite many backward steps and false moves.

From now on, there was more or less agreement on the fundamental principle of textual criticism: the establishing of the text is dependent on the history of the text. Furthermore, in practice, the 'textus receptus' was classed as a historical monument. The number of witnesses no longer counted; it was quality which was sought after. And quality itself was assessed by a series of steps: classifying the manuscripts into families, weighing up these different groups by examining their origin and their value and taking the final decision about each variant on the grounds of rational criticism. Something had very definitely changed since the first edition of Erasmus.

That does not mean that the specialists were in complete agreement, even on the most important issues. In particular, the opposition between the theories of Westcott – Hort and von Soden on the history of the text raised problems which are still not resolved in the next fifty-year period. At least, interest now began to focus on the variants of the text before AD 250. Some scholars believed that they could see which were the variants from before AD 150, but in the absence of documentary evidence this could only be speculation. There was a vast field open before the critic whose eyes were focused on matters of detail.

THE ERA OF DOCUMENTATION (1935–1990)

For this period, there is a series of bibliographical lists of the main works concerning New Testament textual criticism which should be referred to for further information. They bring the Bibliography of the first edition of this book up to date, and they follow its section divisions. They are to be found in E. Massaux, 'Etat présent de la critique textuelle du Nouveau Testament' (1953); J. Duplacy, *Où en est la critique textuelle du Nouveau Testament?* (1959), as well as in his 'Bulletins de critique textuelle du Nouveau Testament' (1962–77).

This period has been no more successful than the period following von Soden in producing a great critical edition of the New Testament, comparable to that of C. Tischendorf or H. von Soden in their day, and adapted to the scientific demands of the present. Nevertheless, progress in the area of documentation has been considerable: on the one hand, the discovery of new manuscripts, and, on the other, the more systematic analysis of early and medieval manuscripts, together with the drawing up of new lists of Patristic quotations, have all served to make new material available for the critical apparatus. Initially, their impact has been to cause the 'middle' text established by Nestle (see p. 153) to be revised – though only very timidly. The difficulty has been that the analysis of the enormous amount of documentation which has been collected together has presented such problems that they have not yet been overcome. There are difficulties due to the limited capacity of the human memory which the increased use of computer technology should alleviate; but the main difficulties are methodological. Despite some very thought-provoking studies, such as that by R. Kieffer (1968) on John 6 or that already mentioned by M. E. Boismard and A. Lamouille on Acts (see p. 29), the work done in the area of methodology has not succeeded in formulating any clearer conception of the history of the text in the earliest period. Consequently, Westcott–Hort's theory, with a few slight modifications, maintains its supporters and the 'neutral' text remains the basis of the revised popular edition, even though, at the same time, von Soden's chief ideas find themselves confirmed by certain studies, especially in the area of the Latin versions. A great critical edition would make use of a thorough analysis of all the Greek documentation, and would also draw on critical work carried out for each version, in addition to an organised list of the Patristic quotations. But such an edition is only at the very beginning of its preparatory phrase; it is not something which will be ready tomorrow, but it has, at least, made a good start.

DOCUMENTARY PROGRESS

Library research and archaeological excavations have brought to light a good many new documents. The most famous are the Dead Sea Scrolls which are of great importance for the Old Testament but do not concern the New Testament. On the other hand, the latest discovery made on Mount Sinai will perhaps one day be of the foremost importance for the history of the New Testament text, although for the moment little is known about the details. In 1975, in the course of some clearing work at St Catherine's Monastery, there came to light an old storehouse of books, walled-up and forgotten. Hundreds of manuscripts were found in it, often incomplete or even in a fragmentary state; most of them were in Greek but there were others in all the main languages of the early New Testament versions with the exception, it seems, of Coptic. Many of these manuscripts look as though they are biblical or liturgical.

The other most notable discoveries which concern the New Testament are: about forty Greek papyri and, in particular, the Bodmer collection (see pp. 12–13); about sixty Greek uncials in a very fragmentary state, including the only Greek copy of the Diatessaron dating from the third century (see p. 32); the only known Syriac copy of Ephraem's commentary on the Diatessaron (see p. 32); twenty or so Coptic manuscripts as well as many fragments, containing principally the Gospels and Acts and, to a lesser extent, the Epistles (see pp. 37–9); the Gospel of Thomas from the (Coptic) library of Nag Hammadi (see p. 36), which is of more interest for the literary criticism of the Gospels than it is for textual criticism; finally, the oldest Georgian manuscript of any length, the ḫan-meti palimpsest (see p. 41).

At the same time, the lists of manuscripts and quotations have been extended or created: 400 Greek minuscules and some 600 lectionaries have been added to the *Kurzgefasste Liste* ... and in the supplements (see p. 10) edited by K. Aland (V); the list of forty Old Latin manuscripts noted by Gregory has grown to 100 in Beuron where it has further been observed that certain early types of text are only preserved in the form of quotations (see p. 49); the number of Harclean Syriac manuscripts has gone from thirty-five (Gregory 1902–9 (V)) to 130 (Thomas 1979 (V)); for the Old Georgian, the list has changed from consisting of a few elements (not distinguished by Gregory from the manuscripts of the Athonite revisions) to about one hundred, according to B. Outtier (1988). Finally, there is the general catalogue of Patristic quotations compiled in Strasbourg and published in the form of an index, and also the collections of Eastern quotations (those in the *CSCO* notably), which are both useful complements to the documentation of the manuscripts.

PROJECTS FOR A GREAT CRITICAL EDITION

The first idea for the editio maior dates from 1926. Initially, the project was an English one, under the direction of S. C. E. Legg who published in Oxford an edition first of the Gospel of Mark (1935 (V)) and then of Matthew (1940 (V)), both with a critical apparatus that was rich but judged to be inadequate. The project was not continued. It was taken up later by an Anglo-American committee under the name of the International Greek New Testament Project (1952), which intended to edit Luke's Gospel. Extensive documentary and methodological work was undertaken, under the direction of M. M. Parvis, then E. C. Colwell on the American side, and on the English side G. G. Willis, then J. N. Birdsall, and finally J. K. Elliott. But nothing came of it for some time. Long silences alternated with periods of renewed activity. For more than thirty years, the publication of Luke did not materialise. Then, at last, in 1984 the first half of the Gospel of Luke (1 – 12) came out, and in 1987 the second half (13 – 24). The result was disappointing. It was an edition suitable neither for the general public nor for the needs of the specialists. Although displaying a high degree of scholarship, it was lacking on the level of methodology and of no interest for the history of the text. The idea of editing the 'textus receptus', which allowed the critical apparatus to be kept smaller, made it, at the same time, very difficult to use. Moreover, the variants were not selected with sufficient thoroughness, which means that they are of very unequal value, while the Greek manuscripts, which were selected by means of the Claremont Profile Method (see p. 70), represent only a very small proportion of the mass of those that exist for Luke's Gospel. And, in the absence of an explanatory introduction, it is impossible to know whether the witnesses which were not selected contain significant variants or not. If the goal was to create a 'new Tischendorf' in the sense of a work of great scholarship, then it has to be acknowledged that the goal has been achieved. If the purpose was rather to make a critical edition which would gather together as much information as possible relating to the early history of the Greek New Testament text, then the work needs to be done all over again, starting with a different foundation: in particular, that provided by the methodological insights of J. Duplacy (see pp. 71 – 3), as well as the presentation of the various text types in horizontal, parallel lines as in the *Vetus Latina* edition (see pp. 29 – 30). But it is premature to want to embark on a general edition of the Greek text as long as there are not good critical editions of the versions.

The periodical silences of this first attempt at an 'editio maior' encouraged the birth of another project on the Continent: the *Novi Testamenti graeci editio maior critica*, which was to be short-lived (1968 – 78). The cause can be seen to lie in the inability of the team to work together despite their bringing complementary skills to the task. All the conditions for success were there: the three co-editors had chosen to begin with the Catholic Epistles which have far fewer witnesses than the Gospels; and, what was more, they shared considerable expertise. The first co-editor, K. Aland, together with the Institut für Neutestament-liche Textforschung which he had founded in Münster, was there to play the part of successor to both Gregory for the list of the Greek New Testament manuscripts, and Nestle for the popular edition of the Greek New Testament (see p. 153); moreover, as part of an international team, he had successfully produced a revision of Nestle's Greek text for the United Bible Societies (see p. 166).

The second co-editor, J. Duplacy, joined the team as a scholar experienced in research into questions of method and the history of the text; his role was to take the place of Vaganay (whose manual he was preparing to re-edit in a considerably amplified form), sharing Tischendorf's interest in the Patristic quotations and certain of von Soden's ideas on the history of the text. Under the auspices of the French Centre national de la recherche scientifique, he assembled the French members of the team and worked with them in three directions: the catalogue of Patristic quotations with the Centre d'analyse et de documentation patristique, not long set up in Strasbourg; the early liturgical use of the Bible; and the language of the Catholic Epistles, with the idea of deriving arguments based on internal criticism for the selection of variants.

Finally, the third co-editor, B. Fischer, was then director of the Vetus Latina Institut in Beuron which, for the previous twenty years, had been editing the most remarkable critical edition of an early version ever attempted; the co-editors (and his eventual successors), W. Thiele and H. J. Frede, shared, together with Duplacy, many of von Soden's notions of the history of the text. And yet, the project failed. K. Aland, in Münster, was unwilling to move beyond the Claremont Profile Method to incorporate Duplacy's new and conclusive ideas (see pp. 71 – 3). Like the Anglo-American team, the project was hindered by the amount of documentation which was certainly kept up to date but which was unmanageable for analysis. One thing, at least, that came out of the project was that it became very clear that, for the preparation of a great critical edition of the Greek New Testament, critical editions of the early versions could play an important part; and this does not only mean the first versions (Latin, Syriac, Coptic). To improve the editions of the early versions was one of the assignments which two new research teams took upon themselves: the Centre de documentation sur les manuscrits de la Bible, set up by C.-B. Amphoux in 1982 in Montpellier (called the Centre Jean Duplacy from 1988), and the Centre de recherches sur la Bible latine, set up in 1983 in Louvain, under the direction of P. Bogaert and R. Gryson.

POPULAR EDITIONS

During this period the editions of Vogels and Merk have been re-edited (see p. 159), the ninth edition of Merk including variants from the Bodmer papyri (1964). In addition, there have been other new editions. J. M. Bover's edition (Madrid, 1943 – (III)) has a very limited apparatus, but the text itself often includes 'Caesarean' or 'Western' readings.

The editions of the Bible societies, however, are the ones which have become widely accepted for popular use. A dozen or so new editions of Nestle's New Testament were made, the first ones by Erwin Nestle and the later ones by K. Aland: the text remained unchanged but new discoveries were added to the critical apparatus, which was nonetheless somewhat limited, the text taking up most of the page. The twenty-fifth edition (1963) mentioned the Bodmer papyri for the first time.

From 1963 onwards, K. Aland worked on a revision of the 'middle' text established by Nestle (see p. 165). The new text was the work of an international committee made up of K. Aland, M. Black, B. M. Metzger, A. Wikgren and, after the first edition, C. M. Martini. The first edition was published in 1966 by the United Bible Societies (*The Greek New Testament*). The apparatus contains very few variant readings but, for each one, a large number of witnesses is regularly given. The choice of variants is based on the majority vote of the committee, and the proportion of votes obtained is indicated by a letter placed at the head of each variation unit. The most notable effect of this combination of philological and democratic processes is that the previous choices tend to be repeated. In the third edition (1975), which was preceded by the publication of a 'companion book' by B. M. Metzger (1975; see p. 88) commenting on the selection of each variant, the conformity of the text with the 'Alexandrian' type, the one preferred by Westcott – Hort as the 'neutral' text, is even greater. The revised edition of 1983[3a] does not alter the situation.

It is the text of the 1975 edition which was used, sometimes with different punctuation, for the twenty-sixth edition of Nestle (Stuttgart, 1979) prepared by K. Aland and the Münster Institute. New minuscules were added to the apparatus, the number of variation units mentioned was increased, and an extremely useful system of sigla was inserted in the text to refer to variant readings in the apparatus. But, at the same time, Aland made some unfortunate decisions. Certain witnesses are left out of the apparatus altogether, such as the versions other than the Latin, Syriac or Coptic ones which are wrongly regarded as 'secondary' (Introduction, p. 59*). Interest is focused on the papyri and Greek uncials: the Fathers are given only occasional mention, the minuscules play an auxiliary role and the lectionaries are neglected. Nor does the apparatus show the groups of witnesses which attest a particular type of text. Disregarding the progress made in the domain of documentation, the critical apparatus has been constructed in order to justify the text which, to all intents and purposes, is presented as equivalent to the original text, for it is said only of those readings enclosed in brackets that they 'are of doubtful authenticity with regard to the original text' (Introduction, p. 44*). The concern not to trouble simple minds with an uncertain or reworked text is no doubt a laudable one, but is it right to alter history? For what is implied to be the original text is in fact probably a text established in Egypt around the year AD 200, doubtless with some earlier readings but also some innovations, at which point the earlier readings are relegated to the apparatus or not given at all if they are only attested by the witnesses which have already been excluded from the apparatus. Nevertheless, thanks to the wealth of documentation available to the editors, this popular edition is still the least bad. And so, as long as it is used with care, the apparatus is of some value.

Thus, the agreement reached by the Bible societies for a revised Greek text will guarantee for a long time to come the stability of the new 'textus receptus' which, essentially, is that established by Lachmann (see pp. 146 – 7). It is the text which is used in the *Synopsis quattuor evangeliorum* (edited by K. Aland (1966 – (III)), after the ninth edition (Stuttgart, 1976); the current edition, the thirteenth (1985), includes in its apparatus new material from the Nestle – Aland twenty-sixth edition. As for the Synopsis of A. Huck (1892 (III)), which was first of all revised by H. Lietzmann and H. G. Opitz (1936[9]) and then recast by H. Greeven (Tübingen, 1981), the present text is a little different, but it basically still tends to give preference to the Egyptian text, a text which dates from after AD 200.

THE QUESTION OF THE HISTORY OF THE TEXT

It would not be possible, in just a few pages, to attempt to cover all the many studies written in the last fifty years which touch in one way or another on issues connected with textual criticism. The most important ones have been carefully reviewed by Duplacy in his 'Bulletins' (see p. 162). Generally on very specific points, they nonetheless mark an undeniable step forward within their own limited domain, whether it be, for example, a better knowledge of the manuscripts (especially the minuscules), of the quotations (see especially Boismard 1950) or of the history of the text after the fourth century. But, despite the contributions of G. D. Kilpatrick, A. F. J. Klijn, W. Thiele, J. Duplacy and many more, there is a stumbling block that remains, that is the history of the text before AD 200. There are only indirect witnesses for this period: a few Patristic quotations, early variants preserved in the Greek or in some versions which can be dated with some uncertainty using internal criticism, versions of the Diatessaron which are of varying degrees of trustworthiness, and that is about all. On this meagre foundation, two contradictory theories about the history of the text still find supporters: the theories of Westcott – Hort (see pp. 149 – 51) and of von Soden (see pp. 155 – 7).

Until around 1960, the main question on which scholars were divided was in essence the following: is the text of Codex Vaticanus a recensional text or not? The supporters of Westcott – Hort said 'no', those of von Soden said 'yes'. But at the same time there was the problem of the 'Western' text: why were there so many variants? When did they occur? Which were the variants which produced the others? On this point, no hypothesis has yet been put forward to explain the facts. It is simply observed that, however far back one goes, there is always some witness to the 'Western' text. The discovery of the Nag-Hammadi manuscripts (1945) and the textual study of the Gospel of Thomas disclosed a certain link between the Apocryphal writings and these 'Western' witnesses. Could the variants, therefore, be theological?

Some tended to think so (see p. 93), but there is a lack of convincing evidence. Could they be due to the influence of the Diatessaron? For a long time that was the explanation given, in spite of the fact that they existed before Tatian. The truth of the matter is that Biblical scholars had come to a dead end: new documents confirmed the early age of the 'Western' readings, but no explanation for their existence had been found.

The discovery of the Bodmer papyri, in particular P^{75}, seemingly released the blockage by appearing to present an answer to the problem. But, in fact, it only served to hinder careful thought on the matter, providing as it did an argument in favour of the non-recensional nature of Codex Vaticanus; for, though probably a century older, the text of P^{75} for Luke and John is exceptionally close to that of Codex Vaticanus. Thus it was that after the period of stagnation came the recession. For many people, the question of the original text was henceforth resolved: Codex Vaticanus was indeed its best representative. The existence of the 'Western' text was not ignored, but its enigmatic quality was forgotten and it was stated without any evidence that it must, after all, be later than B.03. The old theory of the 'neutral' text gained ground, it became more or less the inevitable choice. It was on these assumptions that the editions of the Bible societies were made (the editorial committee of the new 'textus receptus' has no convinced supporter of the 'Western' text), and also that most exegetes work without any further concern. And yet the facts were there. The 'Western' text is widely attested in the second century, even before AD 150, whereas P^{75} is probably no earlier than AD 230. Because of this, some scholars persist in maintaining that the remarkable agreements between P^{75} and B.03 are not sufficient reason to deny that the 'Western' text is pre-recensional, that is the type of text closest to the primitive text without being identical to it. But since there is room for doubt, it is the documents themselves which will decide. That is why Duplacy, who had originally thought of writing a history of the text before AD 200, eventually decided to devote his energy to the vast work of documentation and did not ever manage to return to his initial project.

Thanks to the collecting of documentary information, it is possible today to see why this stagnation occurred (even in those critics who never ceased believing in the earlier date of the 'Western' text compared with the other types), and thus escape from the present impasse. All textual research after Westcott – Hort has been carried out with the two following presuppositions:

1. the biblical text is a written text and, as such, is governed by the rules of written documents;
2. the biblical text belongs to the literary genres of narrative and wisdom literature, that is, it is made up of independent literary units which can be regarded separately from one another and understood in isolation, and which furthermore relate real events or events that are presented as real by the authors.

If these two postulations were withdrawn, the perspectives of textual criticism could be profoundly altered,

1. if the biblical text follows other rules than those of written documents it could be treated, for example, as governed by the rules of oral literature. There is no anachronism in that, and Marcel Jousse has provided a great deal of material which would enable this possibility to be investigated by fresh research;
2. if the biblical text is not primarily made up of narrative and wisdom literature, what is it made up of? Philo of Alexandria, the Gnostic writers, the Fathers of the Church themselves, all freely engage in an understanding of Scripture which involves finding hidden meaning, only accessible to the initiate. Perhaps the New Testament belongs to a literary genre which was not for the ordinary reader. Or, to put it more precisely, before the New Testament acquired its final revised character as we know it, it may perhaps have been born in a culture where Scriptural writings belonged to a didactic literary genre specifically addressed to those of a certain level of religious sophistication.

It is on these new principles that the history of the text before AD 200, as it has been set out earlier (see pp. 91 – 7), depends. The future work of textual criticism in this respect is to check if the principles are well-founded, if they explain any more facts than the other assumptions concerning the nature of the text. We may well be very near to being able to explain what the New Testament looked like in the years immediately following the writing of each of its books. But this is still only a hypothesis. If the conception of the text as described here is accurate, then the 'Western' text would represent those witnesses which are closest to the text as it was originally conceived by its authors; this text would subsequently have been forgotten and transformed until it became the recensional text which we possess. There is no question about the legitimacy of this text since it has been adopted by the Church, in different forms but all basically similar to each other, since the middle of the second century. On the basis of this hypothesis, those who, following on from von Soden's exceptional insights, have upheld the primitive character of the 'Western' text have, by their persistence in the face of opposition and technical difficulties, been the pioneers of what could be, in the not too distant future, a radical new conception of first-century Christianity.

Thus, a major contribution of the last fifty years will have been the productive increase in documentary research, now seen as indispensable to the creation of a great critical edition of the New Testament. This research must continue, for it is far from having reached its goal yet. At the present time, there exists no critical edition, either of the text in Greek or in any other language, which makes full use of all the documentation available in one area (manuscripts and quotations). The model to be copied in this respect is the Vetus Latina edition (see pp. 29 – 30), but it still lacks the Catholic Epistles and the shorter Pauline Epistles. As with the Vetus Latina edition, what should be aimed at is the presentation of each text type in horizontal lines one above the other and with their variants, their manuscripts, and the quotations which support them, and, for the Eastern languages, a literal translation (perhaps in Latin) so as to make them more widely accessible. Then, and only then, would it be possible to envisage bringing together in one single apparatus both the Greek witnesses and the witness of the versions. On the other hand, the main preoccupation of the years to follow could equally well be literary rather than documentary. It could well happen that the view which we suggest of the history of the text before AD 200 may be confirmed, and that the principles which we have just laid down should turn out to be well-founded, or at the very least not be contradicted by documentary evidence. If this happens, then in order for textual criticism to progress towards the creation of a great critical edition it would have to be backed up by serious research into the literary genre of the New Testament writings, not only the text as we read it now which has been reasonably well studied but also the text of the earlier types, in particular the pre-recensional text. By virtue of the new questions emerging from the current assembling of documentary information, textual criticism is perhaps opening up the way for a new history of form criticism.

Bibliography

I MANUSCRIPTS CITED WITH THEIR NUMBER

Roman numerals in the date column refer to centuries. Numbers in bold type indicate main representatives of the text types. Numbers in brackets preceded by 'ex' at the end of an entry refer to a previous system of numbering.

frag. = fragment

Date	Number	Location and catalogue number
II	*Greek*	
	P^{52}	Manchester, J. Rylands Libr., Gr. P. 457
c. 200	**P^{46}**	Dublin, A. Chester Beatty, Pap. II
		Ann Arbor, Univ. of Michigan, inv. 6238
	P^{66}	Geneva, Bibl. Bodmer, P. Bod. II
		Dublin, A. Chester Beatty
	0189	Berlin, Staatl. Museen, P. 11765
III	*Greek*	
	P^{4}	Paris, Bibl. Nat., suppl. Gr. 1120
	P^{5}	London, Brit. Libr., Pap. 782/2484
	P^{12}	New York, Pierpont Morgan Libr., Pap. Gr. 3
	P^{22}	Glasgow, Univ. Libr., 2-X.1 (frag.)
	P^{45}	Dublin, A. Chester Beatty, Pap. I
		Vienna, Österr. Nat. Bibl., Pap. G. 31974
	P^{47}	Dublin, A. Chester Beatty, Pap. III

172

P⁴⁸	Florence, Bibl. Laurenziana, PSI 1165
P⁶⁴	Oxford, Magdalen Coll., Gr. 18
	Barcelona, Fundación S. Lucás Ev., P. Barc. 1 (ex: P⁶⁷)
P⁷⁵	Geneva, Bibl. Bodmer, P. Bod. XIV.XV
0212	New Haven (Conn.), Yale Univ., P. Dura 10
0220	Boston, Leland C. Wyman

Coptic
sa(1)   Jackson (Miss.), Univ. of Mississippi (Codex Crosby)

c. 300   *Greek*:

P¹⁸	London, Brit. Libr., Pap. 2053 vᵒ (frag.)
P⁷⁸	Oxford, Ashmolean Mus.
0162	New York, Metropol. Mus. of Art, 09-182-43

IV   *Greek*

P⁶	Strasbourg, Bibl. Nat. Univ., Pap. Cop. 379–384 (Gr.–Cop.)
P⁷²	Geneva, Bibl. Bodmer, P. Bod. VII.VIII.IX
S.01	London, Brit. Libr., add. 43725 (Sinaiticus)
B.03	Rome, Bibl. Vaticana, Vat. Gr. 1209 (Vaticanus)
0169	Princeton (N.J.), Theol. Semin., Pap. 5
0171	Florence, Bibl. Laurenziana., PSI 2.124
	Berlin, Staatl. Museen, P.11863
*l*1604	Oxford, Bodleian Libr., Cop.f.5.(P) (Gr.–Cop.)

Latin
it(3)   Vercelli, Bibl. Capitolare (Vercellensis, a)

Syriac
syˢ   Sinai (Mt), Mon. Hag. Aikaterinēs, Syr. 30 (Sinaiticus)

Coptic

sa(2)	Berlin, Staatl. Museen, P. 15926
bo(1)	Geneva, Bibl. Bodmer, P. Bod. III
ac(1)	= P⁶
ac²(1)	Cambridge, Brit. and Foreign Bible Soc., MS 137
fay(1)	Ann Arbor, Univ. of Michigan, inv. 3521

c. 400   *Greek*

P⁵⁰	New Haven (Conn.), Yale Univ. Libr., P.1543
D.05	Cambridge, Univ. Libr., No. II 41 (Bezae, Gr.–Lat.)

057 Berlin, Staatl. Museen, P. 9808
059 Vienna, Österr. Nat. Bibl., Pap. G. 36112
    Vienna, Österr. Nat. Bibl., Pap. G. 39779 (ex: 0215)
0160 Berlin, Staatl. Museen, P. 9961

Latin
it(1) Turin, Bibl. Naz., G.VII.15 (Bobbiensis, k)
it(2) Trent, Mus. Naz. (Palat. 1185) (Palatinus, e)
it(4) Verona, Bibl. Capitolare, VI(6) (Veronensis, b)
it(5) = D.05

Coptic
sa(3) Geneva, Bibl. Bodmer, P. Bod. XIX
mae(1) Princeton (N.J.), W. H. Scheide (Codex Scheide)

V *Greek*
A.02 London, Brit. Libr., Royal I D.VIII (Alexandrinus)
C.04 Paris, Bibl. Nat., Gr.9 (Ephraemi rescriptus)
I.106 Washington, Smithsonian Inst., Freer 06.275
    (Freerianus II)
Q.026 Wolfenbüttel, Herzog-August Bibl., Weiss. 64
    (Guelferbytanus B)
T.029 Rome, Bibl. Vaticana, Borg. Cop. 109/T 109 (Bergianus,
    Gr. – Cop.)
    New York, Pierpont Morgan Libr., M 664 A
    Paris, Bibl. Nat., Cop. 129,7 fol.35, 129,8 fol.121.122.
    140.157 (ex: 0139)
    Paris, Bibl. Nat., Cop. 129,9 fol.49.65, 129,10 fol.209
    (ex: 0113)
    Paris, Bibl. Nat., Cop. 129,9 fol.76 (ex: 0125)
W.032 Washington, Smithsonian Inst., Freer 06.274 (Freerianus I)

Latin
it(8) Paris, Bibl. Nat., Lat. 17225 (Corbeiensis II, ff^2)

Syriac
sy^c London, Brit. Libr., Add. 14451 (Curetonian)

Coptic
sa(4) Barcelona, Semin. Papir. Fac. Teol., P Palau 181–
    182
sa(5) Barcelona, Semin. Papir. Fac. Teol., P Palau 183
mae(2) New York, Pierpont Morgan Libr., G.67 (Codex Glazier)
mae(3) Milan, Istit. Papirologia, Cop.1

c. 500	*Latin*	
	vg^s	St Gallen, Stiftsbibl., 1395 (ex: 292) (Sangallensis)
		St Gallen, St Paul in Kärnten, 25.4.21a
		Zürich, Staatsarchiv, A.G.19,II
		Zürich, Zentralbibl., C 43 / C 79b / Z XIV 5

Georgian

geo(1)   Tbilisi, K.K. Sax. Xelnac'erta Inst., A 89/A 844 (Han-meti palimpsest)

VI   *Greek*

D.06   Paris, Bibl. Nat., Gr.107, 107 AB (Claromontanus, Gr.–Lat.)

E.08   Oxford, Bodleian Libr., Laud 35 (Laudianus, Gr.–Lat.)

H.015   Paris, Bibl. Nat., Coislin 202/suppl. Gr. 1074 (Coislinianus)

Athos (Mt), Mon. Meg. Lauras

Kiev, Central Nauk. Bibl. Akad., Petrov 26

Leningrad, Gosud. Publ. Bibl., Gr.14

Moscow, Gosud. Istor. Mus., 563

Moscow, Gosud. Bibl. Lenina, Gr. 166, 1

Turin, Bibl. Naz., A.1

N.022   Leningrad, Gosud. Publ. Bibl., Gr.537 (Purpureus Petropolitanus)

Athens, Byz. Mous., frag.21

Rome, Bibl. Vaticana, Vat. Gr. 2305

Lerma (Alessandria), A. Spinola

London, Brit. Libr., Cotton. Tit. C.XV

New York, Pierpont Morgan Libr., 874

Patmos, Mon. Iōannou, 67

Salonica, Archaiol. Mous.

Vienna, Österr. Nat. Bibl., Theol. Gr.31

0.023   Paris, Bibl. Nat., Suppl. Gr.1286 (Sinopensis)

P.024   Wolfenbüttel, Herzog-August Bibl., Weiss. 64 (Guelferbytanus A)

R.027   London, Brit. Libr., Add. 17211 (Nitriensis)

Z.035   Dublin, Trinity Coll., K.3.4 (Dublinensis)

Φ.043   Tirana, Archiv. Nat., 1 (Beratinus)

060   Berlin, Staatl. Museen, P. 5877

070   Oxford, Clarendon Press, b.2

London, Brit. Libr., Add. 34274 (ex: 0110)

London, Brit. Libr., Or.3579 B (ex: 0202)

		Paris, Bibl. Nat., Cop. 129,7 fol.14.72, 129,8 fol.89.90.

Paris, Bibl. Nat., Cop. 129,7 fol.14.72, 129,8 fol.89.90.
139.147–154, 129,9 fol.87, 129,10 fol.119–124.156.
164 (ex: 0124)
Vienna, Österr. Nat. Bibl., Pap. K. 15 (ex: 0180)
Vienna, Österr. Nat. Bibl., Pap. K. 2699 (ex: 0178)
Vienna, Österr. Nat. Bibl., Pap. K. 2700 (ex: 0179)
Vienna, Österr. Nat. Bibl., Pap. K. 9007 (ex: 0190)
Vienna, Österr. Nat. Bibl., Pap. K. 9031 (ex: 0191)

080   Alexandriæ, Bibl. Patriarcheiou, 496
Leningrad, Gosud. Publ. Bibl., Gr. 275

*l*1276   Cambridge, Univ. Libr., Tay. Schech. coll 16.98
*l*1347   Verona, Bibl. Capitolare, I(1)
*l*1354   Cambridge, Univ. Libr., Add. 1875, (Gr.–Heb.)

Latin
it(10)   Brescia, Bibl. Civica Queriniana (Brixianus, f)
it(50)   = D.06
it(55)   Paris, Bibl. Nat., Lat. 6400 G (Floriacensis, h)
it(75)   = E.08
vg^F Fulda, Landesbibl., Bonif. 1 (Fuldensis)
vg^M Milan, Bibl. Ambrosiana, C.39 inf
vg^Z London, Brit. Libr., Harley 1775

Gothic
(1)   Uppsala, Univ. Bibl. (Argenteus)

c. 600   *Greek*
P^3 Vienna, Österr. Nat. Bibl., Pap. G. 2323
P^{44} New York, Metropol. Mus. of Art, inv. 14-1-527

Coptic
sa(6)   Dublin, A. Chester Beatty, A

VII   *Greek*
P^{74} Geneva, Bibl. Bodmer, P. Bod. XVII
0188   Berlin, Staatl. Museen, P. 13416

*l*1353   (ex: Rome, Bibl. Vaticana, Borg. Cop. 2) (Gr.–Cop.)

Coptic
sa(7)   Dublin, A. Chester Beatty, B

c. 700   *Latin*
it(11)   Berlin, Staatsbibl., Breslau 5 (Rhedigeranus, 1)

VIII	*Greek*	
	P⁴¹	Vienna, Österr. Nat. Bibl., Pap. K. 7541–48 (Gr.– Cop.)
	E.07	Basle, Öffentl. Bibl. Univ., A.III.12 (Basileensis)
	L.019	Paris, Bibl. Nat., Gr. 62 (Regius)
	046	Rome, Bibl. Vaticana, Vat. Gr. 2066
	*l*1602	New York, Pierpont Morgan Libr., 615 (Gr.–Cop.) Freiburg-im-B., Univ. Bibl., 615
	Latin	
	vg^A	Florence, Bibl. Laurenziana, Amiat. I (Amiatinus)
c. 800	*Greek*	
	Ψ.044	Athos (Mt), Mon. Meg. Lauras, B'52 (Athusiensis)
	Coptic	
	sa(8)	New York, Pierpont Morgan Libr., M.569
	sa(9)	New York, Pierpont Morgan Libr., M.5
	sa(10)	New York, Pierpont Morgan Libr., M.570
	sa(11)	New York, Pierpont Morgan Libr., M.571
	sa(12)	New York, Pierpont Morgan Libr., M.572
	Arabic	
	(1)	Rome, Bibl. Vaticana, Borg. Arab. 95
IX	*Greek*	
	D^abs	Leningrad, Gosud. Publ. Bibl., Gr.20 (Sangermanensis, Gr.–Lat.)
	F.09	Utrecht, Bibl. Rijksuniv., 1 (Codex Boreeli)
	F.010	Cambridge, Trinity Coll., B.XVII.1 (Augiensis, Gr.–Lat.)
	G.011	London, Brit. Libr., Harley 5684 (Seidelianus I) Cambridge, Trinity Coll., B.XVII.20
	G.012	Dresden, Sächs. Landesbibl., A.145b (Boernerianus, Gr.–Lat.)
	H.013	Hamburg, Staats. Univ. Bibl., 91 in scrin. (Seidelianus II)
	K.017	Paris, Bibl. Nat., Gr.63 (Cyprius)
	K.018	Moscow, Gosud. Istor. Mus., S. 97, V. 93 (Mosquensis)
	L.020	Rome, Bibl. Angelica, 39 (Angelicus)
	M.021	Paris, Bibl. Nat., Gr.48 (Campianus)
	P.025	Leningrad, Gosud. Publ. Bibl., Gr.225 (Porphyrianus)

U.030 Venice, Bibl. Marciana, 1397 (I.8) (Nanianus)
V.031 Moscow, Gosud. Istor. Mus., S.399, V. 9 (Mosquensis)
Δ.037 St Gallen, Stiftsbibl., 48 (Sangallensis, Gr.–Lat.)
Θ.038 Tbilisi, K.K. Sax. Xelnac'erta Inst., Gr.28 (Koridethi)
Λ.039 Oxford, Bodleian Libr., Auct. T. infr. 1.1 (Tischendorfianus III)
Π.041 Leningrad, Gosud. Publ. Bibl., Gr.34 (Petropolitanus)
Ω.045 Athos (Mt), Mon. Dionysiou, 55 (Athusiensis)
0136 Leningrad, Gosud. Publ. Bibl., Gr.281 (Gr.–Arab.)
Sinai (Mt), Mon. Hag. Aikaterinēs, Harris 9 (ex: 0137)
33 Paris, Bibl. Nat., Gr.14
461 Leningrad, Gosud. Publ. Bibl., Gr.219
565 Leningrad, Gosud. Publ. Bibl., Gr.53
566 Leningrad, Gosud. Publ. Bibl., Gr.54/282
892 London, Brit. Libr., Add.33277

*l*46 Naples, Bibl. Naz., Vien.2

Latin
it(66) Leningrad, Gosud. Publ. Bibl., Q.v. I 39 (Corbeiensis, ff)
it(76) = d^{abs}
it(77) = G.012
it(78) = F.101

Georgian
geo(2) Mestia, Ist'oriul-etnograpiul Muz., 1 (Adysh MS)

Arabic
ar(1) Sinai (Mt), Mon. Hag. Aikaterinēs, Arab.72
ar(2) Sinai (Mt), Mon. Hag. Aikaterinēs, Arab.151
ar(3) = 0136

c. 900 *Greek*
1424 Maywood (Ill.), Theol. Semin., Gruber 152

X *Greek*
S.028 Rome, Bibl. Vaticana, Vat. Gr. 354
X.033 Munich, Univ. Bibl., fol. 30 (Monacensis)
Γ.036 Oxford, Bodleian Libr., Auct. T. infr. 2.2 (Tischendorfianus IV)
36ᵉ Paris, Bibl. Nat., Coislin 20
262 Paris, Bibl. Nat., Gr.53
1143 Berat, Metropol. Bibl. (Alex. 2)

1582	Athos (Mt), Mon. Batopediou, 949
1739	Athos (Mt), Mon. Meg. Lauras, B'64
1891	Jerusalem, Kathol. Orthod. Patriarcheion, Saba 107
	Leningrad, Gosud. Publ. Bibl., Gr.317
2193	(ex: Athos, Mon. Iberōn, 247)

Georgian

geo(3)	Tbilisi, K.K. Sax. Xelnac'erta Inst., A 89/A 509 (Codex Ksani)
	Leningrad, Gosud. Publ. Bibl., Georg. 8–9
geo(4)	Athos (Mt), Mon. Iberōn, Georg. 83 (Opiza MS)
geo(5)	Leningrad, Gosud. Publ. Bibl., Georg. 212 (Tbet' MS)
geo(6)	Tbilisi, K.K. Sax. Xelnac'erta Inst., H 1660 (Codex Džruč)
geo(7)	Tbilisi, K.K. Sax. Xelnac'erta Inst., A 1453 (Codex Parhal)
geo(20a)	Athôs (Mt), Mon. Iberōn, Georg.42
geo(22)	Sinai (Mt), Mon. Hag. Aikaterinēs, Georg. 58-31-60
geo(23)	Sinai (Mt), Mon. Hag. Aikaterinēs, Georg. 39
geo(24)	Tbilisi, K.K. Sax. Xelnac'erta Inst., H 1346 (Kranim MS)
geo(50)	Tbilisi, K. Marx Sax. Sažaro Bibl., 40 (Kala Lectionary)

Slavonic

sl(1)	Leningrad, Gosud. Publ. Bibl., Glag. 1 (Zographensis)

c. 1000   *Ethiopic*

eth(1)	Aduwa, Abba Garima Mon., 1
eth(2)	Aduwa, Abba Garima Mon., 2
eth(3)	Aduwa, Abba Garima Mon., 3

XI   *Greek*

7[p]	Basle, Univ. Bibl., A.N.III.11
28	Paris, Bibl. Nat., Gr.379
81	London, Brit. Libr., Add. 20003
	Alexandria, Bibl. Patriarcheiou, 59
104	London, Brit. Libr., Auct. D. infr. 2.17
124	Vienna, Österr. Nat. Bibl., Theol. Gr. 188
174	Rome, Bibl. Vaticana, Vat. Gr. 2002
230	Escorial, Bibl. s. Lorenzo, Y.III.5
323	Geneva, Bibl. Publ. Univ., 20
431	Strasbourg, Grand Sémin., 1

700	London, Brit. Libr., Egerton 2610
788	Athens, Ethnikē Bibl., 74
899	Uppsala, Univ. Bibl. Gr.4
945	Athos (Mt), Mon. Dionysiou, 124 (37)
1012	Athos (Mt), Mon. Iberōn, 1063 (68)
1175	Patmos, Mon. Iōannou, 16
1243	Sinai (Mt), Mon. Hag. Aikaterinēs, Gr.261
1448	Athos (Mt), Mon. Meg. Lauras, A'13
2138	Moscow, Nauk. Bibl. Gor'kogo, 1
2147	Leningrad, Gosud. Publ. Bibl., Gr.224
2298	Paris, Bibl. Nat., Gr.102

Georgian

vg(1)	Athos (Mt), Mon. Iberōn, Georg. 92

Slavonic

sl(2)	Moscow, Gosud. Bibl. Lenina, Φ 87/1689 (Marianus)

c. 1100   *Greek*

256	Paris, Bibl. Nat., Arm.9 (Gr.–Arm.)
1735	Athos (Mt), Mon. Meg. Lauras, B'42

Armenian see 256 *Supra*

XII   *Greek*

1eap	Basle, Univ. Bibl., A.N.IV.2
1r	Harburg (Schloss), Ött-Wall. Bibl., I.1.40.1
2e	Basle, Univ. Bibl., A.N.IV.1
2ap	Basle, Univ. Bibl., A.N.IV.4
7e	Paris, Bibl. Nat., Gr.71
22	Paris, Bibl. Nat., Gr.72
36a	Oxford, New Coll., 58
57	Oxford, Magdalen Coll., Gr.9
119	Paris, Bibl. Nat., Gr.85
120	Paris, Bibl. Nat., Suppl. Gr. 185
157	Rome, Bibl. Vaticana, Urbin. Gr.2
326	Geneva, Bibl. Publ. Univ., 20
346	Milan, Bibl. Ambrosiana, S. 23 sup.
543	Ann Arbor, Univ. of Michigan, 15
579	Paris, Bibl. Nat., Gr. 97
713	Birmingham, Selly Oak Coll., Peckover, Gr.7
826	Grottaferrata, Bibl. della Badia, A'α'3
828	Grottaferrata, Bibl. della Badia, A'α'5

	872	Rome, Bibl. Vaticana, Vat. Gr. 2160
	876	Ann Arbor, Univ. of Michigan, 16
	983	Athos (Mt), Mon. Esphigmenou, 29
	1071	Athos (Mt), Mon. Meg. Lauras, A'104
	1241	Sinai (Mt), Mon. Hag. Aikaterines, Gr. 260
	1278	Manchester, J. Rylands Libr., Gr. 17
	1611	Athens, Ethnikē Bibl., 94
	2652	Athens, Ethnikē Bibl., 103

Latin

it(6) Paris, Bibl. Nat., Lat. 254 (Colbertinus, c)

c. 1200 *Greek*

1689 Athens, Ethnikē Bibl. (Prodromosy' 10)

1799 Princeton (N.J.), Univ. Libr., Garrett 8

XIII *Greek*

6	Paris, Bibl. Nat., Gr. 112
13	Paris, Bibl. Nat., Gr. 50
118	Oxford, Bodleian Libr., Auct. D. infra. 2.17
206	London, Lambeth Palace, 1182
273	Paris, Bibl. Nat., Gr. 79
383	Oxrford, Bodleian Libr., Clarke 9
614	Milan, Bibl. Ambrosiana, E.97 sup.
1108	Athos (Mt), Mon. Esphigmenou, 64
1292	Paris, Bibl. Nat., Suppl. Gr. 1224
1505	Athos (Mt), Mon. Meg. Lauras, B'26
1604	Athos (Mt), Mon. Batopediou, 976
1758	Lesbos, Mon. Leimōnos, 195
1852	Uppsala, Univ. Bibl., Gr.11
2492	Sinai (Mt), Mon. Hag. Aikaterinēs, Gr.1342

*l*547 Rome, Bibl. Vaticana, Vat. Gr. 1217

Latin

it(51) Stockholm, Kgl. Bibl. (Gigas liber)

Ethiopic

eth(4) Paris, Bibl. Nat., Eth 22 (Zotenberg 32)

XIV *Greek*

4ᵉ	Paris, Bibl. Nat., Gr.84
131	Rome, Bibl. Vaticana, Vat. Gr. 360
209	Venice, Bibl. Marciana, 394

	429	Wolfenbüttel, Herzog-August Bibl., Aug. 16.7.4°
	603	Paris, Bibl. Nat., Gr. 106 A
	630	Rome, Bibl. Vaticana, Ottob. Gr. 325
	1394	Athos (Mt), Mon. Pantokratoros, 47
	1581	Athos (Mt), Mon. Batopediou, 949
	1698	Athens, Ethnikē Bibl., 2508
	1765	London, Brit. Libr., Add. 33214
	1831	Athens, Ethnikē Bibl., 119
	1832	Athens, Ethnikē Bibl., 89
	1890	Jerusalem, Kathol. Orthod. Patriarcheion, Panag. Taphou 462

c. 1400	*Greek*	
	2495	Sinai (Mt), Mon. Hag. Aikaterinēs, Gr. 1992

XV	*Greek*	
	4ᵃᵖ	Basle, Univ. Bibl., A.N.IV.5
	69	Leicester, Town Mus., 6.D.32/1
	130	Rome, Bibl. Vaticana, Vat. Gr. 359
	1518	London, Lambeth Palace, 1181 (lost)
	Ethiopic	
	eth(5)	Paris, Bibl. Nat., Eth. 21 (Zotenberg 35)
	eth(6)	Paris, Bibl. Nat., Eth. 26 (Zotenberg 42)

XVI	*Greek*	
	61	Dublin, Trinity Coll., A 4.21
	522	Oxford, Bodleian Libr., Canon. Gr. 34
	Ethiopic	
	eth(7)	Paris, Bibl. Nat., Eth. 24 (Zotenberg 41)

II NAMES OF THE LIBRARIES IN FULL

Aduwa (Ethiopia), Abba Garima Monastery: eth (1), (2), (3)

Alexandria (Egypt), Bibliothēkē tou Patriarcheiou: 080, 81

Ann Arbor (Mich.), University of Michigan, University Library, Department of Rare Books: P⁴⁶, 543, 876, fay(1)

Athens, Byzantinon Mouseion: N.022

Athens, Ethnikē Bibliothēkē tēs Hellados: 788, 1611, 1689, 1698, 1831, 1832, 2652

Athos (Mt), Monē Batopediou: 1581, 1582, 1604

Athos (Mt), Monē Hagiou Dionysiou: Ω.045, 945

Athos (Mt), Monē Esphigmenou: 983, 1108

Athos (Mt), Monē tōn Iberōn: 1012, 2193, geo(20a), geo(vg)

Athos (Mt), Monē Megistēs Lauras: H.015, Ψ.044, 1071, 1448, 1505, 1735, 1739

Athos (Mt), Monē Pantokratoros: 1394

Barcelona, Fundación S. Lucás Evangelista: P^{64}

Barcelona, S. Cugat del Vallés, Seminario de Papirologia de la Facultad Teologica: sa(4), (5)

Basle, Universitätsbibliothek: 1^{eap}, 2e, 2^{ap}, 4^{ap}, 7^p

Berat (Albania), Bibliothēkē tēs Metropoleōs: 1143

Berlin, Staatliche Museen Berlin–Dahlem: 057, 0160, 0171, 0189, sa(2)

Berlin, Staatsbibliothek der Stiftung Preussischer Kulturbesitz: it(11)

Birmingham, Selly Oak College: 713

Boston, Leland C. Wyman: 0220

Brescia, Biblioteca Civica Queriniana: it(10)

Cambridge (GB), Trinity College: F.010, G.011, H.013

Cambridge (GB), University Library: D.05, *l*1276, *l*1354
                              (British and Foreign Bible Society): $ac^2(1)$

Dresden, Sächsische Landesbibliothek: G.012

Dublin, A. Chester Beatty Library: P^{45}, P^{46}, P^{47}, sa(6), (7)

Dublin, Trinity College: Z.035, 61

Escorial, Biblioteca del Real Monasterio S. Lorenzo: 230

Florence, Biblioteca Mediceo-Laurenziana: P^{48}, 0171, vg^A

Freiburg-im-Breisgau, Universitätsbibliotek: *l*1602

Fulda, Landesbibliothek: vg^F

Geneva, Cologny, Bibliothèque Bodmer: P^{66}, P^{72}, P^{73}, P^{74}, P^{75}, sa(3), bo(1)

Geneva, Bibliothèque Publique et Universitaire: 326

Glasgow, University Library: P^{22}

Grottaferrata, Biblioteca della Badia: 826, 828

Hamburg, Staats- und Universitätsbibliothek: H.013

Harburg (Schloss), Fürstlich Öttingen-Wallerstein'sche Bibliothek: 1^r

Jackson (Miss.), University of Mississippi: sa(1)

Jerusalem, Katholicon Orthodoxon Patriarcheion: 1890, 1891

Kiev, Centralnaja Naučnaja Biblioteka Akademii: H.015

Leicester, Town Museum: 69

Leningrad, Gosudarstvennaja Publičnaja Biblioteka im. M. E. Saltykova-Ščedrina: H.015, N.022, Γ.036, Π.041, 080, 0136, 461, 565, 566, 1891, 2147, D^{abs}, it(66), geo(3), (5), sl(1)

Lerma (Alessandria, Italy), Biblioteca A. Spinola: N.022

Lesbos, Monē tou Leimōnos: 1758

London, British Library: P^5, P^{18}, S.01, A.02, G.011, N.022, R.027, 070, 81, 104, 700, 892, 1765, vg^z

London, Lambeth Palace: 206 (1518)

Bibliography

Manchester, John Rylands Library: P^{52}, 1278

Maywood (Ill.), Theological Seminary of the Evangelical Lutheran Church: 1424

Mestia (Svaneti), Ist'oriul-etnograpiul Muzeumi: geo(2)

Milan, Biblioteca Ambrosiana: 346, 614, vg^M

Milan, Istituto di Papirologia della Università degli Studi: mae(3)

Moscow, Gosudarstvennaja Biblioteka SSSR im. V. I. Lenina: H.015, sl(2)

Moscow, Gosudarstvennyj Istoričeskij Musej: H.015, K.018, V.031

Moscow, Naučnaja Biblioteka im. A.M. Gor'kogo Moskovskogo Universiteta: 2138

Munich, Universitätsbibliothek: X.033

Naples, Biblioteca Nazionale: *l*46

New Haven (Conn.), Yale University, Beinecke Rare Book and Manuscript Library: P^{50}, 0212

New York, Metropolitan Museum of Art: P^{44}, 0162

New York, Pierpont Morgan Library, P^{12}, N.022, T.029, *l*1602, sa(8), (9), (10), (11), (12), mae(2)

Oxford, Ashmolean Museum: P^{78}

Oxford, Bodleian Library: E.08, Γ.036, Λ.039, 118, 383, 522

Oxford, Clarendon Press: 070

Oxford, Magdalen College: P^{64}, 57

Oxford, New College: 36^a

Paris, Bibliothèque Nationale, Département des Manuscrits: P^4, C.04, D.06, H.015, K.017, L.019, M.021, O.023, T.029, 070, 4e, 6, 7e, 13, 28, 33, 36e, 119, 120, 262, 273, 579, 603, 1292, 2298, it(6), (8), (55), Eth (4), (5), (6), (7)

Patmos, Monē tou Hagiou Iōannou tou Theologou: N.022, 1175

Princeton (N.J.), H. Scheide Collection: mae(1)

Princeton (N.J.), University Library: 1799

Rossano, Curia arcivescovile, Tesoro della Cattedrale: Σ.042

Salonica (Thessalonica), Archaiologikon Mouseion: N.022

St Gallen, Stiftsbibliothek: Δ.037

Sinai (Mt), Monē tēs Hagias Aikaterinēs: 0136, 1241, 1243, 2492, 2495, geo(22), (23), arab(1), (2)

Stockholm, Kungliche Biblioteket: it(51)

Strasbourg, Bibliothèque Nationale Universitaire: P^6

Strasbourg, Grand Séminaire: 431

Tbilisi, K.S. Kekelidzis Saxelobis Xelnac'erta Instituti: Θ.038, Geo(1), (3), (6), (7), (24)

Tbilisi, K. Marksis Saxelobis Sažaro Biblioteka: geo(50)

Tirana, National Archives: Φ.043

Trent, Museo Nazionale: it(2)

Turin, Biblioteca Nazionale: H.015, it(1)

Uppsala, Universitetsbibliotek: H.015, 899, 1852, goth(1)
Utrecht, Bibliotheek Rijksuniversiteits: F.09
Vatican City, Biblioteca Angelica: 39
Vatican City, Biblioteca Apostolica Vaticana: B.03, N.022, S.028, T.029, 046, 130, 131, 174, 630, 872, *l*1353, *l*547
Venice, Biblioteca Nazionale Marciana: U.030, 209
Vercelli, Biblioteca Capitolare: it(3)
Verona, Biblioteca Capitolare: *l*1347, it(4)
Vienna, Österreichische Nationalbibliothek: P³, P⁴¹, P⁴⁵, N.022, 059, 124
Washington, Smithsonian Institute, Freer Gallery of Art: I.016, W.032
Wolfenbüttel, Herzog-August Bibliothek: P.024, Q.026, 429

III THE PRINTED EDITIONS

	Date	*Edition*
XVI	*Greek text*	
	1514–	Complutensian Polyglot, Ximenes of Cisneros (published 1520), Alcalá
	1516–	Erasmus (1519², 1522³, 1527⁴, 1535⁵), Basle
	1534	S. de Colines, Paris
	1546	R. Estienne (1542², 1550³ 'Regia'), Paris; (1551⁴), Geneva
	1565–	Th. de Bèze (1604⁹), Geneva
	1571	Royal Polyglot, Plantin (1568–72), Antwerp
	Latin version	
	1514–	= Complutensian Polyglot (vg)
	1551	= Estienne's 4th edition (vg)
	1571	= Antwerp Polyglot (vg)
	1590–	Clementine Vulgate, Sixtus V and Clement VIII (1592², 1598³ vg^cl), Rome
	Syriac version	
	1555	J. A. Widmanstetter, Vienna (sy^p)
	1569	I. Tremelius, Geneva (sy^p)
	1571	= Antwerp Polyglot (sy^p)
	Ethiopic version	
	1548–9	Petrus Ethypos, Rome (eth^ro)
	Arabic version	
	1590	(Gospels), G. B. Raimundi, Rome

XVII   *Greek text*

1624–	B. and A. Elzevir (1633², 'textus receptus') Leiden
1630–3	Polyglot, Le Jay (1628–45, complete Bible), Paris
1657	Polyglot, B. Walton (1654–7, Prolegomena and collations), London
1658	Etienne de Courcelles, Amsterdam
1675	J. Fell, Oxford

Latin and Syriac versions

1630–3	= Paris Polyglot (vg)
1657	= London Polyglot (vg)

Arabic version

1616	T. Erpenius, Leiden
1630–3	= Paris Polyglot
1657	= London Polyglot

Ethiopic and Persian versions

1657	= London Polyglot

Armenian version

1666	A. D. Oskan, Amsterdam

XVIII   *Greek text*

1707	Critical edition (Prolegomena), J. Mill, Oxford
1707	*Evangeliorum harmonia graeco-latina* (Prolegomena), N. Toinard, Paris
1709	E. Wells, Oxford
1711	G. von Mästricht (rules of internal criticism)
1729	W. Mace, London
1734	J. A. Bengel (classification of manuscripts), Tübingen
1751–2	Critical edition (Prolegomena), J. J. Wettstein, Amsterdam (repr. Graz, 1962)
1775–	Critical editions, J. J. Griesbach (1777¹), Halle; (1796–1806²), Halle–London; (1803–7³, Introduction), Leipzig
1776	E. Harwood, London
1782–8	C. F. Matthaei (10 vols.)

Latin version

1743–	Critical edition (3 vols.), P. Sabatier, Rheims; (1751²), Paris (repr. Munich, 1976) (it)

Syriac version

1778–1803 Critical edition (4 vols.), J. White (Gospels, 1778; Acts and Epistles, 1779–1803), Oxford (sy^h)

Coptic version

1716   D. Wilkins, Oxford (bo)

Armenian version

1789   J. Zohrab, Venice

Georgian version

1709   Edition of the Gospels, Tbilisi

1742–3   Moscow Bible

XIX *Greek text*

1830–36   J. M. Scholz, Leipzig

1831–   Critical editions, K. Lachmann (1842–50, Prolegomena), Berlin

1841–   *Editio octava critica maior*, C. Tischendorf (vols. I and II, 1869–72; and vol. III, Prolegomena by C. R. Gregory, 1884[1]–1894[2]), Leipzig

1857–9   S. P. Tregelles, London,

1872   *Bibliotheca Novi Testamenti Graece*, E. Reuss, Brunswick

1881   *The New Testament in the original Greek* (2 vols.), B. F. Westcott–F. J. A. Hort, London

1886   *The resultant Greek Testament*, R. F. Weymouth, London

1892–   *Synopsis*, A. Huck (1936[9] + H. Lietzmann–H. G. Opitz; 1981[13] + H. Greeven), Tübingen

1894–1900 *Das Neue Testament. Textkritische Untersuchungen und Texterstellung*, B. Weiss, Leipzig

1895–1902 (Acts, Luke, John) F. Blass, Leipzig

1897   F. Schjøtt

1898   J. M. S. Baljon

1898–   *Novum Testamentum Graece*, popular edition, Eb. Nestle (1927[10] + Er. Nestle; 1963[25] + K. Aland; 1979[26] new text (= UBS), amplified apparatus), Stuttgart

Latin version

1889–1954 *Novum Testamentum ... secundum editionem sancti Hieronymi* (3 vols.), J. Wordsworth–H. I. White, Oxford (vg^{WW})

Bibliography

Coptic version

1898–1905   *The Coptic versions of the New Testament in the Northern dialect* (4 vols.), G. Horner, Oxford (repr. Osnabrück, 1969) (bo)

Ethiopic version

1826   T. Pell Platt, London (eth^{PP})

XX   *Greek text*

1904–   Popular edition, British and Foreign Bible Society, (1958 edn., G. D. Kilpatrick), London

1910–   A. Souter (1947^2), Oxford

1913   *Die Schriften des Neuen Testaments in ihrer ältesten erreichbaren Textgestalt*, H. von Soden (I/1–4, 1902–10, Berlin; II, 1913, Göttingen)

1916   (Acts) Th. Zahn

1920   H. J. Vogels, Düsseldorf (1955^4, Freiburg-im-Breisgau)

1926   (Acts) 'The text of Acts', J. H. Ropes (vol. III in *The beginnings of Christianity*, ed. F. J. Foakes Jackson–K. Lake), London

1933   (Acts) *The Acts of the Apostles*, A. C. Clark, Oxford.

1933   A. Merk (1964^9), Rome

1935–40   (Matthew, Mark) S. C. E. Legg, Oxford

1943–   J. M. Bover (1968^5), Madrid

1963–   *Synopsis quattuor evangeliorum*, K. Aland (1985^{13}), Stuttgart

1966–   *The Greek New Testament*, United Bible Societies, ed. K. Aland – M. Black – C. M. Martini – B. M. Metzger – A. Wikgren (= UBS, 1968^2, 1975^3, 1983^{3a}), Stuttgart

1984–7   (Luke) *The New Testament in Greek: The Gospel according to St. Luke*, International Greek New Testament Project (IGNTP), (vol. I, chs. 1–12, 1984; vol. II, chs. 13–24, 1987), Oxford

1985   (Acts) *Le Texte occidental des Actes des Apôtres, reconstitution et réhabilitation*, M. E. Boismard–A. Lamouille, Paris

Latin version

1938–   (Gospels) *Itala: das Neue Testament in altlateinischer Überlieferung*, A. Jülicher, vol. I: Matthew (1972^2), vol. II: Mark (1970²), vol. III: Luke (1976²), vol. IV: John (1963²)

1956 –   *Vetus Latina, die Reste der altlateinischen Bibel*, vol. XXIV/ 1: Ephesians (H. J. Frede, 5 fasc., 1962 – 4); vol. XXIV/2: Philippians, Colossians (H. J. Frede, 7 fasc., 1966 – 71); vol. XXV/1: 1, 2 Thessalonians, 1, 2 Timothy (H. J. Frede, 11 fasc., 1975 – 82); vol. XXV/2: Titus, Philemon, Hebrews (H. J. Frede, 6 fasc. published, 1983 – 9); vol. XXVI/1: Catholic Epistles (W. Thiele, 7 fasc., 1956 – 9), Freiburg-im-Breisgau (it)

1969 –   *Bibla sacra iuxta Vulgatam versionem*, R. Weber – B. Fischer – J. Gribomont – H. F. D. Sparks – W. Thiele (1975², 1983³), Stuttgart (vg^st)

1989   *Bibla sacra iuxta Vulgatam versionem*, Monachi Pontificale Abbatiae sancti Hieronymi, Rome (vg^r)

Syriac version

1901   (Gospels) E. Pusey – G. H. Gwilliam, Oxford (sy^p)
1904   (Gospels) F. C. Burkitt, 2 vols., Cambridge (sy^c)
1905 – 20   British and Foreign Bible Society (2 vols.), London
1910   (Gospels) A. Smith Lewis, London
1929 – 70   (Gospels) D. Plooij – C. A. Phillips – A. H. A. Bakker (8 fasc.), Amsterdam (Diat^l)
1978   (Revelation) A. Vööbus (*CSCO* 400), Louvain

Coptic version

1911 – 24   *The Coptic versions of the New Testament in the Southern dialect* (7 vols.), G. Horner, Oxford (repr. Osnabrück, 1969) (sa)

Georgian version

1929 – 55   (Gospels) R. P. Blake – M. Brière (*PO* 20/3: Mark; 24/1: Matthew; 26/4: John; 27/3: Luke), Paris
1945 – 56   *Monuments of the Old Georgian language*, vol. II: Gospels (A. Šanidze, 1945); vol. VII: Acts (I. Abuladze, 1950); vol. IX: Catholic Epistles (K. I. Lort'k'ipanidze, 1956), Tbilisi
1955   *L'Ancienne Version géorgienne des Actes des Apôtres d'après deux manuscrits du Sinaï*, G. Garitte, Louvain

Ethiopic version

1920 – 6   F. de Bassano (1934²), Asmara

Bibliography

1989 *Novum Testamentum æthiopice: The synoptic Gospels*, vol. I, *General introduction*; vol. II, *Edition of the Gospel of Mark*, R. Zuurmond, Stuttgart

Slavonic version
1927–36 *Kritické studie staroslovanského textu biblického* (6 vols.), J. Vajs, Prague
1948 (Acts) F. Pechuska, Prague

Nubian version
1982 *Griffith's Old Nubian Lectionary*, *Studia et textus* 8, G. M. Browne, Rome–Barcelona
1988 'Old Nubian texts from Qasr'Tbri'm', *Egypt Exploration Society* 1, G. M. Browne–J. M. Plumley

IV CRITICAL EDITIONS OF PATRISTIC WRITINGS
(See also List of abbreviations, pp. 13–14)

Die apostolischen Väter, ed. F. X. Funk–K. Bihlmeyer, 2nd edn., Tübingen, 1956
Corpus apologetarum christianorum (9 vols.: I–V, Justin, 3rd edn. 1876–81; VI–IX, 1851–72), ed. I.C. Th. Otto, Jena
Sancti Irenaei ... Adversus haereses, ed. W. W. Harvey, Cambridge, 1857

(Catenae)
K. Staab, *Paulus-Kommentare aus der griechischen Kirche aus Katenenhandschriften*, Münster, 1933
J. Reuss, *Matthäus-, Markus- und Johannes-katenen ...* (Münster, 1941); *Matthäus-Kommentare aus der griechischen Kirche aus Katenenhandschriften* (*TU* 61, Berlin, 1957); *Johannes-Kommentare ...* (*TU* 89, Berlin, 1966); *Lukas-Kommentare ...* (*TU* 130, Berlin, 1984)
(Pelagius) *TextS*, 9(1–2), ed. A. Souter, Cambridge, 1922–6
(Tyconius) *TextS*, 3(1), ed. F. C. Burkitt, Cambridge, 1894
(Ephraem) *St Ephraim's quotations from the Gospels* (*TextS*, 7(1), ed. F. C. Burkitt, Cambridge, 1901
An eulogy of James, the brother of the Lord (*Studies and Text* 44), ed. J. Noret, Toronto, 1978

Section V

Date

Greek manuscripts

1894   C. R. Gregory, *Prolegomena*, in *Novum Testamentum Graece* (Tischendorf 1841 – (III)), vol. III

1900 – 9   C. R. Gregory, *Textkritik des Neuen Testamentes*, vols. I and III, Leipzig (supplements: *Zur Liste der neutestamentlichen Handschriften*, vols. I – IV (E. von Dobschütz, 1924 – 33) and V – VI (K. Aland, 1954 – 7), *ZNW*)

1902   H. von Soden, *Die Schriften des Neuen Testaments*, I: *Untersuchungen*, vol. I, Berlin

1908   C. R. Gregory, *Die griechischen Handschriften des Neuen Testaments, Versuche und Entwürfe*, vol. II, Leipzig

1963   K. Aland, *Kurzgefasste Liste der griechischen Handschriften des Neuen Testaments*, vol. I: *Gesamtübersicht* (*Arbeiten zur Neutestamentlichen Textforschung* 1), Berlin – New York (supplements: *Id.*, *Materialen zur Neutestamentlichen Handschriften*, vol. I (*Arbeiten zur Neutestamentlichen Textforschung* 3), 1969, pp. 22 – 37; and *Bericht der Stiftung zur Förderung der Neutestamentlichen Textforschung*, Münster, 1972, 1974, 1977, 1982, 1985, 1988)

1966   K. Treu, *Die griechischen Handschriften des Neuen Testaments in der UdSSR*, Berlin

1969   J. Noret, 'Manuscrits grecs du Nouveau Testament', *Anal. Boll.* 87, pp. 460 – 8

1976   K. Aland, *Repertorium der griechischen christlichen Papyri*, vol. I: *Biblische Papyri* (*Patristische Texte und Studien* 18), Berlin – New York

1976   J. van Haelst, *Catalogue des papyrus littéraires juifs et chrétiens* (*Papyrologie* 1), Paris

Manuscripts of the versions

1898 – 1924 G. Horner, in *The Coptic versions of the New Testament*: vols. I and III (bo); vols. III, V, VI, VII (sa)

1902 – 9   C. R. Gregory, *Textkritik des Neuen Testamentes*, vols. II and III, Leipzig

1919 – 33   A. Vaschalde, 'Ce qui a été publié des versions coptes de la Bible', *RB* 28 (1919) – 31 (1922) and *Le Muséon* 43 (1930) – 46 (1933), (10 articles). (Supplement: W. C. Till, 'Coptic Biblical texts pubished after Vaschalde's lists', *BRJL* 42 (1959 – 60), pp. 220 – 40

1944   G. Graf, in *Geschichte der christlichen arabischen Literatur*, vol. I (*Studi e Testi* 118), Vatican City, pp. 85 – 195

Bibliography

1959   E. F. Rhodes, *An annotated list of Armenian New Testament manuscripts*, Tokyo

1979   J. D. Thomas, 'A list of manuscripts containing the Harclean Syriac version of the New Testament', *TRNE* 2(2), pp. 26–32

1986–9   F. J. Schmitz–G. Mink, *Liste der koptischen Handschriften des Neuen Testaments*, I: *Die sahidischen Handschriften der Evangelien* (2 vols.), Berlin–New York

1987   A. Boud'hors, *Catalogue des fragments coptes. Bibliothèque Nationale, Département des Manuscrits*, vol. I: *Fragments bibliques nouvellement identifiés*, Paris

1988   B. Outtier, 'Essais de repertoire des manuscrits des vieilles versions géorgiennes du Nouveau Testament', *LOAPL* 1, pp. 173–9

forthcoming   A. Desreumaux, *Répertoire des bibliothèques contenant des manuscrits syriaques*, Paris

Patristic Quotations

1975–   *Biblia patristica, index des citations et allusions bibliques dans la littérature patristique*, ed. Centre d'analyse et documentation patristique (Strasbourg), Paris (vol. I: *Des origines à Clément d'Alexandrie et Tertullien*; vol. II (1977): *Le IIIe siècle, Origène excepté*; vol. III (1980): *Origène*; vol. IV (1980): *Eusèbe, Cyrille, Epiphane*)

VI EDITIONS AND COLLATIONS OF THE PRINCIPAL MANUSCRIPTS

Greek manuscripts

$P^{45.46.47}$ F. G. Kenyon, *The Chester Beatty Biblical Papyri*, vols. I–III (illustrations in separate vols.), London, 1933–7

P^{66} V. Martin, *Papyrus Bodmer II, Jean 1–14*, suppl. *Jean 14–21*, Geneva, 1956–8; complete edition with facsimile, 1962

P^{72} M. Testuz, *Papyrus Bodmer VII–IX, Jude, 1–2 Pierre, Psaume 33(34)*, Geneva, 1959

P^{74} R. Kasser, *Papyrus Bodmer XVII, Actes, Jacques, Pierre, Jean et Jude*, Geneva, 1961

P^{75} V. Martin–R. Kasser, *Papyrus Bodmer XIV–XV, Luc (3–24) et Jean (1–15)*, Geneva, 1961

S.01   C. Tischendorf, *Novum Testamentum Sinaïticum*, Leipzig, 1863
    K. Lake, facsimile edition, Oxford, 1911

A.02   F. G. Kenyon, facsimile edition, London, 1909

B.03   Vatican library, facsimile edition, Milan, 1904
    Vatican library, facsimile edition (Introduction by C. M. Martini), Vatican City, 1968

C.04	C. Tischendorf, *Codex Ephraemi Syri Rescriptus*, Leipzig, 1843 – 5
D.05	F. H. Scrivener, *Bezae Codex Cantabrigiensis*, Cambridge, 1864 (repr. Pittsburgh, 1978) Facsimile edition, Cambridge, 1899
D.06	C. Tischendorf, *Codex Claromontanus*, Leipzig, 1852
E.07	R. Champlin, *Fam. E and its allies in Matthew* (*S & D* 28), Salt Lake City, 1966 J. Geerlings, *in Mark* (*S & D* 31), *in Luke* (*S & D* 35), Salt Lake City, 1968
E.08	C. Tischendorf, *Codex Laudianus*, Leipzig, 1870
F.010	F. H. Scrivener, *An exact transcript of the Codex Augiensis*, Cambridge, 1859 (collations of many mins. inc. 69, 206, 1518)
G.012	Facsimile edition (Introduction by A. Reichardt), Leipzig, 1909
H.015	M. H. Omont, *Notice sur un très ancien manuscrit grec en onciales des Epîtres de Paul, conservé à la Bibliothèque Nationale*, Paris, 1889
K.018, L.020, P.025	See min. 2344
W.032	H. A. Sanders, facsimile edition, Ann Arbor (Mich.), 1912 H. A. Sanders, *The New Testament manuscripts in the Freer Gallery*, vol. I: *The Washington Manuscript of the Four Gospels*, New York, 1912
Θ.038	G. Beerman – C. R. Gregory, *Die Koridethi Evangelien*, Leipzig, 1913
Π.041	S. Lake, *Family Π and the Codex Alexandrinus* (*S & D* 5), Salt Lake City, 1936 (collations of K.018, 72, 178, 265, 489, 1079, 1219, 1346, 1478, 1500, 1816, in particular)
Ω.045	See min. 1739
0212	C. H. Kraeling, *A Greek fragment of Tatian's Diatessaron from Dura* (*S & D* 3), London, 1935
f¹	K. Lake, *Codex 1 of the Gospels and its allies* (*TextS* 7(3)), Cambridge – London, 1902
f¹³	K. Lake, *Family 13, the Ferrar Group* (*S & D* 11 (Mark)), London, 1941 J. Geerlings, *S & D* 19 (Matthew), vol. 20 (Luke), vol. 21 (John), Salt Lake City, 1961 – 2
574	E. C. Colwell, *The Four Gospels of Karahissar*, Chicago, 1936
579	A. Schmidtke, *Die Evangelien eines alten Unzialcodex nach einer Abschrift* ... Leipzig, 1903
700	H. C. Hoskier, *Collation of Cod. Ev. 604*, London, 1890
1739	K. Lake – S. New, *Six collations of New Testament manuscripts*, Cambridge (Mass.), 1932 (mins. 1241 and 1739; also Ω.045, 543, 1342, 1175)

Bibliography

2138   A. Valentine-Richards, *The text of Acts in Cod. 614 and its allies*, Cambridge, 1934 (mins. 614, 383, 431, 1518, 876)

     K. W. Clark, *Eight American Praxapostoloi*, Chicago, 1941 (mins. 876, 1799, 2412; also 223, 1022, 1960, 2401, 2423)

2344   M. Davies, *The text of the Pauline Epistles in MS. 2344 (S & D* 38), Salt Lake City, 1968 (collations of K.018, L.020, P.025, 69, 330, 436, 462, 2344, 2400)

*l*547   J. Geerlings, *The Ferrar Lectionary (S & D* 18), Salt Lake City, 1959

Latin manuscripts

it(1,k) J. Wordsworth – W. Sanday – H. J. White, *Old Latin Biblical Texts* 2, Oxford, 1886

     C. Cipolla, facsimile edition, Turin, 1913

it(2,e) C. Tischendorf, *Evangelium Palatinum*, Leipzig, 1847

it(3,a) A. Gasquet, *Collectanea biblica latina*, vol. III, Rome, 1914

it(4,b) E. S. Buchanan, *Old Latin Biblical Texts* 6, Oxford, 1911

it(6,c) H. J. Vogels, *Evangelium Colbertinum*, Bonn, 1953

it(8,ff^2) E. S. Buchanan, *Old Latin Biblical Texts* 5, Oxford, 1907

it(11,l) H. J. Vogels, *Collectanea biblica latina*, vol. II, Rome, 1913

it(51,gig) J. Belsheim, *Die Apostelgeschichte und die Offenbarung Joh ... aus dem 'Gigas Librorum'* ..., Christiania (Oslo), 1879

it(55,h) E. S. Buchanan, *Old Latin Biblical Texts* 5, Oxford, 1907

it(66,ff) J. Wordsworth, 'The Corbey St. James (ff)', *Studia Biblica* 1, Oxford, 1885

vg^F E. Ranke, *Codex Fuldensis*, Marburg – Leipzig, 1868

vg^S C. H. Turner, *Oldest manuscript of the Vulgate Gospels*, Oxford, 1931 (suppl.: P. Lehman, in *Zentralblatt für Bibliothekwesen* 1 (1933), pp. 50 – 76; A. Dold, *ibid.*, pp. 709 – 17 and *Bib* 22 (1941), pp. 105 – 47; B. Bischoff, *Studi e Testi* 121, Vatican City, 1946, pp. 407 – 36 and *Mittelalterliche Studien* 1, Stuttgart, 1966, pp. 101 – 11

Syriac manuscripts (and Diatessaron)

Diat^a P. A. Ciasca, *Tatiani evangeliorum harmoniae arabice*, Rome, 1888

     A. S. Marmardjii, *Diatessaron de Tatien, texte arabe* ..., Beirut, 1935

Diat^e L. Leloir, *Saint Ephrem, commentaire de l'Evangile concordant, texte syriaque* (MS Chester Beatty 709), Dublin, 1963

Diat^f E. Ranke, see above (Latin manuscripts: vg^F)

Diat^l D. Plooij *et al.*, see above (1929 – 70 (III))

Diat^p G. Messina, *Diatessaron persiano*, Rome, 1951

Diat^t V. Todesco – A. Vaccari – M. Vatasso, *Il Diatessaron in volgare italiano*, Vatican City, 1938, pp. 175 – 368

Diat^v *Ibid.*, pp. 1 – 171

sy^c   F. C. Burkitt, see above 1904 (III))

sy^s   A. Hjelt, facsimile edition, Helsingfors, 1930

           A. Smith Lewis, see above (1910 (III))

sy^pal   A. Smith Lewis, *A Palestinian Syriac lectionary*, London, 1897 (suppl. Cambridge, 1907)

           A. Smith Lewis, *The Palestinian Syriac lectionary*, London, 1899

           A. Smith Lewis, *Codex Climaci rescriptus*, Cambridge, 1909

           H. Duensing, *Christlich-palästinisch-aramäische Texte und Fragmente*, Göttingen, 1906

Coptic manuscripts

sa(2)   F. Hintze–H. M. Schenke, *Die Berliner Handschrift der sahidischen Apostelgeschichte* (*TU* 109), Berlin, 1970

sa(3)   R. Kasser, *Papyrus Bodmer XIX, Matthieu 14–28 et Romains 1*, Geneva, 1962

sa(4)   H. Quecke, *Das Lukasevangelium sahidisch* (P Palau 181), Barcelona, 1977

           H. Quecke, *Das Markusevangelium sahidisch* (P Palau 182), Barcelona, 1972

sa(5)   H. Quecke, *Das Johannesevangelium sahidisch* (P Palau 183), Barcelona, 1984

sa(6–7)   H. Thompson, *The Coptic version of the Acts of the Apostles and the Pauline Epistles in the Sahidic dialect*, Cambridge, 1932

bo(1)   R. Kasser, *Papyrus Bodmer III, Jean et Genèse 1–4* (*CSCO* 177–8), Louvain, 1958

ac(1)   F. Rösch, *Bruchstücke des ersten Clemensbriefes*, Strasbourg, 1910

ac^2(1)   H. Thompson, *The Gospel of St John, according to the earliest Coptic manuscript*, London, 1924

fay(1)   E. M. Husselman, *The Gospel of John in Fayumic Coptic*, Ann Arbor, 1962

mae(1)   H. M. Schenke, *Das Matthäusevangelium in mittelägyptischen ... (cod. Scheide)* (*TU* 127), Berlin, 1981

mae(2)   (unpublished, but collations in:)

           Th. C. Petersen, 'An early Coptic manuscript of Acts', *CBQ* 26 (1964), pp. 225–41

           E. J. Epp, 'Coptic manuscript G^67 and the role of Codex Bezae as a Western witness in Acts', *JBL* 85 (1966), pp. 197–212

mae(3)   T. Orlandi, *Lettere di San Paolo in copto-ossirinchita ...*, Milan, 1974

Gothic manuscripts

goth(1)   *Codex Argenteus Upsaliensis*, facsimile edition, Uppsala, 1927

goth(2–5)   J. de Vries, *Wulfilae codices Ambrosiani*, Turin–Florence, 1936

Georgian manuscripts

geo(1)   L. Kazaia, facsimile edition, Tbilisi, 1984
geo(2)   A. Khakhanov–E. Takaischvili, facsimile edition, Moscow, 1916
geo(3)   I. Imnaisvili, Tbilisi, 1949–50
geo(4–5)   R. P. Blake–M. Brière, see above (1929–55 (III))
geo(6)   A. Šanidze, Tbilisi, 1945
geo(22–23) G. Garitte, see above (1955 (III))

Arabic manuscripts

0136–0137 A. Smith Lewis, *Catalogue of the Syriac manuscripts in the Convent of St Catherine on Mount Sinai* (*Studia Sinaitica* 1), London, 1894, pp. 105f. (Arabic text of Gr. – Arab. uncial)
ar(2)   H. Staal, *An Arabic manuscript of the Pauline Epistles* (*S & D* 40), Salt Lake City, 1969

Slavonic manuscripts

sl(1)   V. Jagić, *Quattuor evangeliorum codex glagoliticus olim Zographensis nunc Petropolitanus*, Berlin, 1879 (repr. 1954) (corrections made by L. Moszynski in B. M. Metzger 1977, p. 405, n. 4)
sl(2)   V. Jagić, *Quattuor evangeliorum versionis paleoslovenicae codex Marianus glagoliticus*, Berlin, 1883, (repr. 1960)

VII WORKS CONCERNING MANUSCRIPTS AND NEW TESTAMENT TEXTUAL CRITICISM

Achtemeier P. J. 1990 '*Omne verbum sonat*: the New Testament and the oral environment of late Western antiquity', *JBL* 109, pp. 3–27
Aland B. 1985 *Die neuen neutestamentlichen Handschriften von Sinai (Bericht der Stiftung zur Förderung der neutestamentlichen Textforschung)*, Münster, pp. 76–89
    1986 *Das Neue Testament in syrischer Überlieferung: I Die grossen katholischen Briefe* (*ANTF* 7), Berlin–New York
    1989 'Die Rezeption des neutestamentlichen Textes in den ersten Jahrhunderten', in Sevrin 1989 (ed.), pp. 1–38
Aland K. 1967 *Studien zur Überlieferung des Neuen Testaments und seines Textes*, Berlin
    1969 (ed.) *Materialen zur neutestamentlichen Handschriftenkunde*, Berlin
    1969 'Novi Testamenti graeci editio maior critica', *NTS* 16, pp. 163–77
    1970 'Bemerkungen zu den gegenwärtigen Möglichkeiten textkritischer Arbeit aus Anlass einer Untersuchung zum Cäsarea-Text der katholischen Briefe', *NTS* 17, pp. 1–9
    1972 (ed.) *Die alten Übersetzungen des Neuen Testaments, die Kirchenväterzitate und Lektionare* (*ANTF* 5), Berlin
    1987 *Text und Textwert der griechischen Handschriften des Neuen Testaments, I:*

Die katholischen Briefe, Bd. 1. *Das Material (ANTF* 9); Bd. 2. *Die Auswertung* (*ANTF* 10); Bd. 3. *Die Einzelhandschriften (ANTF* 11), Berlin

Aland K. – Aland B. 1982 *Der Text des Neuen Testaments*, Stuttgart (1989²); (Eng. trans. by E. F. Rhodes, Grand Rapids, 1989²)

Alexander L. 1990 'The living voice: scepticism towards the written word in early Christian and in Graeco-Roman texts', in Clines *et al.* (eds.), pp. 221–47

Amphoux C.-B. 1978 'Les Manuscrits grecs de Jacques d'après une collation de 25 lieux variants', *RHT* 8, pp. 247–76

1981a 'La Parenté textuelle de sy^h et du gr. 2128 dans Jacques', *Bib* 62, pp. 259–71

1981b 'Le Texte des épîtres catholiques. Essais de classement des états de texte, préparatoires à une histoire du texte de ces épîtres', *Thesis*, Paris-Sorbonne

1981c 'Quelques témoins grecs des formes textuelles les plus anciennes de l'Epître de Jacques: le groupe 2138 (ou 614)', *NTS* 28, pp. 91–115

1981/2 'Note sur le classement des manuscrits grecs de 1 Jean', *RHPR*, pp. 125–35

1987 'La Révision Marcionite du Notre Père de Luc (11, 2–4) et sa place dans l'histoire du texte', in Gryson–Bogaert (eds.), pp. 105–21

1988a 'Parabole Matthéenne du fils prodigue: la version du Codex Bezae (D.05 du Nouveau Testament)', *LOAPL* 1, pp. 167–71

1988b 'Un indice de variation pour le classement des états d'un texte', *RHT* 18, pp. 279–99

1990 'Les Contextes de la parabole des deux fils: Matthieu 21, 28–32', *LOAPL* 3, pp. 215–48.

(forthcoming) 'Le Chapitre 5 de Luc: les variantes de l'histoire du texte au second siècle'

Amphoux C.-B. – Outtier B. 1984 'Les Leçons des versions géorgiennes de Jacques', *Bib* 65, pp. 365–76

Anderson H. – Barclay W. 1965 (eds.) *The New Testament in historical and contemporary perspective. Essays in memory of G. H. C. Macgregor*, Oxford

Arbache S. 1975 'Le Tétraévangile Sinaï arabe', Dissertation, Louvain

Atiya A. S. 1967 'Codex Arabicus (Sinai Arabic MS. No. 514)', in Lehmann-Haupt (ed.), pp. 25–85

Awoniyi J. P. 1981 'The classification of the Greek manuscripts of the Epistle of James', Dissertation, Andrews University (Mich.)

Baarda T. 1975 'The Gospel quotations of Aphrahat the Persian Sage: I: Aphrahat's text of the Fourth Gospel' (2 vols.), Akademisch Proefschrift, Free University, Amsterdam

1989 '"A staff only, not a stick" – Disharmony of the Gospels and the Harmony of Tatian', in Sevrin 1989 (ed.), pp. 311–33

Baarda T. – Hilhorst A. – Luttikhuizen G. P. – van der Woude A. S. 1988 (eds.) *Text and testimony. Essays in honour of A. F. J. Klijn*, Kampen

Bibliography

Bar-Asher M. 1977 'Palestinian Syriac studies. Source-texts, traditions and grammatical problems', Thesis (in Hebrew), Jerusalem

Baron S. W. 1956–7 *Histoire d'Israel. Vie sociale et religieuse* vol. I and II, Paris

Barrett C. K. 1979 'Is there a theological tendency in Codex Bezae?', in Best–Wilson (eds.), pp. 15–27

Bataille A. 1955 *Les Papyrus*, vol. II of *Traité d'études byzantines*, Paris

Baumstark A. 1930 'Zum georgischen Evangelientext', *OC* 3/4, pp. 1–14

Bédier J. 1913 *Le Lai de l'ombre*, Préface, Paris

   1928 'La Tradition manuscrite du lai de l'ombre. Réflexions sur l'art d'éditer les anciens textes', *Romania* 54, pp. 161–96, 321–56

   1929 *La Tradition du 'Lai de l'ombre', réflexions sur l'art d'éditer les anciens textes*, Paris

Bengel J. A. 1742 *Gnomon*

Bentley R. 1720 *Proposals for printing a critical edition of the New Testament*, reproduced in Gregory 1894 (V), pp. 231–40

Berger S. 1879 *La Bible au XVIᵉ siècle*, Paris

   1893 *Histoire de la Vulgate pendant les premiers siècles du Moyen Age*, Nancy/Paris

Best E. –Wilson R. McL. 1979 (eds.) *Text and interpretation: Studies in the New Testament presented to Matthew Black*, London – New York

'Bible' (Articles) 1960 'Orientales de la Bible (Versions)', *DBS* 6, cols. 807–84

   1980 'Bibelübersetzungen', *TRE* 6, pp. 161–216, 228–66

   1987 *La Bible de A à Z*. Vol. VI: *Histoire du texte biblique* (Articles from the *Dictionnaire encyclopédique de la Bible*), Turnhout

Birdsall J. N. 1959 'A Study of MS 1739 of the Pauline Epistles and its relationship to MSS 6, 424, 1908, and M', PhD Thesis, Nottingham

   1969 'A report of the textual complexion of the Gospel of Mark in MS 2533', *Nov T* 11, pp. 233–9

   1970 'The New Testament text', in *The Cambridge history of the Bible*, vol. I: *From the beginnings to Jerome*, P. R. Ackroyd–C. F. Evans (eds.), Cambridge, ch. 11, pp. 308–77

   1971 'Khanmeti fragments of the Synoptic Gospels from MS Vind. Georg. 2', *OC* 55, pp. 62–89

   1983 'Introductory remarks on the Pauline Epistles in Georgian', *SP* 18, pp. 281–91

   1984 'The Euthalian material and its Georgian versions', *OC* 68, pp. 170–95

   1986 'The geographical and cultural origin of the Codex Bezae Cantabrigiensis: a survey of the status quaestionis, mainly from the palaeographical standpoint', in Schrage (ed.), pp. 102–14

   1988 'The Georgian version of the Acts of the Apostles', in Baarda *et al.* (eds.), pp. 39–45

Birdsall J. N. –Thomson R. W. 1963 (eds.) *Biblical and Patristic studies in memory of R. P. Casey*, Freiburg-im-Breisgau

Blanchard A. 1989 *Les Débuts du codex*, Turnhout

Blass F. 1895 *Acta Apostolorum sive Lucae ad Theophilum liber alter. Editio philologica apparatu critico, commentario perpetuo, indice verborum illustrata*, Göttingen

1898 *Philology of the Gospels*, London

Boismard M.E. 1950 'Critique textuelle et citations patristiques', *RB* 57, pp. 388–408

1953 'Problèmes de critique textuelle concernant le 4ᵉ évangile', *RB* 60, pp. 347–71

1957 'Le Papyrus Bodmer II' (= P^{66}), *RB* 64, pp. 363–98

Bonnassieux F.J. 1906 *Les Evangiles synoptiques de Saint Hilaire de Poitiers*, Lyons

Bouvarel-Boud'hors A. 1986 'Fragments coptes–sahidiques du Nouveau Testament à la Bibliothèque Nationale de Paris', International colloquium *Bible et informatique: le texte*, Paris – Geneva, pp. 389–98

1988 'Fragments du Nouveau Testament fayoumiques à la Bibliothèque Nationale', *LOAPL* 1, pp. 95–116

Bowyer W. 1772 *Conjectures on the New Testament collected from various authors*, London

Brecht M. 1980 (ed.) *Text, Wort, Glaube: Studien zur Überlieferung, Interpretation und Autorisierung biblischer Texte. Kurt Aland gewidmet (Arbeiten zur Kirchengeschichte 50)*, Berlin

Carder M. 1969 'A Caesarean text of the Catholic Epistles?', *NTS* 16, pp. 252–70 (for a critique, see Aland 1970)

Cazeaux J. 1983 *La Trame et la chaîne ou les structures littéraires et l'exégèse dans cinq des traités de Philon d'Alexandrie*, Leiden

Chase F.H. 1893 *The Old Syriac element in the text of Codex Bezae*, London

1895 *The Syro-Latin text of the Gospels*, London

Clark A.C. 1914 *The primitive text of the Gospels and Acts*, Oxford

1918 *The descent of manuscripts*, Oxford (repr. 1969)

Clines D.J.A. – Fowl S.E. – Porter S.E. 1990 (eds.) *The Bible in three dimensions: essays in celebration of forty years of Biblical studies in the University of Sheffield (Journal for the Study of the Old Testament, Supplement series 87)*, Sheffield

Collomp P. 1931 *La Critique des textes*, Paris

Colwell E.C. 1952 *What is the best New Testament?*, Chicago

1968 'The International Greek New Testament Project', *JBL* 87, pp. 187–97

1969 *Studies in methodology in textual criticism (New Testament Tools and Studies 9)*, Leiden

Conybeare F.C. 1926 'The Commentary of Ephrem on Acts' (Eng. trans.), in Foakes-Jackson–Lake (eds.), vol. III, pp. 373–453

Corssen P. 1892 *Der Cyprianische Text der Acta Apostolarum*, Berlin

Dain A. 1975 *Les Manuscrits*, Paris (3rd edition)

D'Alès A. 1923 'Vetus romana', *Bib*, pp. 53–90

Daniels B.L. – Suggs M.J. 1967 (eds.), *Studies in the history and text of the New Testament in honor of K. W. Clark*, Salt Lake City

Bibliography

De Bruyne Dom D. 1915 'Etude sur les origines de notre texte latin de S. Paul *RB* 12, pp. 358–92

1921 'Bulletin d'ancienne littérature chrétienne, section B ("Littérature non biblique")', *Revue Bénédictine*

De Labriolle P. 1920 *Histoire de la littérature latine chrétienne*, Paris (1947³)

Delebecque E. 1986 *Les Deux Actes des Apôtres*, (*Collection études bibliques* 6), Paris

Delobel J. 1985 'Luke 6:5 in Codex Bezae: The Man who worked on the Sabbath' in *A cause de l'Evangile: Mélanges offerts à Dom J. Dupont*, pp. 453–77

1989 'The Lord's Prayer in the textual tradition, a critique of recent theories and their view on Marcion's role', in Sevrin (ed.), pp. 293–309

Descamps A. – De Halleux A. 1970 (eds.) *Mélanges bibliques en hommage au R. P. Béda Rigaux*, Gembloux

Desreumaux A. 1979 'Les Matériaux du syro-palestinien', Thesis, Paris

Devreesse R. 1928 'Chaînes exégétiques grecques', *DBS* 1, cols. 1084–1233

1942 'Le Christianisme dans la province d'Arabie', *RB* 51, pp. 110–46

1954 *Introduction à l'étude des manuscrits grecs*, Paris

1955 *Les Manuscrits grecs de l'Italie méridionale*, Vatican City

Duplacy J. 1959 *Où en est la critique textuelle du Nouveau Testament?*, Paris

1962–77 'Bulletins de critique textuelle', 1: *RSR* 50 (1962), pp. 242–63 and 564–98; 51 (1963), pp. 432–62; 2: *RSR* 53 (1965), pp. 257–84; 54 (1966), pp. 426–76; 3: *Bib* 49 (1968), pp. 515–51; 51 (1970), pp. 84–129; 4: *Bib* 52 (1971), pp. 79–113; 53 (1972), pp. 245–78; 5: *Bib* 54 (1973), pp. 79–114; 58 (1977), pp. 259–70 and pp. 542–68

1965 'Histoire des manuscrits et histoire du texte du Nouveau Testament', *NTS* 12, pp. 124–39 (= Duplacy 1987, pp. 39–54)

1969 'Le Texte "occidental" des épîtres catholiques', *NTS* 16, pp. 397–9 (= Duplacy 1987, pp. 119–21)

1970 'Les Lectionnaires et l'édition du Nouveau Testament grec', in Descamps–Halleux (eds.), pp. 509–45 (= Duplacy 1987, pp. 81–117)

1971–4 'L'Inventaire général des citations patristiques de la Bible grecque', *VC* 25, pp. 157–60; 26 pp. 313–18; 27, pp. 316–20; 28, pp. 304–7

1973 'P⁷⁵ et les formes les plus anciennes du texte de Luc', in F. Neirynck (ed.), *L'Evangile de Luc, problèmes littéraires et théologiques: Mélanges Cerfaux*, (*BETL* 32), Gembloux, pp. 111–28; 1989², pp. 21–8 (= Duplacy 1987, pp. 151–68)

1975 'Classification des états d'un texte, mathématiques et informatique: repères historiques et recherches méthodologiques', *RHT* 5, pp. 249–309 (= Duplacy 1987, pp. 193–257)

1979 'La Pratique de l'ordinateur dans la critique des textes', *Préalables philologiques à la classification automatique des états d'un texte*, International CNRS colloquium 579 (March 1978), Paris, pp. 23–33 (= Duplacy 1987, pp. 279–92)

1980 'Les "Regulae Morales" de Basile de Césarée et le texte du Nouveau

Testament en Asie-Mineure au IVe siècle', in Brecht (ed.), pp. 69–83 (= Duplacy 1987, pp. 293–307)

1981 'La Préhistoire du texte en Luc 22, 43–44', in Epp–Fee (eds.), pp. 77–86

1987 *Etudes de critique textuelle du Nouveau Testament, presented by J. Delobel* (*BETL* 78), Leuven

Duplacy J. – Amphoux C.-B. 1980 'A propos de l'histoire du texte de 1 Pierre', *Lectio Divina* 102, pp. 155–73 (= Duplacy 1987, pp. 309–27)

Durand A. 1911 'Le Texte du Nouveau Testament', in *Etudes*, vol. 126, pp. 289–312; 'Théorie actuelle', in vol. 127, pp. 297–328, Paris

Ehrman B. D. 1987a 'Methodological developments in the analysis and classification of New Testament documentary evidence', *Nov T* 29, pp. 22–45

1987b 'The use of group profiles for the classification of New Testament documentary evidence', *JBL* 106, pp. 465–86

Elliott J. K. 1976 (ed.) *Studies in New Testament language and text: essays in honour of George D. Kilpatrick on the occasion of his sixty-fifth birthday* (*Supplements to Novum Testamentum* 44), Leiden

1986 'An examination of the text and apparatus of three recent Greek synopses', *NTS* 32, pp. 557–82

1988 'Why the International Greek New Testament Project is necessary', *RQ* 30, pp. 195–206

1989a *A bibliography of Greek New Testament manuscripts* (*Society for New Testament Studies, Monograph series* 62), Cambridge

1989b 'L'Importance de la critique textuelle pour le problème synoptique', *RB* 96, pp. 56–70

1990 (ed.) *The principles and practice of New Testament textual criticism: collected essays of G. D. Kilpatrick* (*BETL* 96), Leuven

Epp E. J. 1966 *The theological tendency of Codex Bezae Cantabrigiensis in Acts*, Cambridge

1967 'The Claremont Profile Method for grouping New Testament minuscule manuscripts', in Daniels–Suggs (eds.), pp. 27–38

1989 'Textual criticism', in Epp–Macrae (eds.), pp. 75–126

Epp E. J. – Fee G. D. 1981 (eds.) *New Testament textual criticism: its significance for exegesis. Essays in honour of Bruce M. Metzger*, Oxford

Epp E. J. – Macrae G. W. 1989 (eds.) *The New Testament and its modern interpreters*, Pennsylvania–Georgia

Fee G. D. 1968 'Codex Sinaiticus in the Gospel of John: a contribution to methodology in establishing textual relationships', *NTS* 15, pp. 22–44

1971 'The text of John in Origen and Cyril of Alexandria: a contribution to methodology in the recovery and analysis of Patristic citations', *Bib* 52, pp. 357–94

1974 'P^{75}, P^{66} and Origen: the myth of early textual recension in Alexandria', in Longenecker–Tenney (eds.), pp. 19–45

Bibliography

Ferrar W. H. 1877 *A collation of four important manuscripts of the Gospels*, ed. T. K. Abbott, Dublin

Finegan J. 1975 *Encountering New Testament manuscripts*, London

Fischer B. 1963 'Ein neuer Zeuge zum westlichen Text der Apostelgeschichte', in Birdsall–Thomson (eds.), pp. 33–63

1972 'Das Neue Testament in lateinischer Sprache: der gegenwärtige Stand seiner Erforschung und seine Bedeutung für die griechische Textgeschichte', in Aland K. (ed.) 1972, pp. 1–92

1986 *Beiträge zur Geschichte der lateinischen Bibeltexte*, Freiburg-im-Breisgau

1988–9 *Die lateinischen Evangelien bis zum 10. Jahrhundert, I: Varianten zu Matthäus* (1988), *II: Varianten zu Markus* (1989), Freiburg-im-Breisgau

Foakes-Jackson F. J.–Lake K. 1920–33 (eds.) *The beginnings of Christianity*, Pt. I, *The Acts of the Apostles* (5 vols.), London

Follieri H. 1969 *Codices graeci Bibliothecae Vaticanae selecti …, exempla scripturarum* IV, Vatican City

Frede H. J. 1961 *Pelagius, der irische Paulustext, Sedulius Scottus*, Freiburg-im-Breisgau

1964 *Altlateinische Paulus-Handschriften*, Freiburg-im-Breisgau

Friedrichsen G. W. S. 1926 *The Gothic version of the Gospels*, Oxford

1939 *The Gothic version of the Epistles*, Oxford

Froger Dom J. 1968 *La Critique des textes et son automatisation*, Paris

Gardthausen V. 1911–12 *Griechische Paleographie*, 2nd edn., Leipzig

Greenlee J. H. 1964 *Introduction to New Testament textual criticism*, Grand Rapids (Mich.)

1985 *Scribes, scrolls and Scriptures*, Grand Rapids (Mich.)

Gregory C. R. 1911 *Vorschläge für kritische Ausgabe des griechischen Neuen Testaments*, Leipzig

Gribomont J. 1957 'Les Règles Morales de Saint Basile et le Nouveau Testament', *TU* 64, pp. 416–26

1960 'L'Eglise et les versions bibliques', *La Maison-Dieu* 62, pp. 41–68

Griffiths J. G. 1969 'Numeral taxonomy and some primary manuscripts of the Gospels', *JTS* 20(2), pp. 389–406

1973 'The interrelations of some primary manuscripts of the Gospels in the light of numeral analysis', *TU* 112, pp. 221–38

Gryson R. 1988 'La Vieille-latine, témoin privilégié du texte du Nouveau Testament', *RTL* 19, pp. 413–32

1990 'La Version gothique des évangiles. Essai de réévaluation', *RTL* 21, pp. 3–31

Gryson R.–Bogaert P. 1987 (eds.) *Recherche sur l'histoire de la Bible latine*, (*Cahiers RTL* 19), Louvain-la-Neuve

Haenchen E.–Weigandt P. 1968 'The original text of Acts?', *NTS* 14, pp. 469–81

Harlfinger D. 1980 (ed.) *Griechische Kodikologie und Textüberlieferung*, Darmstadt

Harris J. Rendel 1891 *Codex Bezae, a study of the so-called Western text of the New Testament, TextS* 2
1893a *Stichometry*, London
1893b *On the origin of the Ferrar Group*, Cambridge
1894 *Four lectures on the Western text of the New Testament* London
1900 *Further researches into the history of the Ferrar Group*, London
Hatch W. H. P. 1932 *The Greek manuscripts of the New Testament at Mt Sinai*, Paris
1934 *The Greek manuscripts of the New Testament in Jerusalem*, Paris
1939 *The principal uncial manuscripts of the New Testament*, Chicago
1951 *Facsimiles and descriptions of minuscule manuscripts of the New Testament*, Cambridge (Mass.)
Hausleiter J. 1891 'Die lateinische Apokalypse der alten afrikanischen Kirche', *Forschungen zur Geschichte des neutestamentlichen Kanons*, 4(1) (ed. Th. Zahn), Leipzig, pp. 1–224
Havet L. 1911 *Manuel de critique verbale*, Paris (repr. Rome, 1967)
Head P. 1990 'Observations on early papyri of the Synoptic Gospels, especially on the "Scribal Habits"', *Bib* 71, pp. 240–7
Hedley P. L. 1934 'The Egyptian texts of the Gospels and Acts', *Church Quarterly Review* 118, pp. 24–39
Heidenreich J. 1900 *Der neutestamentliche Text bei Cyprian*, Bamberg
Heimerdinger J. 1988 'Actes 8,37: la foi de l'eunuque éthiopien', *ETR* 63, pp. 521–8
Hirunuma T. 1962 *New Testament textual criticism*, Tokyo (in Japanese)
1966– *Studia textus Novi Testamenti*, Tokyo (monthly journal in Japanese)
1987 *New Testament textual studies: the process of the development of the discipline*, Tokyo (in Japanese)
1989 *The praxis of New Testament textual studies: how to use apparatus criticus*, Osaka (in Japanese)
Hoskier H. C. 1914 *Codex B and its allies*, London
1929 *Concerning the text of the Apocalypse*, 2 vols., London
Hug J. L. 1808 *Einleitung in die Schriften des Neuen Testaments* (1847[4]), Stuttgart
Irigoin J. 1958–9 'Pour une étude des centres de copie byzantins', 1–2, *Scriptorium* 12, pp. 208–27; 13, pp. 177–209
1963 'Les Manuscrits grecs de 1931 à 1960', *Lustrum*, 7, pp. 7–93
1977 'Quelques réflexions sur le concept d'archétype', *RHT* 7, pp. 235–45
Jacquier E. 1913 *Le Texte du Nouveau Testament*, vol. II of *Le Nouveau Testament dans l'église chrétienne*, Paris
Jousse M. *Le Style oral rythmique et mnémotechnique*, Paris (1981[2])
Junack K. – Gütting E. – Nimtz U. – Witte K. 1989 *Das Neue Testament auf Papyrus*, vol. II: *Die paulinischen Briefe, 1: Römer, 1–2 Korinther* (*ANTF* 12), Berlin
Kasser R. 1965 'Les Dialectes coptes et les versions coptes bibliques', *Bib* 45, pp. 63–74

Keck L. E. – Martyn T. L. 1966 (eds.) *Studies in Luke – Acts: essays presented in honor of Paul Schubert*, Nashville

Kenyon F. G. 1901 *The text of the Greek Bible*, London (1975³, ed. A. W. Adams)

Kerchensteiner J. 1964 'Beobachtungen zum altsyrischen Actatext', *Bib* 45, pp. 63 – 74

1970 *Der altsyrische Paulustext CSCO* 315, Louvain

Kieffer R. 1968 *Au-delà des recensions? L'évolution de la tradition textuelle dans Jean 6, 52 – 71*, Lund

Kilpatrick G. D. 1934 'Western text and original text in the Gospels and Acts', *JTS* 44, pp. 24 – 36

1944 'Western text and original text in the Epistles', *JTS* 45, pp. 60 – 5

1963 'An eclectic study of the text of Acts', in Birdsall – Thomson (eds.), pp. 64 – 77

1965 'The Greek New Testament text of today and the *textus receptus*', in Anderson – Barclay (eds.), pp. 189 – 206

1969 'Some problems in New Testament text and language' in Best – Wilson (eds.), pp. 198 – 208

1972 'Some thoughts on modern textual criticism and the Synoptic Gospels', *NTS* 19, pp. 275 – 92

1986 'The two texts of Acts', in Schrage (ed.), pp. 188 – 95

Klijn A. F. J. 1949 *A survey of the researches into the Western Text of the Gospels and Acts*, Utrecht

1966 'In search of the original text of Acts', in Keck – Martyn (eds.), pp. 103 – 111

1969 *A survey of the researches into the Western Text of the Gospels and Acts (1949 – 69)* (*Supplements to Novum Testamentum* 21), Leiden

Kraft B. 1924 *Die Evangelienzitate des heiligen Irenäus*, Freiburg-im-Breisgau

Kremer J. 1979 *Les Actes des Apôtres: tradition, rédaction, théologie*, Gembloux

Lagrange M.-J. 1925a *Evangile selon Saint Jean*, Paris

1925b 'L'Origine de la version syro-palestinienne des évangiles', *RB* 34, pp. 481 – 504

1929 *Evangile selon Saint Marc* (4th edn.), Paris

1933 'Projet de critique textuelle rationnelle du Nouveau Testament', *RB* 42, pp. 481 – 98

1935 *Critique textuelle*, vol. II: *Critique rationnelle*, Paris

Lake K. 1933 *The text of the New Testament*, 6th edn. (S. New), London

Lake K. – Blake R. P. 1923 'The text of the Gospels and the Koridethi Codex', *HTR* 16, pp. 267 – 86

Lake K. – Blake R. P. – New S. 1928 'The Caesarean text of the Gospel of Mark', *HTR* 21(4), pp. 207 – 404

Lake K. – Lake S. 1934 – 5 *Dated Greek minuscule manuscripts to the year 1200*, 11 vols., Boston

Lefebvre G. 1904 *Bulletin de l'Institut français d'archéologie orientale* 4, pp. 1–5, Cairo

Lehmann-Haupt H. 1967 (ed.) *Homage to a bookman: essays on manuscripts, books and printing written for Hans P. Kraus*, Berlin

Leloir L. 1958 *L'Evangile d'Ephrem d'après les œuvres éditées*, CSCO 180, Louvain
1966 *Ephrem de Nisibe: commentaire de l'évangile concordant au Diatessaron*, SC 121
1967 *Citations du Nouveau Testament dans l'ancienne tradition arménienne, 1 Matthieu*, CSCO 283–4, Louvain

Lietzmann H. 1933 *An die Römer*, 4th edn., Tübingen, pp. 1–18

Longenecker R. N. – Tenney M. C. 1974 *New dimensions in New Testament study*, Grand Rapids

Lyonnet S. 1934 'La Version arménienne des évangiles et son modèle grec: Matthieu', *RB* 43, pp. 69–87
1938 'La Première Version arménienne des évangiles', *RB* 47, pp. 355–82
1950 *Les Origines de la Version arménienne et le Diatessaron* (*Biblica et orientalia* 13), Rome

Marava-Chatzinicolaou A. – Touphexi-Paschou C. 1978 *Catalogue of the illuminated Byzantine manuscripts of the National Library of Greece*, vol. I: *Manuscripts of the New Testament texts, 10th–12th century*, Athens

Marichal R. 1961 'La Critique des textes', *L'Histoire et ses méthodes* (Pleiade Encyclopaedia), Paris, pp. 1247–1366

Martin J. P. P. 1883–6 *Introduction à la critique textuelle du Nouveau Testament*, 7 vols., Paris

Martin V. – De Budé G. 1927 *Eschine, Discours*, vol. I

Massaux E. 1953 'Etat présent de la critique textuelle du Nouveau Testament', *NRT* 75, pp. 703–26
1963 'Le Texte de 1 Pierre du papyrus Bodmer VIII' (= P^{72}), *ETL* 39, pp. 616–71

Mees M. 1970 *Die Zitate aus dem Neuen Testament bei Clemens von Alexandria*, Bari

Metzger B. M. 1955 *Annotated bibliography of the textual criticism of the New Testament, 1914–1939*, Copenhagen
1963 *Chapters in the history of New Testament textual criticism*, Leiden
1968 *The text of the New Testament*, 2nd edn., Oxford
1975 *A textual commentary to the Greek New Testament*, 2nd edn. London–New York
1977 *The early versions of the New Testament*, Oxford
1981 *Manuscripts of the Greek Bible*, Oxford

Milne S. H. 1926 *A reconstruction of the Old Latin text or texts of the Gospels used by St Augustine*, Cambridge

Molitor J. 1953–9 'Das Adysh-Tetraevangelium, neu übersetzt und mit altgeorgischen Paralleltexten verglichen', *OC* 37, pp. 30–5; 38, pp. 11–40; 39, pp. 1–32; 40, pp. 1–15; 41, pp. 1–21; 42, pp. 1–18; 43, pp. 1–16

1965–6 'Die altgeorgische Version der katholischen Briefe ins Lateinische übertragen', *OC* 49, pp. 1–17; 50, pp. 37–45

1966–8 'Die georgische Version der Apokalypse (von 978) ins Lateinische übertragen', *OC* 50, pp. 1–12; 51, pp. 1–28; 52, pp. 1–21

Montfaucon B. 1708 *Palaeographia graeca*, Paris (repr. 1970)

Omont H. 1890 *Fac-similés des manuscrits grecs datés de la Bibliothèque Nationale, du IXe au XIVe siècle*, Paris

Parker D. 1982 'A "dictation theory" of Codex Bezae', *JSNT*, pp. 97–112

Parvis M. M. – Wikgren A. 1950 *New Testament manuscript studies*, Chicago

Pattie T. S. 1979 *Manuscripts of the Bible*, London

Pelekanidis S. M. – Christou P. C. – Tsioumis C. – Kadas S. N. 1974–9 *The treasures of Mt Athos: Illuminated manuscripts*, 3 vols., Athens

Pernot H. 1938 *Recherches sur le texte original des évangiles*, Paris

Perrot C. 1963 'Un fragment christo-palestinien découvert à Khirbet-Mird', *RB* 70, pp. 506–55

Petersen Th. C. 1964 'An early Coptic manuscript of Acts: an un-revised version of the so-called Western text', *CBQ* 26, pp. 225–41

Politis L. 1980 'Nouveaux manuscrits grecs découverts au Mt Sinaï', *Scriptorium* 34, pp. 5–17

Possinus P. 1673 *Catena graecorum Patrum in evangelium secundum Marcum* (with collations by Caryophilus including the first of Codex Vaticanus), Rome

Quentin Dom H. 1922 *Mémoire sur l'établissement du texte de la Vulgate*, Rome – Paris

1926 *Essai de critique textuelle*, Paris

Renoux C. 1985 *La Chaîne arménienne sur les épîtres catholiques*, vol. I: *La Chaîne sur l'épître de Jacques* (*PO* 193) Turnhout

Reynolds L. D. – Wilson N. G. 1974 *Scribes and scholars*, 2nd edn., Oxford

Richards W. L. 1977 'The classification of the manuscripts of the Johannine Epistles', *Dissertation*, Missoula (Montana)

Robertson A. T. 1925 *An introduction to the textual criticism of the New Testament*, London

Roller O. 1933 *Das Formular der paulinischen Briefe*, Stuttgart

Rönsch H. 1871 *Das Neue Testament Tertullians*, Leipzig

Salonius A. H. 1927 'Die griechischen Handschriften des Neuen Testaments in den Staatlichen Museen zu Berlin', *ZNW* 26, pp. 97–119

Sanday W. – Turner C. H. – Souter A. 1923 *Novum Testamentum sancti Irenaei*, Oxford

Schäfer K. T. 1929 *Untersuchungen zur Geschichte der lateinischen Übersetzung des Hebräerbriefs*, Freiburg-im-Breisgau

Schäfers J. 1917 *Evangelienzitate in Ephräms des Syrers Kommentar zu den paulinischen Schriften*, Freiburg-im-Breisgau

Schmid J. 1955–6 *Studien zur Geschichte des griechischen Apokalypse-Textes*, 2 vols., Munich

Schmitz F. J. 1982 'Neue Fragmente zur bilinguen 070', *Bericht der Stiftung zur Förderung der Neutestamentlichen Textforschung*, Münster, pp. 71–92

Schrage W. 1986 (ed.) *Studien zum Text und zur Ethik des Neuen Testaments: Festschrift zum 80; Geburtstag von Heinrich Greeven*, Berlin–New York

Schüssler K. 1969 (ed.) 'Epistularum catholicarum versio sahidica', Dissertation, Münster

Scrivener F. H. 1894 *A plain introduction to the criticism of the New Testament*, 4th edn (E. Miller), London

Semler J. S. 1765–7 *Hermeneutische Vorbereitung*, vol. III/1, Halle
Wetstenii libelli ad crisin atque interpretationem Novi Testamenti, Halle
Apparatus ad liberalem Novi Testamenti interpretationem, Halle

Sevrin J. M. 1989 (ed.) *The New Testament in early Christianity* (*BETL* 86), Leuven

Simon R. 1689 *Histoire critique du texte du Nouveau Testament*, Rotterdam (Eng. trans. London, 1689)
1690 *Histoire critique des versions du Nouveau Testament*, Rotterdam (Eng. trans. London, 1692)
1693 *Histoire critique des principaux commentateurs du Nouveau Testament*, Rotterdam
1695 *Nouvelles observations sur le texte et les versions du Nouveau Testament*, Paris

Sloane C. O'C. 1967 'Catenae', *New Catholic Encyclopaedia*, Washington, vol. 3, pp. 244–6

Souter A. 1930 *The text and canon of the New Testament*, 3rd edn., London

Stramare T. 1987 *La Bibbia 'Vulgata' dalle origini ai nostri giorni, Collectanea Biblica Latina*, Rome

Streeter B. H. 1927 *The Four Gospels. A study of origins*, 2nd edn., London

Tarchnischvili 1959 *Le Grand Lectionnaire géorgien de l'Eglise de Jérusalem*, *CSCO* 188–9; 204–5, Louvain

Thiele W. 1965 *Die lateinische Texte des I. Petrusbriefes*, Freiburg-im-Breisgau

Tov E. 1982 'Criteria for evaluating textual readings: the limitations of textual rules', *HTR* 75, pp. 429–48

Treu K. 1961 'Zur vermeintlichen Kontraktion von ΙΕΡΟΣΟΛΥΜΑ in 0188, P.13416', *ZNW* 52, pp. 278–9

Turner C. H. 1927 'A textual commentary on Mark 1', *JTS* 28

Turner E. G. 1968 *Greek papyri, an introduction*, Princeton (N.J.)
1971 *Greek manuscripts of the ancient world*, Oxford

Turyn A. 1972 *Dated Greek manuscripts of the 13th and 14th centuries in the libraries of Italy*, Springfield (Ill.)

Vardanian A. 1930 *Euthalius Werke, Untersuchungen und Texte*, Vienna

Vatican 1972 *Il libro della Bibbia* (exhibition catalogue), Vatican City

Vogels H. J. 1919 *Beiträge zur Geschichte des Diatessarons im Abendland*, Münster
1920 *Untersuchungen zur Geschichte der lateinischen Apokalypse-Übersetzung*, Düsseldorf

Bibliography

1922 'Die Lukaszitate bei Lucifer von Calaris' and 'Die Johanneszitate bei Lucifer von Calaris', *TQ* 103, pp. 23–37 and pp. 183–200

1926a 'Codex Bezae als Bilingue', *Bulletin of the Bezan Club* 2, pp. 8–12

1926b *Evangelium Palatinum*, Münster

1928 *Vulgatastudien*, Münster

1929 *Codicum Novi Testamenti specimina*, Bonn

1955 *Handbuch der neutestamentlichen Textkritik*, 2nd edn., Bonn

Voicu S. J. – D'Alisera S. 1981 I.M.A.G.E.S. (*Index in manuscriptorum graecorum edita speciminal*), Rome

von Harnack A. 1916a *Zur Revision der Prinzipen der neutestamentlichen Textkritik*, Leipzig

1916b 'Porphyrius, "Gegen die Christen"', Abhandlungen der Kön. Preuss. Akad. der Wissenschaft, Phil. Hist. Kl.1., Berlin

1924 *Marcion, das Evangelium von fremden Gott, TU* 45, 2nd edn., Leipzig (repr. 1960)

1931 *Zur neutestamentlichen Textkritik*, Berlin

von Soden H. 1902–10 *Die Schriften des Neuen Testaments in ihrer ältesten erreichbaren Textgestalt*, vol. I: *Untersuchungen*, Berlin

1909 *Das lateinische Neue Testament in Afrika zur Zeit Cyprians*, Leipzig

1927 'Der lateinische Paulustext bei Marcion und Tertullian', in R. Bultmann – H. von Soden (eds.), *Festgabe für Adolf Jülicher zum 70. Geburtstag*, pp. 229–281, Tübingen

Vööbus A. 1954 *Early versions of the New Testament*, Stockholm

Weiss B. 1897 *Der Codex D in der Apostelgeschichte*, Leipzig

Weitzmann K. 1964 'Manuscripts', *Byzantine art and European art*, pp. 291–356, 540–52, 571–87, Athens

Westcott B. F. – Hort F. J. A. 1881 *The New Testament in the original Greek*, Introduction, Cambridge

Willard L. C. 1971 'A critical study of the Euthalian apparatus', Dissertation, Yale University, New Haven (Conn.)

Willis W. H. 1961 *Proceedings of the Ninth International Congress of Paleography*, pp. 382–9, Oslo

Wisse F. 1982 *The Profile Method for classifying and evaluating manuscript evidence, S & D* 44, Grand Rapids

Wittek M. 1967 *Album de paléographie grecque*, Gand

Zahn Th. 1916 *Die Urausgabe des Lucas*, Leipzig

Zaphiris G. 1970 *Le Texte de Matthieu d'après les citations de Clément d'Alexandrie*, Gembloux

Zotenberg H. 1877 *Catalogue des manuscrits éthiopiens de la Bibliothèque Nationale*, Paris

Zuntz G. 1945 *An ancestry of the Harklean New Testament*, London

1953 *The text of the Epistles*, London

Index of modern authors and editors

209

Index of modern authors and editors

211

Index of ancient authors